THE NOVELS OF PÉREZ GALDÓS

THE NOVELS OF PÉREZ GALDÓS

The Concept of Life as Dynamic Process

BY

SHERMAN H. EOFF

WASHINGTON UNIVERSITY STUDIES
NOVEMBER, 1954
SAINT LOUIS

CONTENTS

INTRODUCTION

THE critic who undertakes an extensive study of a writer like Benito Pérez Galdós (1843-1920) is confronted with a stimulating task. The literary output of this distinguished Spaniard, consisting largely of contemporary and historical novels, is vast in quantity and rich in meaning. Pre-eminent in his own country, Galdós must also be considered one of the most vital and one of the most representative novelists of the nineteenth century in Europe. None of his contemporaries dedicated himself to his profession more earnestly than he, or participated more intelligently in the intellectual and literary movements of the age. When, as a youth of nineteen, he left his home in the Canary Islands to study at the University of Madrid, he turned sympathetically to the advanced thought of the day. Deciding a few years later on the novel as a career, he came gradually to fuse literary creed with some of the dominant philosophical and scientific ideas of his century. This was a century in which the concept of change and growth, especially under the impact of developments in the biological and social sciences, assumed a prominent position. In novelistic art it was the age of realism, which in its essential meaning was an effort to bring literature as close to life as possible. For a writer who, like Galdós, felt himself in step with the intellectual and literary trends of his generation, the motto might well have been: art is life, and life is process.

The image of natural process in the novels of Galdós can be recognized and appreciated if the stories of some of his maturest works are visualized as organic developments in which plot and characterization merge. This particular view of the novelist has enough newness about it to justify a detailed presentation. Its relevancy pertains especially to the contemporary, or social, novels, and to these the present inquiry is confined. Here, after all, is the place to become most intimately acquainted with Galdós. His historical novels (*Episodios Nacionales*) may be popularly favored among Spanish-speaking peoples, but surely his importance in literary history will rest primarily on those works of which *Doña Perfecta, Fortunata y Jacinta, Angel Guerra*, the *Torquemada* series, and *Misericordia* are outstanding examples.

The paramount objective in this study is, essentially, to interpret Galdós' portrayal of life by way of an examination of his novelistic method. The term "method" is used with special reference to structural framework or basic plot movement, as distinguished from "technique" or the surface manner that gives the basic form its finished appearance. Primary emphasis thus will rest upon an understanding of the fundamental structural form in which the author molds the material constituting his subject. In broad terms, Galdós finds his "subject" in the individual's frictional relationship with society. He looks upon this subject enthusiastically, regarding it both as suitable for the novel and as an unescapable premise for any speculation on man's ultimate destiny. The foremost task, therefore, is to explain how the author's conception of this interrelationship is made manifest in his development of plot. This task involves answering, with respect to the novels individually, what appears to be but is not a simple question: what is the story? Interpretation of a novel's essential meaning is made to wait upon an answer to this fundamental question. The approach here indicated reverses the usual procedure, for scholarly studies on Galdós have most frequently discussed his ideas and his attitude toward the local Spanish scene, while touching but lightly on his literary form.

Since Galdós was clearly a broad-minded thinker who had his country's interest at heart, and since his works contain much information on Spanish life in the nineteenth century, it is not surprising that he is represented above all as a liberal who studiously confronted the social conditions of his day and sought to counteract the prejudices of a formalistic, authoritarian society. There is no reason to minimize the importance of this view, but there is much more to Galdós than his role as social historian and progressive leader. He felt very strongly the responsibility of imparting ideas, sometimes to the detriment of his art; but he also felt that his mission as artist came first, and he succeeded in developing a decisive form, in which he molded a picture of life that overshadows the specific problems and circumstances of social living in Spain. The vitality and solidity of his novels derive in large part from his depiction of the life process itself, especially as it pertains to the individual. Here is where his real literary importance and his essential "message" are to be found.

At the heart of Galdós' method is the study of individual character. As a mere youth, years before he had decided upon his career, he showed his aversion to the "novel of action," which was popular in the 1860's and appeared widely in serial form ("la novela por entregas"); and as he developed his own plans for the novel, he was determined to concentrate upon character portrayal rather than the narration of exciting events. In this respect, of course, he was following the lead of earlier nineteenth-century realists who grounded their separate narratives in the portraiture of a central personage. Nor did Galdós allow the depiction of customs and types more than incidental importance. He made use of social conditions—important to be sure as background for character development—but in none of his works is the primary objective a delineation of the contemporary scene, such as one finds in the "novel of customs." The emphasis is upon characterization, with special attention to the social factors that help to shape individual lives.

For this reason it is of the highest importance to determine how characterization in the novels is integrated with plot development. To do so it is necessary to penetrate the surface or descriptive view of the principal characters and envisage them as growing personalities, not as static quantities observed within fixed situations. If the novels are examined from this point of view, it will be found that, in almost every one, personality growth is an integral part of the narrative movement, and consequently a basic element of the "story." Thus the novelist's creative talent should appear in a new light, and his social, moral, and philosophical ideas should take on new meaning.

Galdós is frequently referred to as a psychological novelist. It is more exact to call him a socio-psychological novelist or a literary social psychologist, for he is interested more in the formative influence of social relations, as regards the individual, than he is in the intricate workings of the mind. His technique is often more descriptive of outward manifestations than interpretative of deep-lying motives. Nevertheless, he visualizes personality in its broad functional aspects and records his interpretation in one comprehensive treatment. In an important respect it is proper to call his portrayal dynamic. From the vantage point of the present day, the socio-psychological factors with which he deals may seem elementary. It may be said that he draws heavily upon the common fund of knowledge which is based on observation, such, for example, as the effects of family circumstances upon a person's behavior.

The elementary nature of his psychological knowledge, however, does not keep the novels from being substantial and firmly constructed representations of life.

Galdós' method was a gradual development, which began with indecisiveness as to narrative plan, crystallized soon into one predominant form, underwent minor changes in the face of the reading public's weariness with long-drawn-out realistic novels, and exhibited finally certain marks of disintegration during the author's old age. His life perspective also followed a course of gradual expansion and growth, affected by the scientific and metaphysical thought of his day, by his own experiences, and by his constant observation of human nature in other people and in himself. Consequently, it seems desirable to maintain as far as possible a chronological view within each of the several phases of our discussion. The plan is undesirable in some respects, since on any single occasion it precludes the comprehensive examination of a specific novel from a variety of viewpoints, and at the same time incurs the danger of repetitiousness because of numerous references to a given work. Despite these disadvantages, the goal of an over-all picture of continuity seems preferable to a list of all-inclusive analyses chronologically arranged, particularly with respect to the novelist's moral and philosophical growth; and though his method varies little once it is decided upon, it can be understood best when visualized within the compass of an entire career.

The novels of Galdós are sometimes heavy with supplementary material, but the reader who penetrates their outer layer is rewarded with a vitalizing representation of human experience grounded in a firm narrative structure. Hence the importance of comprehending each story as a unified narrative movement in which organic structure and psychological portrayal combine to produce an artistic finality. In brief, the object of this study is to learn what the novelist's narrative plan is, how he visualizes personality and merges it with plot development, and what, on the basis of this investigation, his perspective of life is. This is another way of saying that the goal is to define Galdós' stature as a novelist by examining the design that he follows as he molds his conception of the individual-social relationship into novelistic form.

I

THE NARRATIVE PLAN

G ALDÓS showed considerable indecisiveness with regard to questions of form during his apprenticeship in the novel, embracing the years 1867 to 1873. While this was also an important formative period of the young novelist's outlook upon life, priority is given in this chapter to the author's choice and development of a method, which itself changes as general objectives become more clearly defined. Briefly stated, the development begins with a decision to exploit the possibilities of a psychological study of character in relation to its social background, crystallizes momentarily in a plot of dramatic situation, changes to chronological narration of a protagonist's experiences, and then resumes partially an earlier practice by way of a mixture of the dramatic and the chronological plans. Although there are shifts of emphasis in the course of the developing method, at no time is character portrayal relegated to a secondary position with respect to happenings. For this reason, it is necessary to keep in mind the psychological nature of the novels, and this chapter, therefore, introduces the conception of the Galdosian novel as being a story of personality.

When Galdós began to write novels, he was preoccupied with the question of choosing between a historical and a social objective. *La Fontana de Oro* (1867-1868) is essentially a historical novel, and the characters, largely surface delineations, are on somewhat the same level as local landmarks which fit into the picture of a given political epoch. The one exception is doña Paulitas. Her portrayal is limited to one brief moment of her life but includes basic causes of her behavior and a close view of her emotional and physical manifestations when she experiences a tense conflict between love for Lázaro, the protagonist, and the necessity of living up to the nunlike reputation which she has acquired in a sanctified atmosphere of seclusion. Doña Paulitas is merely incidental in *La Fontana de Oro,* but she is representative of what comes to be the major pattern of Galdós' characterization: the recording of a person's psychological reactions in close relation to the social background in which the person's behavior has been conditioned.[1]

With *El audaz* (1871), Galdós makes a definite advance toward utilizing social-psychological material for the basis of his narratives. Although he is obviously groping in this novel as he tries to combine historical and social objectives, the psychology of both the central characters presents complicating elements for the plot. The characterization of the young revolutionist Muriel is overshadowed by heavy attention to political background, in which personal motivations are insufficiently integrated with the sequence of events. But it is clear that the author wanted to show how youthful hardships and injustice to Muriel's father produced in the son an inflexibility which, directed toward personal ascendancy and social vengeance, leads to his downfall. The personality of Susana, daughter of an aristocrat and in love with the plebeian Muriel, is much more thoroughly portrayed. Though bearing the imprint of class prejudice, Susana's arrogance is tempered by a spirit of rebellion against convention, which causes her to disregard many of the traditional rules of conduct. The author carefully follows in his heroine the conflict between ideas imposed by a rigid social order and those based upon an independent sense of dignity and worth. Susana's portrayal receives relatively little space, especially in the latter part of the novel, but it is consistently traced, even to the catastrophic night of Muriel's failure and madness, when the heroine succumbs under the weight of conventional law and chooses suicide in preference to facing her family and her social group after having deserted them to follow her lover.

El audaz would have been Galdós' first psychological novel had its narrative been concentrated upon the love story of the main characters. As it is, it reveals a divided purpose and a resultant structural weakness. After the novelist decides to pursue the historical and social objectives separately, however, his contemporary novels gain artistically, becoming, primarily, studies in personality, in which the plot itself is an unfolding closely related to the characters' psychology.

It is easy to trace the course which Galdós followed in developing the narrative method most suited to his novelistic aims. There is a kind of plot that places a person in a situation which of itself demands decisive action and forces him to reveal his personality as he tries to extricate himself from a set of circumstances chosen by the author. In such a case the importance of the characterization, if it is psychological portrayal, will lie in the protagonist's reactions to the one immediate and dominating problem with which he is faced. This narrative form is essentially a plot of dramatic situation. It lends itself especially to the portrayal of character as seen in one climactic stage of its formation. Or again, a person may be visualized as moving along, perhaps casually most of the time, in an ordinary course of events in which arise the sundry situations that are probable in an extensive view of an individual's life. In this case the individual is led on by the necessity of living up to various circumstances of the moment, which nevertheless grow cumulatively in force and organization and assume a pattern of successive climactic episodes. This form, which may appropriately be called a biographical plot, is best suited to the portrayal of developing personality over a long period of time. The two kinds of plot here described typify, separately or in combination, all of Galdós' social novels. The first is adopted decisively in *Doña Perfecta* (1876), and the second comes gradually to be the novelist's favorite method.

Of all of Galdós' novels, *Doña Perfecta* is structurally the most compact. It is an intense drama held within narrow limits of time, place, and personal motivations. The dramatic problem, which centers upon a mother's opposition to her daughter's marriage to a man of religious beliefs incompatible with her own, emerges quickly and develops rapidly as the battle of will against will leads to hatred and culminates in murder. With a prior conditioning of ecclesiastic rigidity and provincial narrow-mindedness, doña Perfecta immediately finds an opponent in her nephew Pepe, a freethinker with a marked tendency to brutal frankness. Rosario, the daughter in love with Pepe, enforces the latter's will to fight, even though she is completely dominated by her mother; while the priest don Inocencio, in a parallel though more important role, hovers in the background, inciting doña Perfecta to determined action and infuriating Pepe with calculated sarcasm.

The author's technique is one of progressive dramatic preparation along a single line of action. Caballuco's hostility to Pepe at the outset, don Inocencio's presence beside Rosario as Pepe arrives at his aunt's home, mention early in the story of the lawsuits with reference to Pepe's land, all point to impending trouble. As the intensification toward climax and catastrophe grows, all is excluded that does not bear on the central axis of the plot. Even the descriptive material pertaining to the countryside, the minor character types, and incidental scenes contribute to the background theme of provincial obscurantism, and harmonize with the intellectual inflexibility of doña Perfecta.

Though merged with the plot, the novel's ideological purpose accounts for its artistic weakness. Because of his own hostility to what doña Perfecta stands for, the author abruptly and persistently brings about unprovoked attacks upon Pepe from the moment that the latter sets foot in his aunt's house; and he deliberately, almost mechanically, accentuates his hero's difficulties, partly by overemphasis on his liberalism and partly by manipulation of events. The lawsuits, for example, are obviously invented for the sole purpose of instigating trouble for Pepe. If Galdós had allowed the conflict to develop gradually out of a slowly emerging incompatibility, his handling of plot and character would have seemed more natural. As it is, the novel reveals—to its detriment—the author's ideological passion in both its technique and its style.

The characterization of doña Perfecta, nevertheless, more than counterbalances the novel's technical flaws. The portrait of her personality overshadows all else in the story and bears strong testimony to the assertion that Galdós' fundamental strength as a novelist is psychological. The emotional disturbance begins in the protagonist as conflict between two desirable but mutually exclusive goals: one, a peaceful family relationship in which her established reputation for piety will remain undisturbed; and the other, the endorsement of and submission to her worship of ecclesiastic formulas, the indispensable basis of her integrity. The psychological picture is that of a struggle for emotional security on the part of one whose values force her into a violent defensive behavior, which passes through a state of ferment and frustration, and ends in a firm co-ordination of auxiliary motives toward the enforcement of her will. The plot follows the course of a developing passion of hate in an individual who personalizes a small segment of human nature trimmed down to one dominant compulsion. With justification the novel is said to have the classical stamp upon it.

Galdós never again in his novels achieved the compactness and tenseness of *Doña Perfecta*. His new orientation was in an important sense a turn to the realistic method, which at first, however, bore definite marks of romanticism. The transition begins with *Gloria* (1876-1877).

In Part I of *Gloria* a few events are chosen to provide a dramatic conflict between love and religious training. A young man (Daniel) is shipwrecked and brought to the home of a young woman (Gloria). The two fall in love but decide to part because of a difference in religious beliefs. At the time, the young man does not reveal what his religion is. Later he returns for the purpose of aiding a friend in trouble, finds an opportunity to urge his love upon the young woman, spends the night with her, and then discloses that he is a Jew, thus posing a problem of potentially tragic consequences. Depending heavily upon coincidence, especially in connection with the flood that washes away a bridge and keeps Gloria's father away from home, the author manipulates his plot so as to insure drama by making his heroine the victim of accidental happenings. Even so, he does not neglect characterization. Gloria is placed in a sufficiently large and varied number of circumstances to make her appear to be representative of a broad segment of human nature. Still more important, her portrayal has within itself the rudiments of a story, in that it shows how indoctrination with dogmatic religious beliefs emerges in moments of stress to distort natural inclinations.

Part II, written several months after the completion of Part I, is essentially an account of the correction of a mistake, and stresses more the effect of circumstances upon character than it does the drama of a given situation. The only events of real dramatic possibility are the sudden and ruthless intervention of Daniel's mother when her son is on the verge of carrying out his pretense of espousing Catholicism, and the final scene, in which Gloria pays one last visit to her child and dies in the presence of her lover.

Daniel, who at first was scarcely more than the symbol of a forbidden religious faith and an occasion for the conflict in Gloria between love and environment, comes to life in Part II, revealing in some detail his own conflict between love and moral responsibility on the one hand, and racial fervor on the other. Gloria, who was very alert in Part I, becomes meanwhile rather listless, but she remains the central personage in the plot. Galdós has merely altered his method, for the story is now an account of emotional and physical adjustment to the immovable weight of family and religious tradition. Weakened physically and dulled mentally, Gloria becomes more and more passive, while gradually absorbing her aunt's doctrine of martyrdom. The transition, from a spirited demeanor to a kind of stupefied resignation mixed with fanatical mystic zeal, is a psychological story in itself, which takes precedence over the sequence of events. Events serve primarily to bring latent developments to the surface or to effect a change of direction in personality growth. This is the method which Galdós follows in most of his novels subsequent to *Gloria,* though for a few more years he is rather reluctant to part with the dramatic plot which is inherent in a potentially explosive situation.

In *Marianela* (1878) as in the first part of *Gloria,* the happenings combine in climactic sequence to bring tragedy to a person trapped in a hopeless situation. The arrival of the doctor (Teodoro Golfín) to operate on the eyes of the blind boy (Pablo) forewarns of the tragedy which will befall the unfortunate, ugly girl (Marianela: Nela) if her "lover" sees her as she is and not as he imagines her to be. The arrival of Pablo's beautiful cousin (Florentina) is a second warning of the impending calamity, which is soon consummated when the operation proves to be successful and Pablo immediately falls in love with his cousin, leaving Nela to die in abject humiliation.

Such a narrative subject requires careful handling to keep it from degenerating into melodrama, and the author apparently made little effort to forestall the sentimentalism suggested by the situation. His attempts to arouse the reader's sympathy for Pablo, his obvious contraposition of extremes (Florentina's beauty and Nela's ugliness, for example) in order to make his heroine's suffering more poignant, the emotionalism of his attacks on the cold indifference of society, his efforts to create an atmosphere of suspense and mystery, all contribute to a melodramatic effect. Even if the reader does find redeeming features, such as nature description and a delicate sensitivity to the dreamworld of the blind, or becomes interested in the possible symbolic meaning of the story, he can hardly escape the impression that he is confronted with a sentimental outburst on behalf of a child who is mistreated both by nature and by society.

And yet, if *Marianela* is considered from a psychological viewpoint, Galdós appears in a much more favorable light. Pablo, to be sure, is little more than an abstraction embodying intellectual self-sufficiency, worship of beauty, and selfishness. The psychology of Marianela, on the other hand, presents a clear view of progressive movement toward a well-defined finality: An orphan girl, tyrannized by the intense need of being wanted and the feeling of inferiority arising primarily from her hapless physical state, seeks escape in a dreamworld, which is represented first by her companionship with the blind youth and later by the vague religious vision of a world beyond death. When her intent of suicide is thwarted and she is brought back to reality, she faces an unhappy situation with her strongest habitual response: complete surrender to the idea of her own futility, from which she is liberated by an emotional release ending in death. In a sense, then, the novel tells the story of a futile and tragic attempt to create and retain self-esteem on the part of a child hopelessly trammeled by the forces of nature and society. *Marianela,* therefore, conforms with the novelist's growing tendency to build a narrative out of his characters' progressive reaction to a chain of social circumstances.

La familia de León Roch (1878) is a loose combination of biography and dramatic situation. At the outset the protagonist (León Roch), dominated by the ideal of an orderly existence, deliberately chooses a wife (María Egipcíaca) who will, he thinks, insure a peaceful, sober married life. There follows a rather leisurely account of the hero's gradual disillusionment and of his efforts to establish a tolerable relationship at home as his wife comes under the influence of the priest Paoletti. The dramatic situation, and with it a tense moral conflict, develops when the woman (Pepa Fúcar), whom León should have married, reappears. The story ends with León clinging to his ideal of moral orderliness, though bitterly thinking of the vicious clerical influence that has ruined his marriage.

On the surface, therefore, the story presents a chronological account of a man's futile efforts to establish a home in accord with his ideals. The intense portrayal of María Egipcíaca, who turns out to be a turbulent ferment of suppressed sex and of a false mystic zeal kept aflame by the priest, seems to indicate that anticlericalism is the author's main motivation. This impression is enhanced by much collateral material having to do with María's family and associates, presented in such a way as to make León appear a pitiful victim of prejudice against science and independent thinking. But the role of María, like that of Pepa, has the primary purpose of testing León's character. In this connection, the author indulges in amateurish theatrics, announcing the supposed death of Pepa's husband precisely at a moment when León is most susceptible to temptation; and then, by an obviously contrived situation of dramatic reversal, disclosing through Pepa's inopportune appeal to León (immediately after María's death) that her husband is still alive.

This mixture of biography, drama—not to say melodrama—and emotionalism no doubt accounts for the difficulty that critics have had in labeling the novel's unifying narrative theme. The usual reference stresses the author's anticlerical intent and his attack on religious fanaticism, though it is interesting to note that Sáinz de Robles declares that the novel "no es una obra de combate espiritual-religioso," but an account of a "conflicto espiritual-amoroso" centering in the failure of a marriage based only upon an ephemeral sexual attraction.[2] If the narrative is regarded as being essentially biographical, an underlying theme of moral discipline appears, which reveals within an individual the triumph of order over revolution. It cannot be said that this is the novel's sole meaning, but it is the one consistent development from beginning to end, and it is especially important in view of Galdós' continual preoccupation with the individual's involvement in questions of morality.

In these novels "de la primera época," Galdós was not only rebelling against the inhumanity imbedded in a dogma-ridden society; he was also groping for a form that would best enable him to apply his interest in individual psychology to moral and social problems. The plot of dramatic situation, which may have been in part a compromise with a youthful aspiration to be a dramatist, was particularly well suited to passionate ideological attack. After the young novelist's belligerence had cooled off, however, his conception of plot crystallized in a method with which he had been experimenting: the simple chronology of a central personage's experiences, with certain climactic episodes provided here and there for dramatic effect and for designating change of direction in character development.

The decisive orientation to a slow, sometimes tedious, but thorough approach appears in *La desheredada* (1881). In a strict sense, this is Galdós' first realistic novel. Briefly, the narrative of *La desheredada* records events in the life of a woman (Isidora Rufete) who tries in vain to establish her claims to nobility, clinging meanwhile to her illusion of noble birth as her major standard of personal worth, living first with a man of aristocratic name and then with one who is financially able to satisfy her thirst for luxury, and eventually descending to the life of a prostitute when her illusion is irreparably shattered. The novel is plainly didactic in purpose, and it would be little more than a mediocre moralistic tale were it not also the psychological account of a degeneration in character. The descriptive, background material and the picture of social relationships are no substitute for narrative interest in a story that clearly is focused on one person. Nor are the events in this person's life so arranged as to produce dramatic interest in themselves. Only two episodes (Isidora's visit to the Marquesa, whose kinship she claimed, and her eventual imprisonment for a supposed falsification in connection with her claims on the Marquesa's family) are climactically presented. Considered as surface events, they appear in the whole as two widely separated and loosely connected occurrences. The full effect of continuity and progression is experienced only by recognizing the psychological movement, which shows how Isidora subordinates her wholesome inclinations of friendliness, sympathy, and honesty as she tries to prove her nobility; how she is increasingly tyrannized by the love of wealth and luxury; and how her integrity dissolves completely after the final disillusionment following her imprisonment. With the exception of the two decisive episodes mentioned above, the external happenings are scarcely more than occasions for revealing internal development; and even these two episodes are utilized to explain the change in character which follows them.

In one respect *La desheredada* is still a transitional novel. Just as the portrayal of doña Perfecta was an elaboration of one outstanding motive, so the portrayal of Isidora is concentrated on a single motivating force (the worship of a false value). For this reason, the novel has about it that abstractness which is characteristic of stories designed to prove theses. It thus retains some of the argumentative quality so noticeable in the narratives of 1876-1878.[3] *El amigo Manso* (1882) may also be regarded as transitional, both in its thematic abstractness and its combination of dramatic situation and biography.

The chief modification in narrative method to be noted in the novels which follow *El amigo Manso* is the result of a relaxation in thematic demonstration. Social-moral themes are always present in Galdós, but with one or two exceptions, they "go underground" for the next fifteen years. The characters, meanwhile, become more representative of a non-specialized view of human nature, in that their portrayal exhibits not so much the development of a dominant compulsion or a given psychological state as multiple reactions to a variety of circumstances. It may be said, simply, that they are individual Spaniards portrayed with "sympathetic objectivity," and not symbols of Spanish social traits which, in the author's view, are undesirable.[4] Moreover, Galdós broadens the framework of his plots by giving secondary characters important roles of their own. As a result, his novels sometimes appear to emphasize the depiction of society in its collective aspects. With all this broadening and, in some cases, loosening of structure, however, Galdós' major interest continues to be the study of individual personality.

In so far as method is concerned, *El doctor Centeno* (1883) is perhaps the most "plotless" of Galdós' stories; and yet it is fairly typical of the novelist's most fruitful period. The plot is a simple chronology of events in the life of a boy (Felipe Centeno) who sets out to make his way in the world. The main narrative steps are: Felipe's arrival in Madrid with high ambitions for a medical career; his first misfortunes, including service with the priest don Pedro Polo; his service and friendship with the visionary and poverty-stricken Alejandro Miquis, a relationship that constitutes the heart of the novel; termination of this association at the death of Miquis. There are many graphic scenes, numerous well-defined incidental characters, and certain dramatic episodes in the life of the unhappy Miquis. The story bears definite marks of kinship with *Lazarillo de Tormes* and *Don Quijote,* with an echo here and there from some of the tales of Charles Dickens. It thus has a certain charm apart from any thought of a centralized psychological study. To appreciate its meaning fully, however, it is necessary to realize that the author is actually depicting a maturing development in an individual who seeks to realize his own worth. With an initial drive for accomplishment and a pronounced need to belong in a satisfactory social relationship, Felipe consolidates for himself the values of work, perseverance, honesty, and loyalty. His sensible adjustment to a level of accomplishment befitting his own talents, as contrasted with the dreamworld phantasy of Miquis, is a salient feature of the story. Even more important is the presentation of the friendship between the two persons, through which Felipe strengthens his sense of responsibility and, above all, experiences the edifying effects of sympathy and respect. Were it not for this underlying character development, *El doctor Centeno* might be regarded simply as another picaresque novel, recording as it does a series of adventures and misfortunes in the service of masters. Actually, the picaresque resemblance is purely superficial; for Felipe's rise above the average level of his environment is a development altogether contrary to the *pícaro's* facile adaptation to social evils. What takes place within the individual is the most important part of the story.

The structural pattern of *El doctor Centeno* is essentially the same as that of Galdós' maturest and most substantial works, including *Fortunata y Jacinta,* the *Torquemada* series, *Angel Guerra,* and *Misericordia.* The novelist broadens his range of vision and multiplies his secondary characters so as to embrace a large segment of urban life. In varying degree he supplies dramatic episodes having to do with frictional personal relationships; but his interest continues to be focused on the progress of one or two central characters whose "problems" arise from the cumulative vicissitudes of their day-by-day living.

When, out of deference to public taste, Galdós shortened his narratives and turned to the *novela dialogada,* he modified his method in two respects. He sharply curtailed the massive background material relating to setting and incidental characters, and he returned, partly, to the plot of dramatic situation. His intention was to combine the novel and drama in a more intensive psychological portrayal than was possible with the casual movement of his previous method. The result was a hybrid form that lacked the precision and tenseness of drama and added nothing to—if it did not actually dilute—the psychological study. The artistic weakness of these novels is explained primarily by the author's resumption of thematic abstractness. It can also be attributed to his inability to make full use of the slow biographical tempo on which he had depended so heavily in his characterizations. As he turns—reluctantly—away from his former practice, he now tends to follow his main characters separately, trying to visualize each of their personalities as a whole instead of exploiting the potential drama of the situation in which they are involved.

The indeterminateness of the hybrid form, which, incidentally, characterizes a number of Galdós' plays as well as his novels, can be seen in *Realidad* (1889), the first of his *novelas dialogadas*. *Realidad* is above all a philosophical novel, whose meaning, to be discussed in a later chapter, is couched in the psychology of personal relationships. Its structure is of interest in the present connection because it shows Galdós' preoccupation with individual personality, to the disregard of what would usually be considered plot interest. The opportunity for dramatic action lies in the love triangle involving husband (Orozco), wife (Augusta), and wife's lover (Viera), who is also a friend of the husband. The author, instead of interesting himself in the solution of the dramatic problem, uses the love affair as a means of studying the characters individually in the light of their conceptions of truth and morality. Orozco, though participating in the activity befitting his social position, lives intellectually in a world apart from society, engrossed in the contemplation of ultimate reality and bent upon elevating his wife to his own level of spirituality, even after he discovers her infidelity.

Augusta, who respects but does not love Orozco, adheres to a philosophy by which she justifies her earthy, sensuous enjoyment of life, unable to sympathize with the cold otherworldliness of her husband. Viera, who lives an anchorless existence, torn between his pride in an aristocratic name, his Bohemian habits, and the guilt deriving from his betrayal of a friend, eventually terminates his conflict by committing suicide. The chief motivating force in Augusta's life is at first her rebellious independence of conventional standards, which nevertheless gives way to the common adjustment of preserving appearances after the tragic outcome of her illicit love affair. In her relation to her husband, she represents the triumph of earthiness over the supra-earthly attitude of one who personifies abstract metaphysics. Conversely, Orozco illustrates the failure of a self-appointed metaphysician in his efforts to put his theory into practice. Viera's story is primarily one of social maladjustment. Orozco's discovery of the love affair between his wife and Viera is a climactic episode that comes late in the story and brings to a conclusion three interdependent but essentially separate personality plots, in each of which the discovery of the love affair is a final test. The narrative movement in the novel thus follows the private interests of the several personages and converges upon but does not grow out of the conflict inherent in the situation. This structure, of course, is in keeping with the author's primary aim, which is to study questions of reality and morality from a variety of standpoints.

The structure of *La loca de la casa* (1892), Galdós' second *novela dialogada*, is simpler and more clearly defined than that of *Realidad*. The narrative is a slow chronological development growing out of a domestic situation in which a daughter comes to the rescue of her aristocratic and bankrupt father, marries a rich but crude plebeian, and discovers the morally beneficial results of what promised to be an unbearable relationship. The few dramatic scenes are but steps in the developing psychology of the two main characters. In so far as method is concerned, *La loca de la casa* is plainly the incorporation of a situational problem in a biographical plot, of which adjustment to environment is an important component. Much the same can be said for *El abuelo* (1897), except that its narrative is more compactly centered around a single emotional conflict. The last three of Galdós' contemporary novels (*Casandra*, 1905; *El caballero encantado*, 1909; *La razón de la sinrazón*, 1915), all of them in dialogue, are abstract and loosely constructed hybrids, which show definite marks of a decline in creative energy. But they, too, reveal a continued interest in individual psychology. Continuing his early aversion to the "novel of action," Galdós followed throughout his career a method in which the study of personality takes precedence over events.

Up to this point the purpose has been to describe the particular plot design which the novelist employed to satisfy his socio-psychological aims. It now seems desirable to examine one of the novels in detail in order to illustrate more fully the author's biographical method, and to show how an analysis of his method may be used for purposes of interpretation. *Misericordia* (1897) is especially suitable for such an examination because in its structure it is typical of the greatest number and the most substantial of the social novels.

The narrative of *Misericordia* traces the experiences of Benina, a servant, who struggles feverishly to support the household of her impoverished mistress, doña Paca, only to be dismissed by the latter's daughter-in-law, Juliana, when the family inherits some money. On the surface, the novel appears to be a story of ingratitude centering around a woman whose goodness and strength of character overshadow the weakness of her mistress and continue to sustain her after her cruel dismissal. Almost everyone will agree that the focal point of interest in *Misericordia* is Benina, a truly charitable soul, who not only devotes her life to her fellow man, but who in the end is Christian enough to forgive the injustice of which she has been a victim. This view is accurate enough as a starting point. In the necessary elaboration, however, it is important to keep in mind the difference between static and developing character. If Benina is a static character, the emphasis rests largely upon her charitableness, and the significance of the novel can adequately be described in terms of the general situation, that is, the culmination of events in a dramatic episode of injustice and pardon. If Benina is a developing personality, it is necessary to observe in what way her psychological development constitutes a story in itself.

When the protagonist is first introduced, she appears as a sturdy, energetic woman, bearing the marks of an arduous existence, and yet with a certain refinement of manners that sets her apart from the beggars whom she has joined momentarily in a desperate effort to raise some money. Her friendliness and consideration for others are apparent, but they are less noticeable than the determined drive to obtain the means necessary to meet the needs of the family which she serves. The reader is thus immediately made aware of the stringent, materialistic problem of money, which provides the basis for the struggle of an individual—on behalf of others, not on behalf of self—and which accounts for the greater part of the happenings in the story. In these early scenes, as Benina hastens here and there impatiently, drawing upon her ingenuity and perseverance, showing a certain aggressiveness and protective superiority though still humble and tolerant with others, she is at an advanced stage of personality growth.

That the reader may know about this growth, the author pauses for an expository chapter, in which he traces the early history of his heroine. Briefly, the exposition relates how a servant has gradually become indispensable to a family in which she has taken over the role of protector and manager; and how, at the same time, her personality has developed. The dependence of doña Paca and her children has produced in Benina a strong feeling of responsibility for their welfare and an affection for them which is an essential part of her own happiness. Because of this development, Benina's former reaction to an insecure position in society (manifest in her pilfering from her mistress, and then from her own savings for the benefit of her mistress) has changed into a courageous drive to meet the material necessities of life. Doña Paca's poverty and helplessness in practical affairs have, in fact, provided an opportunity for the development of Benina's individuality along three basic lines: the need to belong with others; protective concern for others, necessarily involving self-sacrifice; and practical, managerial ingenuity.

At first glance the greater part of the narrative which follows the expository chapter seems to be merely a descriptive elaboration of the personality first introduced. However, the heroine's "family" expands and her feeling of responsibility broadens and intensifies as she fights a losing battle against material odds. This is the impression received from the disseminated happenings, which seemingly have no progressive or dramatic sequence until near the end of the novel. In her continuous activity, for example, Benina appeals to the parsimonious don Carlos for money; calls for help on her friend, the blind Almudena, whose belief in magic momentarily intrigues her though she is too concerned with immediate necessities to trust in it; takes food to doña Paca's daughter, Obdulia; returns to the home of her mistress, where she explains her long absence by hastily inventing an imaginary priest, don Romualdo; starts out again to borrow money; learns of Ponte's miserable state, takes him to doña Paca's in order to care for him, and suffers the jealous, petulant harangue of her mistress while mothering her as she would a child.

During the course of such typical happenings as these, Benina's personality is expanding. Growing weary in her struggle, she feels the need for relaxation and retreats at times into a dreamworld, almost willing to believe in Almudena's communion with the supernatural, and definitely mystified by the appearance of a real don Romualdo, who seems to be a materialization of the imaginary priest who had become something of a moral support for her. But her concern with the tangible world maintains the upper hand. By dint of her constant efforts, she has expanded two outstanding acquirements. Through courage, self-discipline, and labor, she has developed an adjustability in which resignation takes an active form in self-sacrifice; and her concern for others, which remains always sincere and spontaneous, leads to an unconscious pride in her protective, managerial responsibilities. Her rescue of Ponte from impending starvation marks a stage of crystallization at which self-sacrifice, protective activity, and charity are absolute necessities to her being. When she again resorts to begging, only to be imprisoned in an asylum for beggars (Misericordia), her motherly pride in being needed at home is stronger than her shame at being arrested or her fear of doña Paca's displeasure.

Benina is faced with a supreme test when she returns to her mistress's home in company with Almudena, and finds that Juliana has taken over management of the family now that it has inherited money. In this test the basic components of her personality join in turmoil, revealing pride in her own importance, the need of belonging with the family, resignation, and consideration for other people. The last two in combination weigh most heavily as Benina makes her decision in the face of Juliana's refusal to admit her into the family again unless she deserts Almudena. The heroine's decision to remain with her needy friend is the logical outcome of a climactic test in the life of one who has come increasingly to place love of her fellow man above selfish interests.

The novel might have ended here, with a finality that would have left the emphasis on the cruelty of the world's injustice to an outstanding example of Christian love. The author, however, had something else in mind. For one thing, he wanted the final narrative effect to issue from a dramatic reversal of situation, in which Juliana, indirectly begging forgiveness, seeks Benina's reassurance concerning her children's health. For another, he was thinking of a final stage of personality growth. Another step was thus necessary to round out the story of character development. The immediate aftermath of the climactic scene of injustice is a preparation for change and may best be described as the transition from a ceaseless, almost routine activity on behalf of others to a philosophical contemplation of goodness and conformity with God's will.

Up to the time of her most important decision, Benina has had little time to ponder such abstractions as moral values, having taken for granted that charity and compassion were as spontaneous in others as in herself. Now she sees the necessity of defending them as a matter of principle; for her refusal to abandon Almudena brings with it a sudden realization that goodness is an indispensable guide in her life. Though stunned and angered momentarily, she rises above her defeat, looking upon material things as unimportant, and feeling that she has won a victory by renouncing physical comfort and conventional respectability in favor of kindness to those who need help. From a religious and philosophical viewpoint, her life henceforth will be on a higher plane, though still by way of action and not merely as devotion to an abstract value. In the final chapter of the novel Benina's practical adjustability has settled into a peaceful resignation still accompanied by self-sacrifice; while her urge to protect and manage for others, along with the need of serving and belonging with someone else, has now been fixed upon Almudena. The concluding scene, in which she pardons Juliana, portrays her with what have been her constant traits of humility, gratitude, tolerance, consideration of others' wishes, but it shows a more advanced stage of magnanimity and compassion than has hitherto been evident. Unconsciously Benina has acquired a philosophical equanimity and a simple, unaffected saintliness which now seem to rest upon her like a spiritual reward.

The psychological development in the protagonist, then, may be summarized as a combination of these factors: a practical adjustment to exigencies of the moment becoming a philosophical adjustment to the cruelties of injustice and ingratitude; a sense of responsibility for others developing into a personality need which becomes a drive involving self-sacrifice and pride in the responsibility; and the practice of kindness to a few growing into a personal philosophy of charity toward all. Benina's desire to protect and manage is kept from assuming a selfish nature by her sincerity toward individuals as such—not collectively or in the abstract; by her recognition of her humble social state; and by a basic flexibility in the face of necessity. The last is a prominent adjustive feature in her behavior at the time of her dismissal from doña Paca's, when any danger of selfish pride is abruptly ended. The story records the spontaneous manifestation of two major guides to conduct, altruism and practical confrontation with reality, as they merge in an ascending line of philosophical maturation. In short, it is the story of an increase in spirituality on the part of one whose stamina and virtues are strengthened in the crucible of struggle against materialistic opposition.

The secondary characters in *Misericordia,* particularly doña Paca and Almudena, are of importance in the narrative primarily as a means of bringing out the personality of the protagonist. Though slightly infected with the dreamworld escapism of one of these, Benina is concerned most of all with supplying the material needs of the other, and with mothering both of them. There may be some symbolical significance in the roles of doña Paca, helpless in her enslavement to superficial values; and of Almudena, wretched and despised in the eyes of society, but a brother with all men in the eyes of Benina. Viewed as psychological beings, they are both like children, violently upset and dependent when frustrated, and calm and relaxed when their needs are met; the one with money to satisfy her social vanity, the other with companionship to satisfy his need of affection.

Juliana is potentially a more serious character study. She is an example of overemphasis on efficiency and practicality. Her weakness finally causes her some remorse, but she is given relatively little space in the novel, and her change of heart toward Benina comes suddenly, without the reader's having had a chance to follow her struggle with conscience. In the appearance of a real don Romualdo to take the place of the imaginary priest, the author seemingly wishes to show symbolically how good (on the part of Benina) generates good, bringing into existence a concrete benefit to others. We must remember, of course, that the imaginary don Romualdo was a hasty invention, not an image of goodness, and that the real priest who brings news of doña Paca's inheritance is only an ordinary emissary performing a routine duty. It may be that the author wants to show the irony of the fact that Benina's own goodness resulted, by way of a materialization of her fancy, in a material gain which she could not share.

Almost any novel can be considered comprehensively, and simply, as a "picture" of some given section of life. In this broad sense, *Misericordia* exalts humble things and humble people, and raises to a place of dignity what are generally called commonplace realities.[5] Certainly a part of the reader's satisfaction comes from the author's treatment of miscellaneous scenes and characters. But the background, including a picture of the *barrios bajos* of Madrid, which is drawn with sympathy, humor, and restrained pathos, is but the cloak that envelops the narrative core. Admittedly, there is always justification for seeking an ulterior meaning in Galdós' novels, which is sometimes hidden and sometimes plain to the eye. The question is, how best to arrive at this meaning. Shall the setting, events, personages, and personal relationships be viewed as symbols of the author's generative ideas, or shall the characters first of all be regarded as living creatures whose natural behavior within a network of circumstances constitutes a story on which to base a judgment?

Professor Joaquín Casalduero, with characteristic abstractness, tends to follow the first approach. Thus he interprets *Misericordia*[6] as a presentation of the dual aspect of reality, in which the contraposition of tangible reality and the imagination leads to no tragic consequence because the opposites are connected by a bridge of *misericordia* and *piedad*. Almudena's main function is to raise the sight to the upper, mysterious levels of reality, which, however, must be reached by way of a pure conscience. Benina, who wavers between the real and the imaginary, passes from a lower to an upper level through the mysterious realm of *lo soñado*, a prominent phase of which is the episode of don Romualdo. She does so on the strength of piety and a clean conscience; and in the conclusion, Juliana's asking forgiveness symbolizes the means of attaining the reality of spirit. This suggestive interpretation puts the reader on the alert for the possible conceptual design in the author's mind but fails to get at the heart of the novel, which dwells in the person of Benina herself. Benina rises to spiritual heights, and her purity of conscience is all-important, but her ascent is a natural, laborious climb, which results from an adjustment to reverses and the consolidation of a charitable attitude toward all people, and not from contact with a world of mystery and imagination.

The surest way to define the plot of *Misericordia* is to visualize the resolution of what complications there are in the general situation, but to do so with special attention to the protagonist's character. The following statement of Professor William H. Shoemaker satisfies the first of these conditions: "The ultimate purport of the masterpiece *Misericordia* lies in the inspiring and blessed worldly irony of 'one of the least of these' becoming the first when Benina's Christian charity saves the selfish materialists of her mistress' family."[7] This is a summary of the story essentially from the standpoint of situation. It takes into account the self-sacrifice of a humble servant, her cruel dismissal, and her final benevolent response to Juliana's appeal for help. It therefore correctly defines what happens—that is, what happens on the surface. Will the meaning of the novel not become richer, and perhaps different, when it is interpreted as a story of developing personality? If Benina were a static character, the final narrative effect would depend almost wholly upon the emotion experienced by the reader in the presence of a triumph of Christian charity following close after an episode of injustice; and the conclusion would logically follow that the "message" is an exaltation of charity (in the sense of compassion) as opposed to materialistic, social values.

That this view of *Misericordia* is partially correct seems undeniable, but it directs attention more to the novel's moral tone than it does to the plot movement. On the other hand, the reader becomes aware of an active process of human nature if he observes how Benina actually grows in moral stature as her personality needs lead her increasingly into an expression of her basic trait of consideration for others, and how this trait, while crystallizing as a conscious guide to conduct, entails a deepening of benevolence and compassion. The contemplation of this process brings appreciation of a story that is psychologically dynamic, and at the same time it stimulates thinking in philosophical terms. The goodness of Benina is a growth which strengthens itself by its own activity, just as the strength of muscles increases with exercise. The moral advance, naturally, is grounded on enough virtue and courage to propel the individual forward in a vigorous contest with circumstances. The contest and the advance constitute the story; and a good part of the reader's aesthetic experience must surely be explained by the author's creation of a running stream of personal vicissitudes within an expanding circle of relationships, which swells, with the increasing force of Benina's charitable impulse, into one volumed movement.

The intrinsic significance of *Misericordia* is thus seen to be more than the dramatization of opposition between material and spiritual values. The novel is the story of a spiritualization that carries with it its own reward. It is possible to extend this view in a metaphysical direction by inquiring into the author's theory of spiritual advance, and thus to reach finally an Hegelian conception of human experience. But wherever the interpretation may lead, it should grow out of an analysis of the narrative as a consummate organized movement. For it must be assumed that a novel above all else tells a story; and from the total central experience recorded, it is the critic's responsibility to determine what the story is.

In its most characteristic form, the Galdós novel is a narrative account of the interaction between an expanding personality and a combination of environmental factors, circumstances, and events, which embrace a comparatively long period of time. For this reason it is profitable to regard the novels as if they were essentially biographies of individuals. Heavy emphasis thus falls upon the fundamental of character portrayal. In studying personages that carry the burden of the narrative, however, it is not enough to describe them merely by enumerating a fixed set of traits. It is necessary to know how they function as psychological beings and what impels them through the course of happenings wherein they contribute to an integrated plot. The novelist's conception of personality must therefore be examined in order to appreciate fully how he utilizes his knowledge of psychology in composing his stories.

II

PERSONALITY FORMATION

The Importance of Environment

IN the second half of the nineteenth century, physiological psychology was much in vogue, notably because of the influence of Herbert Spencer, Johannes Müller, and Wilhelm Wundt. Galdós reflects this interest in physiology without giving it undue emphasis. It is appropriate to observe, for example, that like Wundt (*Principles of Physiological Psychology*, 1874), who stressed the relation between anatomy, neurology, and psychology, he observed mental activity as a functioning of the organism to be explained in terms of physiological processes correlated with psychical motivations. It seems evident, withal, that he exercised independence of thought, calling, no doubt, upon his own observation of people.

Galdós is remarkably modern in his understanding of what are commonly taken to be the two basic components of personality: psychobiological factors, including intelligence, physique, and temperament or nervous constitution; and environmental influences. He differs from present-day psychologists primarily in his belief in innate character. Just how far this belief extends it is difficult to say, but it seems clear that he attaches considerable importance to it. He sees doña Perfecta as an example of religious fanaticism deeply rooted in a "naturally" hard heart that adheres to formula rather than simple deeds of kindness (IV, 497).[1] And he apparently would have the reader believe that Fortunata (*Fortunata y Jacinta*), who is sincere and sympathetic at heart, possesses a natural goodness and courage, in contrast, for example, with Mauricia *la Dura* and Juanito Santa Cruz. He never makes a statement to this effect, but the character portrayal supports the assertion, and the author himself declares, in reference to Fortunata's stay in a convent for fallen women:

En esto hay que contar con la índole; con el esqueleto espiritual, con esa forma interna y perdurable de la persona, que suele sobreponerse a todas las transfiguraciones epidérmicas producidas por la enseñanza. (V, 257)

If Galdós' practice did not clearly prove otherwise, the above statement might lead one to think that he discounted the effects of environment.

What the novelist calls "esa forma interna y perdurable de la persona" some psychologists of today would explain as idiosyncratic tendencies or constitutional predispositions. Most of them, in any event, would attribute greatest importance to the individual's early conditioning. Not interested in fine points of distinction, Galdós apparently regarded "strength of character" as being at least partially inherited. This is not an insignificant consideration in view of his faith in man's ability to rise above environment, but in so far as his portrayal of individual character is concerned, it matters little whether he believed that certain traits, such as courage and sincerity, are innate or acquired. A more important subject is the use that he makes of his psychological knowledge in the portrayal of character.

Galdós visualizes personality always as a combination of interlocking forces, including intelligence and physique, but he is less interested in these two than he is in his characters' moral qualities. As a general rule he devotes little space to physical and intellectual traits in his expositional passages; he simply takes them for granted as harmonious parts of the total portraits. At times, however, he deliberately calls attention to his characters' mental equipment. In *Fortunata y Jacinta,* for example, the intellectual talents of Juanito Santa Cruz are deliberately included as an integral part of the personality development. Juanito— whose characterization at first promises to be a substantial one, only to be later neglected—finds himself pulled between the *lozanía* of the *pueblo* and the conventional standards of his own class. Having acquired an habitual irresponsibility as the pampered son of a wealthy family, he tries halfheartedly to embrace a set of solid personal values. But he is superficially disturbed by his conflict and satisfies his ego by an increasing sense of superiority bred of his philosophical sophistication, which hardens eventually into face-saving pride, the major trait with which the author finally and summarily dismisses him. It is clearly understood in the first part of the novel that Juanito was *inteligente* as well as *instruído,* and his case is plainly an illustration of how intellectual potentiality is turned by environmental conditioning into a channel of sophistication and cynicism, thus to be used almost wholly as an evasion of moral responsibility. This portraiture of misplaced natural talent clearly demonstrates the care with which Galdós, even with secondary characters and with little comment on native traits, integrates one component of personality with another in a consistent whole.

Among the hereditary physical and mental constituents of personality, temperament is the one factor most emphasized by Galdós. In this respect the portrait of Rosario, doña Perfecta's daughter, is representative of a prominent phase of the author's physical perspective for the whole of his career. Rosario is a delicate girl whose sensitive nervous constitution gradually gives way under the repressive force of her mother's tyranny. Her portrait is thinly sketched, but the reader is fully conscious of a physical-mental development, climactically presented by the author, as the young woman passes from tearful reactions to fainting spells, nervous illness, delirium, and finally to madness, itself a family disease. Rosario is a prototype of Gloria, not only as a victim of rigid traditions, but also as an example of physical deterioration under emotional stress. In Marianela, too, a fragile constitution breaks under an excessive strain which ends in death.

Temperament continues always to be the psycho-biological feature of most consequence in Galdós' portraiture. It becomes less conspicuous in his late novels—when these are viewed collectively—not because the author ceases to believe in its importance, but because his widening perspective of human relations enables him to portray character from the vantage ground of a broad frame of reference. For the most part, mental and constitutional traits are given a supplementary position only, in character and plot development alike. The temperaments of Eloísa and José María (*Lo prohibido*) help to explain their vehement passions and lack of restraint, but are of purely secondary importance in comparison with environmental conditioning in an atmosphere of collective mediocrity. Fundamental in the personality of Maximiliano Rubín (*Fortunata y Jacinta*), one of Galdós' best portraitures, is his delicate nervous constitution, which partially accounts for his madness. His madness develops, however, only because of the battering force of external causes, including domination by an officious aunt, the slight esteem of acquaintances, and defeat by a virile competitor for his wife's love. In *Angel Guerra*, which was written when Galdós undeniably was preoccupied with values that transcend the material world, the author shows as much interest in the psycho-biological aspects of personality as at any previous time.[2] The central character, sensitive and unstable, eventually makes a wholesome adjustment, largely because of the edifying influence of love for a woman; but he is consistently portrayed throughout the novel as a high-strung youth whose excitability and visions are traceable to a nervous temperament aggravated by his early family relationships.

These various examples are typical of Galdós' proportioned treatment of personality. Physical and nervous causes figure in the total picture, but at no time does the author concentrate upon physiological study. In his early works he observes especially the physical breakdown caused by emotional stress. His emphasis then shifts to an observation of psychical adjustment, and with this, a study of individual morality. Except for description of surface manifestations of emotions (gestures, bodily movement, and the like), he places relatively little weight on physiology.

In his observation of nervous and mental disorders, Galdós reflects the current opinion of his day. As the study of psychiatry in the nineteenth century emerged from the spiritualistic schools of the previous centuries, it became focused upon three main beliefs with respect to mental diseases: (1) hereditary causes or hereditary predisposition, (2) organic lesion or encephalic alterations, and (3) dynamic development under stress of external circumstances.[3] Even in Spain, which lagged behind in psychiatric as well as other sciences, an effort was made to formulate an exact analysis of the different kinds of mental diseases. Around the mid-century much weight was given to temperament, to neurological predisposition to insanity, and to physical condition as causes of nervous disorders. But also noticeable was the recognition that insanity is often closely identified with the insecurity deriving from the vicissitudes of social and professional life or the conditions of home life; in short, that emotional stress from personal and group relationships is an important factor in the study of nervous diseases.[4]

Galdós undoubtedly was interested in psychiatry, but like most of the Spanish doctors, he was a much better describer of the outward manifestations of mental disorders than he was a diagnostician. As a novelist, of course, he felt only a minor responsibility for diagnosis. The subject attracted him, nevertheless, and his views seem to be a repetition of the current psychological and medical opinion of his day. His depiction of the depressive and excitative phases of psychical disturbances, which frequently precede his characters' hallucinations and visions (of Maximiliano Rubín, Angel Guerra, and Nazarín, for example), could have been based upon ideas developed by Wundt.[5] But in reference to basic causes, his knowledge conforms fundamentally with such general explanations as the following from Juan Drumen's *Patología médica* (1850):

Basta que un sujeto sea naturalmente débil o que se encuentre accidentalmente debilitado para que empiecen a desenvolverse en él, aunque en grados diferentes, los fenómenos nerviosos.

El temperamento sanguíneo y una constitución pletórica predisponen a la manía. La frecuencia de la locura está siempre en armonía con profesiones que colocan al hombre en mayor dependencia de las vicisitudes sociales.[6]

The number of nervously unstable characters appearing throughout Galdós' novels is large enough to reveal the novelist's serious interest in abnormal psychology and to show that he attached great significance to temperament and the aggravating effects of social relations as sources of nervous disorders. A thorough analysis of the subject—a separate study in itself—lies outside the limits of the present task; but any separate treatment would necessarily have to take into account the author's conception of environmental influences. For environment is, in Galdós' mind, the most important factor in the formation of personality.

In his treatment of environment, Galdós emphasizes first the set of personal relationships peculiar to each individual, and secondly, the collective ideas of society when viewed as a large unit. Within this complex, the individual is seen to absorb beliefs, acquire attitudes, form habits, both mental and physical, and become in a very considerable degree the product of a particular social medium. There are two different phases to the use that the novelist makes of environmental influences: one phase pertaining to traits acquired by the characters before the narrative begins, and the other to the development and modification of these traits during the progress of the narrative. The first is expositive of personal background, and the second is an indispensable part of the total movement of the story.

The author's interest in the introductory phase of his character study appears on two general levels of importance as regards function in the narrative as a whole. In some of the novels we are aware of personal background primarily as harmonizing with the characters' behavior without its being made to explain their motives. The significance is largely that of descriptive consistency (exemplified in *La de Bringas*, *El doctor Centeno*, and *Halma*) and is scarcely more than the usual nineteenth-century practice of identifying character and setting in a descriptive manner. In a much larger number of the novels, and significantly in the most outstanding, the conditioning prior to the beginning of the narrative action is integrated functionally with the portrayal of progressive modification. It can be seen to exert a directive force during the characters' recorded experiences, which constitute in themselves a continuous formative process of interaction between native properties and surroundings. A story thus becomes substantially an account of the way in which a person meets his difficulties in accord with the equipment bestowed upon him by nature and environment.

With most of the novels it is possible to demonstrate in tabular form how the principal characters' conditioning prior to the beginning of the narrative, in combination with native constitutional traits, harmonizes with, if it does not actually account for, their essential behavior. For purposes of illustration, the central personage of *Miau* (1888) may be used, beginning with a table of personality factors classified according to background, needs and aspirations, and the manner in which the individual responds in his efforts to adjust to circumstances:

BACKGROUND
  Natural:
    physical weakness, nervous instability
  Environmental:
    domination by wife, dependence on bureaucracy, dependence on approval of professional group

NEEDS AND ASPIRATIONS
  relaxation
  independence
  self-assurance
  affection (family)
  security
  expansiveness
  belongingness with professional group

ADJUSTIVE BEHAVIOR
  nervous frustration
  moodiness
  timidity
  passivity
  castigatory defense (suspicious, denunciatory attitude toward others)
  rationalization of responsibility
  retreat from reality

As the novel begins, the basic part of Miau's personality is assumed to have been formed during long years of government employment and a subsequent period of unemployment made even more painful by unpleasant relationships within his family. Although Miau's native temperament partly explains his adjustive reactions, his story is essentially one of maladjustment growing out of the circumstances of home and professional life. A well-meaning and affable, though mediocre, man is ill prepared for a harsh battle with the reality of unemployment because of his lack of stamina and his childish submissiveness, both of which have been engendered or at least furthered by his total dependence upon bureaucracy and a domineering wife. While feebly hoping for reinstatement, he tries to maintain his self-respect by remembering the esteem in which he was once held by his professional group; and he satisfies his need of affection with the love of his grandson Luisito. But his major reaction takes the form of puerile emotionalism, the shifting of responsibility to others, and passive resignation. An intensification of neurotic responses develops out of his inability to surmount his difficulties and leads to insanity, which enables him to achieve a temporary satisfaction in the guise of "philosophical" superiority over his immediate surroundings. Though he regains his sanity, he retains his emotional equilibrium and his feeling of relaxation only because of his decision to commit suicide, his final act of retreat from reality. Indirectly, of course, the novel is a demonstration of the evils of a government system that fosters irresponsibility and a lack of versatility in the individual.

It should be obvious that Galdós' attention to environment is much more than literary convention, but in order to make the point still clearer, it will help to look at a different kind of novel by another author. Juan Valera was not a realist, and yet he frequently employed a realistic method in a superficial manner. This superficial realism is characteristic of *Doña Luz* (1879), which is illustrative of what may be called Valera's classical idealism. The first part of *Doña Luz*—about one fourth of the whole—appears to be an introduction to the study of an individual character in whose formation environment is a significant factor. The aristocratic training of doña Luz and her uncertainty regarding her mother's identity explain the courteous aloofness and determined circumspection in her efforts to compensate for her illegitimate birth. These dominant traits guide her into a life of semireclusion in a provincial town and orient her toward the contemplation of ideal love, a kind of romantic mysticism, which finds occasion for active expression on the arrival of Padre Enrique. Her platonic relations with the latter satisfy her starved emotions and her pride concerning elevated moral and intellectual principles, until she is suddenly made aware of the possibility that Padre Enrique is in love with her.

At this point in his story, Valera changes his method from a character study to a plot of events and coincidence. The arrival of the elegant *diputado* don Jaime coincides with doña Luz's decision to break off her relations with Padre Enrique. Her marriage completes momentarily her withdrawal from the priest, but her subsequent discovery of don Jaime's duplicity turns her again, at the time of Padre Enrique's illness and death, to the platonic relationship. Meanwhile the author, passing superficially over the rapid sequence of events in doña Luz's life, has concentrated his major interest on a description of the priest's emotions, which is not so much a psychological analysis as it is a poetic essay on one of his favorite themes: the Neoplatonic conception of earthly love and beauty as reflections of the Absolute.

In short, it turns out that Valera has used the information on the formative period of doña Luz's personality merely as a mechanical device to set the stage for an event. Since the novel, aside from the expositional section, is not a story of a developing character, the environmental conditioning is of incidental importance to the whole, and was probably included out of deference to novelistic convention. Galdós, by contrast, would have studied the central personality more closely after the expositional part than during it, carrying the background material forward to a careful observation of immediate environmental relationships, and at the same time subordinating events to the total view of character development.

With the exception of the three novels written after 1900 (*Casandra, El caballero encantado,* and *La razón de la sinrazón*), which are hardly representative of the social novels as a whole, Galdós is just as alert to the significance of environment in his late as in his early works. The important consideration in this connection is not the amount of background material, including information on family histories and social conditions, but the use to which this information is put. The novels of the 1880's display at greatest length the nineteenth-century realistic practice of supplying abundant exposition and description of setting. This heavy background material is particularly noticeable in *Fortunata y Jacinta,* but the interest in environmental influence is no greater in this novel than in *Angel Guerra* and *Misericordia,* in which the exposition is abbreviated and delayed. Even when Galdós modifies his technique in the *novelas dialogadas,* sharply curtailing exposition and description, the information on personality background is just as integral to the portraiture as if it were elaborately presented in separate sections of the stories. Notable examples are Federico Viera (*Realidad*) and José María Cruz (*La loca de la casa*). These characters occupy principal roles, but what has been said thus far applies also to the minor characters, in a degree roughly proportionate to their prominence in the plots.

Although Galdós emphasized environment, in general conformity with the ideas of an age that had awakened to its meaning, it must not be assumed that he at any time apotheosized it. He would have been the first to insist upon the consequence of innate qualities of personality, and he would have denied that the same general milieu will produce the same results in different people. He regarded environment as the complex of relationships in which a person is involved, especially those relationships pertaining to family and associates, to social groups, and in lesser degree to society collectively. He placed relatively little stress upon physical surroundings such as favorable or unfavorable housing conditions and material facilities. With his interest thus focused upon social relations, Galdós was always aware that the immediate individual-social complex, including inherent tendencies, is inevitably different for every human being. Moreover, he strikes a balance between the individual and the external world, and he never subscribes to the belief that environment must necessarily triumph over man. He asserts in *El amigo Manso* (1882) "que es ley que el mundo sea nuestro molde y no nuestra hechura" (IV, 1208). But in the same novel he also says,

> ¿Fué un mal o un bien para Irene haber nacido entre escaseces y haber educado en esa negra academia de la desgracia que a muchos embrutece y a otros depura y avalora, según el natural de cada uno? (IV, 1188)

And in *Fortunata y Jacinta* (1886-1887) he seems deliberately to be refuting the deterministic theory when he contrasts the cleanliness and dignity of the young girl Adoración and her aunt with their surroundings (I, IX, *viii*).[7]

The points set forth in the foregoing paragraph are of paramount importance in connection with the question of Galdós' "naturalism,"[8] especially if this term is identified—as logically it must be—with the novels of Galdós' French contemporary, Zola. The Spanish novelist believes as firmly in the power of environment as Zola does, but his interpretation is different. For one thing, the French novelist concentrates upon the physical world rather than the network of personal, social relations. For another, his beliefs conform with an early conception of the theory of evolution that visualizes man essentially as a passive being subject to external forces over which he has little or no control. On both counts, the difference between the two writers is pronounced. A comparison of specific novels will make the distinction clear.

In *L'Assommoir* (1877) Zola proposes to demonstrate the degeneration of a family under the oppressive forces of poverty, ignorance, and drink. He constructs his narrative around Gervaise, the central personage. He shows less interest in the formative period of Gervaise's

personality and in the change in her sense of values and adjustive behavior than in the accumulation of external circumstances which cause
her moral breakdown. The circumstances are presented first as a collective picture of unfavorable conditions in a district for the working classes
in Paris, where fetid physical unpleasantness, poverty, ignorance, and
drunkenness combine to produce an over-all unity of bestiality.

Gervaise is thus forced to test her strength against a collective force
that stands apart from her like a superhuman being. She is basically a
person of strong character, honest, industrious, orderly, idealistic, with
simple domestic tastes, content to live a modest, sensible life. She is
enabled to strengthen these characteristics for a few years in a happy
marriage with Coupeau; but a crucial test comes when her husband,
after an accident which incapacitates him for work, begins to drink and
in fact becomes a drunkard almost overnight.

Gervaise maintains her usual stamina for a long time, but sensuality, her main weakness—which as far as we can tell is of long standing rather than engendered by her immediate surroundings—gains control as she gives in to the sensual pursuit of Lantier. Suddenly she
becomes lazy and indifferent, *embêtée* presumably by her environment.
Her change is understandable in view of the drunkenness of her husband and the miserable conditions in her home. The suddenness of her
reversal of conduct may also be regarded as a natural relaxation of will
after years of tense resistance, but Zola has not followed the psychological preparation for change from within. Instead, he has stressed the
heaviness of the forces from without, as though he were determined to
crush his central character in order to prove his theory. So it is that
unfavorable conditions increase in intensity, the general brutification
becomes greater, and the sympathetic characters decrease in number,
especially after Gervaise's deterioration sets in.

The novel is not an account of psychological development in relation
to surroundings, but the story of a person who breaks under the constant
hammering of adverse circumstances, much like a culprit's breakdown
under the severe treatment of the third degree. Zola does not prove that
environment determines character nor even that it determines the outcome of a person's life. He merely demonstrates that an ordinary human being will give way under constant punishment. Nana, the daughter of Gervaise and Coupeau, on the other hand, is portrayed in close
relation to the surroundings that help to form her character and lead
her into prostitution, but she is an incidental personage. As far as the
narrative core of the novel is concerned, the author produces a vigorous

story of events, dynamically depicting harsh realities, including the rough activity of people at work or in their physical relief from oppressive circumstances. His artistic enthusiasm and his strength lie in his description of the physical world.

By contrast, Galdós is interested only incidentally in the scenic presentation of physical surroundings and the portrayal of life in its external movement, and primarily in an observation of the principal characters' social and moral behavior. In accord with this major interest, he integrates environmental influence with personality development. An examination of *La desheredada,* one of his "naturalistic" novels, will illustrate.

In this novel the author makes clear that the highly sensitive temperament of his protagonist, Isidora Rufete, which is directly related to a family background of insanity, accounts in part for her impractical living. But the story of maladjustment and deterioration is more definitely constructed on the persistency of a set of social values. Isidora is an emotionally unstable woman of refined tastes, sincere and spontaneously friendly, who allows her need of belonging to become fixed upon the worship of social caste. Attendant upon this ideal are her aesthetic tastes, her love of luxury, and her anti-*vulgo* attitude, which hardens into a dominant characteristic of vanity and hauteur. Her sacrifice of the usual virtues pertaining to work, economy, and moral relationship with men continues for some time without serious detriment to the integrity of her personality, because of the steadying force of a firm belief in her noble birth; but her habitual conduct becomes more and more escapist and evasive. As a result of continued disappointments with respect to aristocratic aspirations, it increasingly assumes the form of nervous and castigatory reactions, self-pity, and finally a martyrlike self-punishment. In the prolonged vacillation between reality and illusion, Isidora cultivates in some degree a sense of practical values and tries to embrace a standard of self-respect based upon humility, honesty, and work; but her habit of evasion is too strong for a reversal of adjustment, and her self-esteem continues to rest upon a desperate belief in her noble origin. When this support to her integrity is finally and totally undermined, she reacts hysterically at first and then breaks decisively as she descends rapidly to prostitution, though trying feebly to preserve her self-respect by dissociating herself from the name that has identified her with society. In this last step she follows the escapist pattern of one who has dodged responsibility always, worshiping illusions, and assuming a childish, emotional attitude that culminates in a defiant egoism manifest in a glorified self-punishment.

La desheredada, then, is not the story of a personal contest with a heavy physical force composed of depressive living conditions and biological instincts. It is the story of a person who develops certain basic traits in the form of ideals, attitudes, and adjustive habits from a set of personal relations and the ideas of society at large. In Galdós' novel, environment is a complex of social and moral ideas. As such, it indirectly and partially determines the character's action; but what defeats Isidora, after all, is largely of her own choosing: the pursuit of a false value.

Further contrast between the naturalistic treatment of environment and that found in Galdós can be shown by examining a novel of Blasco Ibáñez, the Spanish writer who most closely follows Zola's lead. *Cañas y barro* (1902) is hardly a novel of character, but it does have some resemblance to a typical Galdosian socio-psychological narrative. If it is judged as such, Tonet is the central character, and it is possible to reconstruct around him a developing story of personality. Growing up as an undisciplined youth, pulled alternately between control by his father and his grandfather, two persons of conflicting ideals, Tonet develops a dominant trait of shiftlessness, which becomes at the same time a lethargic kind of rebellion against a background of poverty and misery. The habit of dodging responsibility grows and makes him an easy prey to domination by the strong-willed Neleta. Having no fixed values aside from sensual pleasure and materialistic ease, he supports his self-esteem by talk of his exploits in war and an occasional assertion of independence by way of hunting trips. His basic adjustment by evasion comes to a culminating point in a rebellious rationalization of blame for the murder of his own child, and a final surrender (in suicide) to his own futility.

A similar environmental background explains Neleta's rebellious and determined aggressiveness, which becomes a drive for material wealth and the domination of others, and which hardens into the fierce pursuit of a goal that completely overshadows her sensuality. Neleta becomes in effect the personification of a single motive, and her personality story assumes the abstractness of a thematic demonstration.

Neither the story of Tonet nor that of Neleta, however, nor of the two together, constitutes the integrated "experience" produced by *Cañas y barro*. Nor do the *cuadro* scenes—artistic units in themselves—assume enough importance to make the story a novel of customs. The novel must be considered as a portraiture of the swamp region, the Albufera, in its relation to the people under its heavy shadow. The Albufera's oppressive influence is seen in Tonet (lethargic irresponsibility which leads to tragedy); in *tío* Toni and *la Borda,* Tonet's father and foster sister (numbness and stupor accompanying their tragic disillusionment with reference to family ties and the futility of their efforts at an orderly, industrious existence); in Neleta (materialistic hardness which brings tragedy to others); and in the brutification seen in collective character. The central aesthetic experience brought vividly to the reader by Blasco Ibáñez radiates from the picture of a mass struggle against a gigantic external force that is largely physical. Lengthy passages that leave an impression of the deadening influence of a heavy physical atmosphere, scenes of the lushness of primitive nature—both external and in the form of the instincts of sex and fear—and the final tragic note of futility as *tío* Toni and *la Borda* bury Tonet, all contribute to a somber overtone in a picture of man caught in the web of an irresistible fate. The picture is localized in a struggle between the Albufera and various persons whose individuality is swallowed up by an all-powerful Nature.

Environment in this novel, then, appears chiefly as a kind of mechanical force separate from man and pushing against him like a huge material object, and this conception constitutes a major point of similarity between Blasco Ibáñez and Zola. Environment in the sense of the formative influence of social and personal relationships, as handled by Galdós, helps to explain why the characters of Blasco Ibáñez are what they are; but the story itself is essentially a narrative of culminating events rather than of culminating psychological development. Sociopsychological motives and adjustive behavior could be forgotten without seriously altering the story of *Cañas y barro.* In *La desheredada,* they make up the indispensable core of the story as a whole.

In speaking of Galdós' naturalism, therefore, a distinction should be made between physical environment and the environment of ideas. It is also necessary to comprehend the novelist's vision of man's ability or inability to rise above his surroundings. With Galdós, the individual's ability to direct his own destiny is qualified by his conditioning in a particular set of circumstances. Thus environment, in a broad sense, is always an unescapable determinant; and it is true that for some fifteen years at the beginning of his career the novelist saw his characters as victims more often than as masters. This outlook, however, was nothing more than a manifestation of the young writer's rebellious attitude toward institutions and social beliefs in Spain—an expression of ideological fervor rather than a special literary manner or philosophic perspective. Isidora (*La desheredada*) is a victim of the worship of social caste, just as doña Perfecta is of ecclesiastic formalism. And José María Bueno de Guzmán, the central character of *Lo prohibido* (1884-1885), is the victim of a national attitude of complacency in the atmosphere of a stagnant *status quo*. On the basis of the author's attention to heredity, environment, and sensuality, *Lo prohibido* is commonly considered one of Galdós' most naturalistic works, but its similarity to a novel of Zola is slight.

The explanation is to be found in the author's treatment of individual character. José María comes to Madrid, after having gained financial independence, and settles down to a life of idleness and ease. He engages one of his cousins (Eloísa) in an illicit love affair, tires of her, tries unsuccessfully to seduce her sister (Camila), and before he dies, wills his money to Camila in a show of penitent reversal of his waywardness. Meanwhile, he has written his memoirs as an exercise in self-instruction and the instruction of others. He thus tries to compensate for his failure in life; for he has been motivated all along by a desire to belong in a peaceful and respectable family relationship, which he has come to identify with the morally responsible Camila, a symbol of the kind of respectability from which he is excluded. His sensuousness, manifest in his quest of that which is prohibited (*lo prohibido*), is more the result of a life of indolence than of the relentless force of primitive nature. José María himself realizes this and makes excuses for his lack of moral stamina, blaming his milieu and the passions "inherited" from his father. In like manner, his hereditary physical weakness in the form of nervous disorders is used as an excuse for self-pity and the evasion of responsibility. The author devotes some space to family history in the introductory part of the narrative, in which he speaks of the abnormal tendencies in the family background; but the novel is not in the least a clinical study. The recurring nervous illness assumes in itself no more importance than a case of chronic rheumatism incidentally referred to. The story is above all the history of an anchorless individual who drifts into moral evasion while hovering wistfully on the doorsteps of moral respectability, and like a *pícaro,* rationalizing his failure in terms of environment and inherent nature. The psychological pattern is much the same as that of the dual personality of moralist and rogue found in Mateo Alemán's *Guzmán de Alfarache.*[9]

In *Lo prohibido* Galdós is interested primarily in the subject of morality as seen against the background of a society steeped in an attitude of static complacency which encourages shiftless behavior in certain people. The weak individual is chosen in this case for the purposes of magnifying evil social attitudes and not of demonstrating the weakness of man collectively in the face of a deified environment. Even with reference to this aspect of the subject, it must be remembered that in his so-called naturalistic period of the 1880's, Galdós did not always present an unhealthy view of individual morality. An example is Felipe Centeno, in *El doctor Centeno* (1883). At the comparatively late date of 1892, on the other hand, *Tristana* exhibits the passivity of an individual under environmental influence. At no time, however, does Galdós use a particular case to generalize upon the inability of the human species to rise above its surroundings. *Guzmán de Alfarache* is more naturalistic than *Lo prohibido*, because Alemán in the throes of his personal turmoil visualizes man in the generic sense as hopelessly victimized by a materialistic world ruled by social evils and the sinfulness inherited from Adam. Galdós interests himself simply in the evasive-conformist behavior of an individual who easily adopts the mediocrity of his society.

That the Spanish novelist was in some degree affected by the naturalism which was crystallized by Zola into a special literary manner is unmistakable, but the fact is of less significance than it is sometimes made to assume. For this reason, it is perhaps excusable to prolong the discussion a bit further and consider certain aspects besides the relationship between character and environment. Along with a "scientific" objective, which actually became a poetic display of energy and fantasy, Zola exhibited in practice several features that were quickly noticed and imitated by his contemporaries. Most important of these are: a prodigious accumulation of factual material relating to the external world, a frank revelation of the crudities and brutalities of life, a tendency to emphasize animalistic characteristics in people, the choice of unconventional subjects for the central narrative, and by no means least of all, a sober "impersonality" in style, which is lacking in humorous relief though not devoid of sympathy. These features were but an extension of the realistic technique and differ from it only in degree.

Galdós followed the trends of his day in the presentation of factual detail on the material world, in reproducing in moderate degree the crudities of life and even the animalistic side of human nature. In this practice he naturally exhibits an affinity with Zola, though probably no more than he does with Balzac. The practice is characteristic of his entire career and is almost as conspicuous in *Nazarín* (1895), a study of religion and mysticism, as in *La desheredada* (1881). Brief scenes of coarse, unpleasant physical phenomena are somewhat more noticeable in the novels of the 1880's but by no means limited to them.

La desheredada, however, does have several specific though superficial marks of similarity with Zola's writings and is the one Galdós novel that can justifiably be called naturalistic. There are certain passages in its introductory part, where the slums of Madrid are described, that definitely recall Zola's unrefined details on comparable districts in Paris. A further point of similarity is the author's attention to physical deterioration in Isidora's brother Mariano. Heredity takes its toll in a progressive development of emotional instability, epileptic attacks, and mental degeneration, which is seen against the background of an unfavorable environment. Mariano, of course, is strictly a secondary character. Neither here nor in any of the novels does a study of hereditary physical weakness constitute in itself the main narrative theme. In spite of these similarities, the fundamental consideration of style must be kept in mind; for Galdós' informal, humorous, and picturesque treatment contrasts with Zola's grimness and reveals a deep-rooted difference in philosophic outlook.

The fact that *La desheredada* tells the story of a woman who becomes a prostitute is a reason sometimes offered for calling it naturalistic. Galdós' contemporaries identified with naturalism such a choice of subject matter,[10] and this guide for classification would in all probability be popularly accepted even to this day. That the central character degenerates is more significant—change in Zola usually means change for the worse—but still does not identify the novel with any special school of writing. Emma Bovary's character deteriorates, too, but certainly Flaubert's novel is far from being naturalistic in the manner of Zola. The indispensable basis for comparison is the cause of degeneration, which in Isidora's case is the inflexible adherence to a false ideal. In this respect, Isidora is much more comparable to Flaubert's heroine than to the central character of *L'Assommoir,* for example.

The fact that Galdós' novels up to 1890, roughly, are somewhat more physiological in treatment than his later works is explained by his early alertness to scientific knowledge and his enthusiasm for exploiting a new field of interest. It does not mean that he believed in the preponderance of the physical over the spiritual man. His naturalism, therefore, should be largely discounted. He was first and always a realist and followed the nineteenth-century trend of stressing the relationship between personality and environment. This development is in fact a fundamental of modern realism, manifest in some writers as a literary convention and in others as an integral part of their narratives. Galdós belongs to the latter group. In his novels environment must be taken to mean the particular set of conditions in which individual personality develops; especially those pertaining to the immediate family and personal relations, and in lesser degree to the social structure of community and nation.

The novelist's attention centers first on the formation of values and habits which the outer, social world, in combination with innate tendencies, has effected prior to the beginning of the narrative. In so far as this expositional material is concerned, it is often little more than general information relating, for example, to an orphan child, a domineering mother, a favorable or unfavorable chance in the world. If the information is presented in a prominent, systematic way, it is treated summarily and does not form a study in itself. Were it not for the fact that Galdós integrates this material with the whole of his characterizations, it could be considered of little importance. At most it is but an introductory step in a carefully observed interrelationship between the character's self-assertiveness and the restraining, molding influence of external, social forces. The body of one of the biographical stories is formed out of an extension and expansion of what is known already to have happened in the personal history.

As seen at the beginning of a Galdosian novel, then, the individual has been equipped by nature with certain qualities of strength and weakness and has assimilated environmental effects by acquiring attitudinal and adjustive habits. Thus prepared, he is launched into a specifically observed contest with circumstances, where he stands on approximately equal terms with the forces that surround him. This contest, in which formative influences continue to be operative, constitutes the personality story. Galdós' major interest, therefore, centers upon the immediate functioning of the individual-social relationship, which is at all times active. Any part of a person's life is suitable for this kind of fictional treatment, since personality is assumed to be always in a process of formation. A narrative which thus pictures environment and personality jointly operative is essentially a study in individual adjustment, an observation of changing values and modified habits—in a word, a depiction of growth.

III

COMPLEXITY OF PERSONALITY

Adjustment and Change

THE literary artist at best can give only a partial view of the sensitivity, complexity, and adaptability of the individual. (The scientist himself in less degree is similarly restricted.) He is forced into a technique of selection, of accentuating certain characteristics and subordinating others. In doing this, he is actually adhering to a pattern of normality and authenticity, for each person controls his essential behavior in accord with a few dominant traits. Novelists and dramatists traditionally portray characters of a relatively simple combination of traits, depending upon an integration of these toward some urgent goal, or a conflict between two or three of them, to produce the impression of a life situation.

The realists of the nineteenth century sought to enhance the impression of conformity with observable reality by broadening the range of character traits through attention to multiplicity and variety. This technique often results in a descriptive presentation of comparatively unimportant features pertaining to looks, mannerisms, tastes, and emotional reactions to numerous circumstances unrelated or incidental to the main narrative problem. It has the effect, however, of impressing the reader with "recognizability" in terms of his everyday experiences and acquaintances. Moreover, the realists' desire to avoid the one-sidedness of Romanticism accounts for their inclusion of attributes that offset or balance each other. In simple terms, this means that the hero or the heroine is not altogether handsome and noble or beautiful and pure. But it does not necessarily follow that the realist takes into account major incongruities in individual character—even when portraying abnormal personalities.

The early realists of the nineteenth century give in general a picture of surface irregularities while presenting congruous psychological portraits having a few dominant and harmonious traits. Their characterizations also tend toward what is typical of a chosen social group. The portraiture of "types" is an extreme consequence of the dual tendency to portray characters in simple, harmonious lines and to use contemporary social life as subject matter. This technique, which dates from at least as far back as Theophrastus, becomes especially prominent in the novel of customs of the nineteenth century. A novelist, of course, may attend to what is representative of contemporary society and still give his characters the stamp of individuality by having them react under particular circumstances in a slightly different manner from others in their social group, or by allowing them to react differently at different times. A "type" portrait automatically results if a character is catalogued under one or two traits representative of a social or biological group and is made always to act in such a way as to display these traits.

Although in real life there is no such thing as a type, there are common aspects of personality, of which a special manifestation may be so emphasized in fiction as to abstract an "individual" from his species and make of him a synthetic representative. Such is the case, for example, when an author restricts his characterization by concentrating, in a descriptive and commentarial manner, on an individual's vanity with respect to personal appearance. Yet the common aspects of ego-ascendance and ego-preservation, which underlie vanity, assume breadth and magnitude when seen to impel the individual toward an urgent personal achievement. In this case the character, still an abstraction, may appropriately be called a "human" type, or a symbol of a basic human compulsion. This kind of characterization has an advantage over the purely descriptive, static delineation of a social specimen, because of the interest attached to the character's efforts to realize an ideal. Under this general classification are found some of the most famous literary portraits—Don Quijote, Emma Bovary, Julien Sorel, for example. The social type moves into the realm of the human type when he is given a role of persistent striving, with his typifying attributes focused on the attainment of a specific goal. In this way, even the penurious man can be made to appear as a symbol of the human urge to preserve one's sense of individual worth.

These facts about character portrayal are especially pertinent to the discussion of a nineteenth-century novelist. For more than half of the century the major tendency in the novel was to view human beings as conforming to general social patterns, and in harmony with the earlier philosophical conception of a fixed and static universe, to describe them as though individual character were consistent and unchanging. As regards characterization, the novelist fulfilled his artistic mission through his talent for descriptive delineation, through concentration upon a person's dominating motives, or through psychological analysis of the person's reactions to specific situations. The personalities in a given novel remained essentially the same throughout the course of the story, the variation being little more than elaboration on static traits. The decisive and sometimes sudden reversal of character in the romantic tradition can be considered an exception to the above statement, but such a change usually appears more as plot manipulation on the part of the author than as a natural personality development.

The new viewpoint in philosophical thought accompanying the rise of the theory of evolution brought to the novel a tendency to look upon personality itself as a developing process having its causes in environment. Hence fictional characters began to show marks of change brought about by their relation to their immediate surroundings. The inclusion in the novel of such general knowledge as the difference in an individual between the time of his youth and his later age, of course, was nothing new in literature. It should be remembered, too, that Cervantes left a picture of modification in personality in his depiction of the Don Quijote-Sancho Panza partnership. But the modernity of the nineteenth-century novelists consisted in their observation of a person's change within an immediate and persistent relationship with the environmental conditions that cause the change by necessitating adjustment. The Spanish picaresque novel anticipates the modern novel of environment and change, but in an almost unconscious way on the part of writers who could not comprehend the possibilities of a new viewpoint. In the nineteenth century, on the other hand, writers were conscious of and even enthusiastic about a new idea which centered especially on man's adjustive capacity. The following remarks of Samuel Butler are indicative of the importance attached by writers of his day to the role of adjustment:

> All our lives long, every day and every hour, we are engaged in the process of accommodating our changed and unchanged selves to changed and unchanged surroundings; living, in fact, in nothing else than this process of accommodation. . . . In quiet, uneventful lives the changes internal and external are so small that there is little or no strain in the process of fusion and accommodation; in other lives there is great strain, but there is also great fusing and accommodating power. A life will be successful or not according as the power of accommodation is equal to or unequal to the strain of fusing and adjusting internal and external changes.[1]

Galdós belongs primarily to the second stage of nineteenth-century realism, in which interest in characterization is focused more upon the close and varying relation between personality and environment than it is upon static aspects of human nature. At the same time, he does not approach the portrayal of complexities and incongruities in personality seen in some modern novelists since the time of Dostoevski. As concerns multiplicity and variety of traits, his characters fall into simple patterns. They are always dominated by a few motives, which, taken together, present an individual as a consistent and comparatively small psychological unit. This simplicity is characteristic of his late as well as his early novels, and of his abnormal as well as his normal personalities. But the novelist strives to achieve balance. At times he does this by calling attention to certain incidental characteristics. An occasional mention of facial irregularities, for example, suffices to make the person representative of the species without detracting from the main task, which is to follow the course of the personal history and to observe what happens to the personality. Galdós also achieves balance by offsetting egoistic against nonegoistic traits within the same character, or by variety in selfish and altruistic, well-adjusted and maladjusted characters within the same novel, thus showing a realistic preoccupation with the necessity of supplying a well-rounded view of human nature.

None of Galdós' main characters is a type in the strict meaning of the word. Doña Perfecta comes nearest to being an exception. In this instance, the author seems to follow a conventional conception of physical types, describing his protagonist as an intellectual person with broad forehead, delicate nose, sallow complexion—a person whose marmoreal beauty is indicative of her coldheartedness. Doña Perfecta can also be considered a social type (religious fanatic), and might have been remembered only as such, were it not for the fact that the author's energy and artistry are focused on the particular manifestations of the fanatical drive to achieve a goal. The psychological picture of this drive relegates to the background the typifying traits, and the protagonist thus becomes a personification of the extremism of which human nature is capable when one or two motives are given unbridled freedom. She is therefore more accurately described as a symbolic portrait, like other famous characters in literature mentioned above under the heading of "human" types. Many of Galdós' incidental characters, of course, are types, who are labeled with a few attitudinal and adjustive traits and are allowed to stand thus delineated each time that they appear. In the case of Licurgo, the servant of doña Perfecta, his cautiousness, his practical, peasant sagacity, and his fondness for proverbs categorize him as an "astute peasant" type, though he shows also the humility and dignity of the servant class. Amarillo and his wife Teresita (*Gloria*) almost wholly personify materialistic social vanity. Don Romero in the same novel is a broader portraiture, though still a type, who might be called an "extrovert" or a "rough, country priest"; but he is individualized somewhat by a variety of traits, among them especially his loyalty to friends, his kindness to Gloria, and his political ambitions. There are variations like these throughout the novels, which show an agreement with the realistic practice of picturing what is typical—a practice, of course, which cannot be assigned exclusively to any one age in the history of fiction.

Such personages form a part of the comprehensive collateral material in Galdós, but the major concern in this study is with the novelist's principal characters, which provide the key to his method and his basic perspective of life. His principal characters afford a picture of the individual impelled by a few outstanding motives—social motives primarily—and gaining fullness and variety through efforts to adjust to circumstances. They are simple personalities, with enough varied surface traits to make them representative, but their realness derives above all from the activity of a select number of motivational interests. A few examples will demonstrate what is meant by this statement.

Although Gloria at first seems to be a rather complex personality, her characterization soon narrows down to the responses attendant upon her obedience to family wishes and religious tradition, and her sympathy for the oppressed. In the conflict between these motives and self-satisfaction in love, the chief reactions are rebellious independence and nervous sensibility, mixed with a conciliatory behavior toward her father and the initial phases of an eventual adjustment by way of resignation and religious fanaticism. In Part II the basic motives are approval by Church and society, family approval, and love of her son. Her rebelliousness persists in her unwillingness to give up her son and enter a convent, but new adjustments appear in the form of passive resignation, castigatory rationalization in reference to Daniel and the Jewish race, mystic zeal with respect to her own martyrdom and the conversion of Daniel, and above all, nervous sensitivity and physical weakening.

In brief, the essential characterization of Gloria consists in a few personal values which act as motives of behavior, and a variety of adjustive responses to the conflict entailed by circumstances. There are several instances of particular emotional manifestations (anger, impatience, wounded ego resulting from public scorn) which contribute to a life situation, but the portrayal of Gloria obviously is not one designed to give a many-sided descriptive view of an individual either in the sense of multiplicity or of complexity. The fullness of the portrait lies in the variable adjustive picture, which is a congruous development around four social motives: family approval, Church approval, sympathy for others, love (of Daniel and son).

Even Fortunata, of all the novelist's creations the one most richly elaborated, is portrayed in conformity with a simple pattern. From the standpoint of multiplicity, however, her portrait presents a full and balanced picture. A classification of Fortunata's traits is given below in detail as an illustration of Galdós' ability in fullness of portrayal when at his best. The table will also reveal some of the fundamental features of the novelist's mode of characterization in reference to adjustment and change.[2]

PHYSICAL AND INTELLECTUAL CHARACTERISTICS
Natural:
    beauty, health, vigor, stable temperament, physical stamina, average intelligence
Environmental:
    naïveté—candor, lack of inhibitions, trustfulness, superstitiousness, inability to comprehend abstract language and ideas
    primitiveness—unpolished manners and speech, impulsiveness, cruelty, fierceness

CONSTANT VALUES
    honesty, sincerity (aversion to hypocrisy)
    loyalty to friends and loved ones
    simple domestic interests (aversion to social formalities)
    admiration of masculine strength and virility
    admiration of physical strength of the *pueblo*
    inclination to refinement (aversion to vulgarity)
    practical, earthy "common sense"
    indifference to materialistic interests (such as money)
    consideration for others (sympathy, compassion, gratitude)
    selflessness in love

CHANGING VALUES (decreasing)
    pride in own physical attractiveness
    vanity in being center of interest

CHANGING VALUES (intensifying)
    sense of justice, fairness to others
    friendliness, companionship
    belongingness (family, home, friends)

ACQUIRED VALUES
    independence of others' management
    dignity in loyalty to one's mate
    dignity in being mother of mate's son
    defense of personal honor in reference to mate
    self-objectivation (recognition of own strength and weakness)
    desire for social improvement (conventional respectability, refinement of manners and speech)
    desire for moral improvement (conformity with moral standards, vague mystic inclination to "saintliness")

ADJUSTIVE BEHAVIOR
  Negative, nonconstructive responses (decreasing)
    callous indifference
    passivity (malleability, indecisiveness, despondent submissiveness to an unhappy lot, distrust of self)
    timidity (social and moral inferiority; the first decidedly decreases)
    refractoriness (in the face of personal difficulties and social injustice)
    castigatory reactions (vengeful resentfulness, scorn of rival's honorability)
    rationalization (blaming fate, Nature, environment, the Rubín family)
    self-pity
    distrustfulness and skepticism
    physical volatility (nervousness, hysteria, lethargy)
    deceptiveness (acquired social veneer; temporary)
  Constructive responses to challenge and competition (developing)
    aggressive courage in defense of personal values
    practical flexibility (in management of Maxi, for example)
    identification of self with others, striving for mutuality (with her rival Jacinta, in particular)
    magnanimity in rivalry

In this, as in any kind of analysis, complete accuracy can only be approximated because of a heavy dependence upon inference. The problem is that of describing psychologically such a situation as Fortunata's when, after leaving doña Lupe's home for the last time, she visits don Evaristo Feijoo, seeking advice and consolation (IV, III, *vi*). She is embarrassed at having to admit her failure to follow her friend's doctrine of practical deceptiveness; she obviously wants to unburden her troubles to a sympathetic listener; she retains sincere affection for one who has been kind to her, and feels compassion for his pitiable physical and mental condition. She also feels embarrassment at having to shout to make don Evaristo understand her, but this can be disregarded as superficial, since it belongs more to the situation than to Fortunata. With reasonable accuracy the chief factors operating in this scene may be classified as follows: loyalty to friends, belongingness (need of a confidant), consideration for others (compassion, gratitude), self-pity, and despondency with respect to an unhappy lot.

The traits listed as "physical and intellectual" afford primarily a static view of the person. Some of them (health, stable temperament, average intelligence) are inferred by the reader rather than openly defined by the author. With the exception of a fluctuation in Fortunata's manners and speech (refinement and reversion to former habits), they are constant traits which tend to typify. And, indeed, Galdós does mean Fortunata to be representative of her social class (the *pueblo*), albeit in a rather idealized manner. Repeatedly he exhibits aspects of Fortunata's naïveté, and his heroine would be nothing more than a *pueblo* type if her numerous and varied reactions to circumstances did not bring out her attributes as an individual. The typifying traits become of secondary interest as the reader follows the course of a personal struggle that reveals multiple attitudes and adjustments, the majority of which pertain to individual rather than class behavior.

The picture of personality as given in the table above reveals an unusually full portraiture, covering as it does some seventy aspects. It must be kept in mind, too, that under each of the subdivisions various manifestations have been combined. These number from as few as two or three in some cases up to as many as thirty in others. Moreover, the number is distributed over the entire range of personality: physical, intellectual, attitudinal, adjustive, emotional. The emotional aspects were not listed separately in the table, since each emotion can be traced to a motive, which in turn is indicative of a trait. But Fortunata's emotional range includes an ample show of sorrow, fear, anger, joy, gaiety, humor, excitement, and serenity. In short, the central character in this case is an unusually broad and well-rounded personality. Of the forty-four comprehensive categories into which one psychologist divides the basic human attributes,[3] only the following are insignificant in Fortunata's portrait: hunger, taste, warmth, coolness, play or sport. Others, such as economy, manipulation, style, are relatively unimportant.

Notwithstanding this evidence of fullness, the portrayal is a simplified view of an individual. Taking the story as a whole, the manifestations of highest incidence center around the following motives and adjustments: belongingness and companionship (friends, loved ones, family), which intensify in the latter part of the novel; consideration for others, honesty, sincerity, selflessness in love, loyalty, all of which are constant; honor and dignity in a one-mate relationship, which is stronger in the latter part of the novel; passivity, which is scarcely noticeable in the concluding part; striving for mutuality with Jacinta (sympathy, moral values), which is most intense in the conclusion. These dominant characteristics are supplemented in the course of the long narrative by the many others, some of them purely incidental: superstitiousness, a liking for the rougher kinds of housework, indifference to money, apprehensiveness and skepticism, nervous frustration, and practical flexibility of the moment in managing (humoring) Maximiliano. The author's attention to these traits shows the inclusiveness of his observation, but it is clear that he visualizes personality as a unified, unifying process functioning in accord with a few dominant traits. The complexity consists primarily in adjustive activity, which undergoes a change of direction as new values materialize, and thus indicates the course of psychological development. When Fortunata's personality is viewed in its progressive, functional aspect, it is seen to be animated by four main forces, which issue from her competition with Jacinta: (1) pride and dignity in her love for Santa Cruz, (2) aspiration to peaceful association with friends and family, (3) passivity and rationalization in her adjustive behavior, which give way in large part to (4) the compensatory move of increasing her self-esteem by identifying herself with Jacinta. The "psychological story" of Fortunata is thus a progressive adjustment to the problems imposed by competition, and entails a wholesome development in the form of a cultivation of personal dignity.

A close observer of human nature who chooses to encompass a considerable span of an individual's life for portrayal might picture changing personality without being aware that he is doing so. It is probable, however, that any writer who is abreast of the psychological knowledge of his age will, if his interest rests primarily in his characters, in some way make conscious use of this knowledge. Galdós seems clearly to have been aware that he was recording in many of his central personages a process of gradual change, which he conceived of in terms of adjustment through the assimilation of environment. He says as much in several places. José María (*Lo prohibido*) remarks,

> . . . la vida es un constante trabajo de asimilación en todos los órdenes; que en el moral vivimos, porque nos apropiamos constantemente ideas, sentimientos, modos de ser que se producen a nuestro lado, y que al paso que de las disgregaciones nuestras se nutren otros, nosotros nos nutrimos de los infinitos productos del vivir ajeno. (IV, 1873)

Angel Guerra recognizes that his manner of behavior, though not his native character, adjusts and changes from contact with external forces:

Yo soy el que ha variado . . . yo no soy el que era . . . Cierto es que no somos dueños de nosotros mismos sino en esfera muy limitada; somos la resultante de fuerzas que arrancan de aquí y de allá. El carácter, el temperamento existen por sí; pero la voluntad es la proyección de lo de fuera en lo de dentro, y la conducta un orden sistemático, una marcha, una dirección que nos dan trazada las órbitas exteriores. (V, 1299)

Looking back over his past experiences, Angel admits that "todo ha sido una manera de adaptación" (V, 1573). In *Tristana* also, on mentioning the reluctance of Horacio, Tristana's lover, to return to Madrid from his Mediterranean home, the author speaks of "la inexorable ley de adaptación" (V, 1623).

Tristana (1892) exemplifies Galdós' interest in the "inexorable law of adaptation." Actually, it is one of the novelist's inferior works, a mere sketch rather than a fully developed story, but it is of interest in this connection because it is the outline of a story of personality adjustment, especially on the part of the two leading characters. It has little aesthetic value, primarily because the author summarizes his narrative too hastily and points to his characters' adjustments and change too overtly. For this very reason, it is a clear-cut example of a method more skillfully employed in many of the other novels.

As the action of the story begins, Tristana has drifted passively and naïvely into being the mistress of don Lope Garrido, a friend of her deceased parents and a man almost three times her own age, to whom her mother on dying had left her in charge. Tristana is a girl of latent spiritual vitality and aesthetic sensitivity, which the author apparently relates to the mother's literary propensities and the fantastic illusions manifest in her temporary abnormality immediately preceding her death. But Tristana has in larger degree an acquired passivity in responsive behavior, which acts both as a deterrent to her idealistic aspirations and as a major form of adjustment to unfavorable circumstances. When, after having been dishonored by don Lope, she awakens to the prosaic state into which she has drifted, she longs for freedom to live her own life and amount to something on her own account. Her urge to independence, however, takes a direction which is itself an indication of docile submission to her unhappy fortune; for she accepts the unwritten social law that a woman once dishonored cannot hope for a normal married life. Taking a lead from don Lope's antimatrimonial attitude, she builds for herself the ideal of independence and accomplishment outside of marriage. She rebels against don Lope's domination enough to enjoy the love of the young painter Horacio; and though her love affair satisfies her need of affection and freedom from despotic surveillance, these motives are overshadowed by an increasing urge for self-realization, which fluctuates between art, music, and other ideals of accomplishment unrelated to love and marriage. At this stage of her development, fantasy dominates her behavior. During her lover's absence from Madrid, she imaginatively exalts him into an abstraction far surpassing reality, and consequently suffers disillusionment on his return. This disillusionment coincides with a marked resurgence of resignation and indifference, which follow the forced amputation of a leg and which henceforth maintain a dominant position. Tristana accepts with little show of feeling the gradual withdrawal of her lover, her own chances of attaining happiness, and don Lope's earnest solicitude. Still aspiring to some kind of exalted self-realization, she plunges into the study of music. But in the course of three years, she gradually retreats from the outside world, loses interest in her personal appearance, turns from music to an ardent interest in the Church, itself a vain search for a substitute source of contentment in the form of *lo ideal*, and eventually resigns herself to a prosaic existence at the side of don Lope. The author, who has watched with curiosity and amusement each step in Tristana's journey of adjustment, questions whether this last stage may not be another transitional plateau in her development rather than the "última metamórfosis" in her search for *lo ideal*.

Galdós probably had in mind as a partial objective a presentation of the vague longings in individual human nature for self-realization, and as incidental to this, the fate of woman in a society where women's freedom is strictly limited.[4] But the novel becomes essentially a demonstration of how a person, given a particular set of natural and environmental traits and placed in a particular set of circumstances, follows a course of natural adjustment. Each step in Tristana's history, which covers some four or five years of her life, is an adjustment which enables her to maintain a workable relationship with the exigencies of her position. The total development is a natural process which entails a modification of the central character's personality by way of a gradual suppression of idealistic aspirations and—one might add—a deadening of her sensitivity to surroundings. In this aspect of passive submission, *Tristana* resembles a typically naturalistic novel, but it must be remembered that the protagonist's submission is as much the result of her illusionistic tendencies and her lack of spiritedness as it is of external environment. Moreover, Galdós reminds us in his concluding remarks about Tristana and don Lope ("¿Eran felices uno y otro? . . . Tal vez.") that happiness may lie precisely in the individual's capacity for adapting himself to circumstances. The adjustment, not the nature of the circumstances, is the important thing.

Tristana is not a heroine fighting against odds and failing because of an unrelenting adherence to an ideal. Like Emma Bovary, she reacts to her prosaic environment by aspiring to glorious self-assertion in pursuit of a romantic ideal that proves to be an illusion. But whereas Flaubert concentrates on following the illusion through to its inevitable tragic end, presenting in Emma not a particular individual but the personification of one aspect of human nature, Galdós is interested primarily in the probabilities surrounding a particular person. The story of Tristana is simply that of a girl who, because of a dishonorable position in society, experiences and then suppresses an urge to independence and self-realization. The emphasis is more on the social mark of dishonor, the source of the urge to self-assertion and the beginning of the adjustive problem, than it is on self-realization as a mark of human nature; and like a teacher who explains a diagram on a blackboard, the author presents to his readers the picture of personality development.

Galdós follows the same technique even more pointedly in his characterization of don Lope Garrido, a more thorough portraiture and a more clear-cut picture of adjustment and change than Tristana. At the beginning of the story don Lope appears strictly as a type: a combination of an unscrupulous Don Juan and a *caballero* of the old school out of step with modern society. His type characteristics, however, recede into the background as he is drawn into the defensive struggle of an old man trying to retain ownership of a young woman. Reacting to his inferior position at first with jealousy and threats, he makes an ever expanding concession to the unavoidable, which enables him to save face and at the same time brings a change in his erstwhile social attitudes. As a substitute for a dampened pride resulting from his weakness in competing with a young lover, he leans upon his perspicacity in discovering Tristana's love affair, thus proclaiming that he cannot be deceived; and he develops this substitute pride into a paternal and patronizing generosity which reaches the point of open co-operation with Tristana in writing letters to her lover and arranging for him to visit her.

While obviously maintaining his pride by way of self-exaltation in the face of a forced retreat, don Lope is also acting as a clever psychologist who knows that Tristana is more in love with love than with Horacio, and that once she has had her fling, she will be disillusioned and hence more easily held to her present relationship with himself. His defensive maneuvers are motivated at first almost entirely by vanity, but he comes to have a sincere love for his ward and a growing dependence upon her. Consequently he follows her in her religious pursuits and finally looks with favor upon marrying and settling down to a simple bourgeois existence in which he can raise chickens and cultivate his own garden. The unprincipled Don Juan, the unbending aristocrat, has been converted into an everyday family man of the middle class.

Although the transitions in the change of personality are rapidly drawn and repeatedly pointed out by the author, don Lope's characterization is more substantial than that of Tristana. The reader learns indirectly of the functioning psychology in Tristana largely from the author's description of what is taking place, but he sees psychology at work in don Lope from a firsthand view of motives and responses discernible in numerous dialogue scenes and descriptions of the character's activities. If Tristana in the major role had been portrayed as effectively as don Lope is in the secondary role, the novel would have attained higher artistic merit. It is interesting, nevertheless, as an example of a method used by Galdós with more care and detail in a number of his better novels. To judge from the author's interest in the curiosities of change in people in accord with particular conditions, the presentation of a typical "case history" seems to have been, if not the main objective, at least the main source of pleasure in writing *Tristana.*

There is evidence that Galdós from the time of his earliest novels saw the advantages of observing personality change. He appears, however, to have recognized its possibilities for novelistic use most clearly after 1885. In doña Perfecta the major change discernible, within the body of the narrative, is an increase of inflexibility, a trait which was already well established, needing only to be tested in order to prove its extremity. In like manner, Marianela's need of belonging with others results in an intensification of abjectness; Felipe Centeno's friendliness and practicalness crystallize into kindly honesty and uprightness; and José María's lack of solid personal values (*Lo prohibido*) leads to an evasion of moral responsibility and a rationalization of his own weakness. A similar kind of "change" is also found in some of the later novels. In *Realidad,* for example, Orozco's ideal of saintly living becomes a hard egoistic pride, which results from his self-imposed task of generating spirituality; and Augusta's only observable development, at the time of the narrative action,[5] is merely the crystallization of a conventional, practical adjustment. In the personality developments that take place in two of the early novels, there is a further reminder not to attribute too much importance to chronology: the evolvement of intransigence and a martyr-mystic complex in Gloria, and Isidora's disintegration in self-respect, both of which are plainly consequential in the plot development. These two characterizations follow the pattern of such later novels as *Fortunata y Jacinta,* where the growing need of social and moral respectability leads to the creation of personal dignity; or in the *Torquemada* series, where the protagonist perforce develops expansiveness, concessiveness, and co-operativeness.

It may be said, then, that personality change in Galdós' characters consists of (1) an intensification of values and a crystallization of latent adjustive traits into solid "axioms" of behavior (*Doña Perfecta, Marianela, El doctor Centeno, Lo prohibido, Realidad*), or (2) a gradual modification of attitudes, redistribution of values, and consequent shift in conduct (*Gloria, Fortunata y Jacinta,* the *Torquemada* series). Isidora (*La desheredada*) exemplifies a combination of the two categories. In the second group the change in personality is clearly defined, for the characters come to have beliefs and ideals which are indispensable to their equilibrium and which at one time in their lives were of negligible importance; or they develop ways of meeting hostile circumstances that are essentially different from their former manner of responding. The development thus includes a basic change in character—greater perhaps than the novelist himself was aware of. Fortunata retains always her primitive fierceness and courage—what Galdós probably considers the "forma interna y perdurable de la persona"—but she unmistakably rises in a moral sense, and it is therefore proper to say that her character, as well as her personality, changes.

From the viewpoint of functional psychology, Galdós' conception of personality is fundamentally the same as that held by social psychologists of the present century. Briefly, this view may be described as that of a dynamic interrelationship between the human organism and the forces from without, to which it tries to respond in such a way as to maintain a state of emotional stability. The innate assertiveness of the individual functions along the primary lines of security, belongingness (with social groups or with some other superindividual unit, such as Nature, God, ethical world order, etc.), novelty of experience, and activity (within the range of capability). It meets with opposition from without and is forced into a modification of responses and the curbing of impulses. The organism tends toward a mastery of environment and in a way reshapes it, becoming thus a determinant by selecting and adapting it so as to be able to live comfortably in it. But the adjustment to the surrounding world entails a process of assimilation wherein the individual unconsciously assumes the roles and attitudes of others and acquires new values and a new order of responses. An individual's values and loyalties have no meaning apart from their reference to some superindividual relationship. External elements thus become integrated with a constantly changing self, whose very individuality is an expression of attitudes acquired within a social process of which it forms a part and to which it is indebted for its existence and its development. In short, individual personality is a continual transformation, a reshaping of attitudes and responses necessitated in the organism's efforts to establish and maintain a harmonious relationship with environment. Each seemingly static period of harmony is but a kind of *modus vivendi* and is constantly subject to disturbance, readjustment, and change.[6]

This conception of personality as an interaction between the individual and the social units with which he is inseparably linked is one of the outstanding features of Galdós' character portrayal. In every case, the main characters find themselves enmeshed in a series of happenings and circumstances which call forth an effort to establish a harmonious relationship with social surroundings. They manifest particular aspirations, find their drives blocked, respond in various ways in accord with habits already acquired, trying to compensate for weaknesses or overcome blockages. They develop substitutes for suppressed values, enjoy moments of repose, acquire new drives which meet with obstacles, and continue unceasingly in an adjustive process, which terminates only because the novel ends. The case of Fortunata is one of the best illustrations of such a process:

> With a mixture of competitive spirit and distrust of self, Fortunata searches for a basis of self-respect in her love for Santa Cruz, finds it by convincing herself of the dignity of her love, realizes the need of a concrete proof of her worth, grasps for support at her physical superiority over Jacinta, develops this support under further stress into a belief that not only is love for the father of her child honorable, but that the contribution of a son to the Santa Cruz family is worthy of their gratitude, and having achieved through defense of a "mutual" possession [fight with Aurora for betraying her friendship in a love affair with Santa Cruz] a self-satisfaction as to her right to friendship with Jacinta, advances to the still higher goal of saintly equality, the ultimate of her striving within the period of time encompassed by the narrative.[7]

The functioning psychology described here, it should be emphasized, depicts predominantly the restless state of mind of one who tries to dominate the forces which challenge his own right to a place in society. The author's depiction of the adjustive process, which is his way of visualizing the complexity of the human being, exhibits, above all, the efforts of the individual to reach a state of stabilization and unification amidst difficult circumstances. There are some cases of deterioration of personality (Isidora, Miau), or of half-hearted, passive adjustment (José María Bueno de Guzmán, Tristana), but these also manifest the striving for orientation and the mastery of frictional elements arising in the conflict between self and society.

Even in the author's portrayal of love between man and woman, the same basic social motives stand out. There are a few examples among the women characters in which love is depicted as an essence unadulterated by complicating social factors. To the point are certain moments in the experiences of Eloísa (*Lo prohibido*), Fortunata, and Dulcenombre (*Angel Guerra*). These few examples give evidence at least that Galdós was capable of handling delicate sentiments artistically; but in no case does the delicate emotional aspect constitute a major narrative theme, for the author characteristically portrays love as being complicated by socio-psychological disturbances, and not as a thing of beauty *per se*.

It is this major concern with social orientation and self-realization that explains Galdós' slight treatment of perhaps the most dynamic of all emotional conflicts: the workings of a guilty conscience. There are several instances in his novels in which individual conscience is put to a test, but in almost every case the conflict is resolved or temporarily calmed by the individual's acceptance of a socially workable course of action. The feeling of guilt takes a very light toll in Galdós' characters. A glance at two of the novels will illustrate.

In *Tormento* the author repeatedly speaks of Amparo's conscience, and the protagonist's sense of guilt for her past sin with her seducer, the derelict priest don Pedro Polo, does motivate her behavior in some degree. At times she tries to rationalize her sin, and at other times, to wash it away by good deeds. Most of all, her sense of guilt disturbs her by demanding that she confess to Caballero before marrying him. But the story of Amparo is that of a timid girl trying desperately to bolster her courage in the face of an unfriendly society, rather than that of a guilty conscience. Her early background and her relationship with the Bringas family have developed in her the dominant trait of a whipped-dog attitude of defeatism, which she constantly tries to overcome. Her fruitless resolutions to confess to Caballero suggest the indecision of a swimmer who repeatedly tests the cold water with his toes and never plunges in for the swim. Three primary motives are at work in her psychology: (1) shame for her sin, combined with a sense of duty to tell Caballero about it, (2) obsession with her lack of courage, and (3) fear that her secret will be discovered. The first is continually subordinated to the second, which in turn is overshadowed by the third. More than once on the point of confessing to Caballero, Amparo is frightened away by the slightest indication that he suspects her past, and the accelerated psychological movement culminates always in terror at the thought of discovery, until Rosalía Bringas finally confronts her with the fact that her secret is known. This is the climactic point of her defeatism, which is temporarily dissolved as she first succumbs in a physical crisis and then attempts suicide.

The final dynamic scene for Amparo, however, comes with her confession to Caballero after he has decided to leave her, and represents her happiest and most scintillating moment: the swimmer has at last been able to plunge into the cold water. She is proud of herself, not because she has satisfied a sense of honor—her confession is nothing more than an admission of something that everyone already knows—but because she has conquered her timidity. Her facile decision to go away with her lover, even though unmarried to him, is an epilogue to the body of the story and indicates the results of her having gained the confidence she lacked. She will be a much stronger character henceforth and in the company of Caballero will be no less moral. The two together, in fact, represent the triumph of two individuals caught in the web of an oppressive, conventional society, though both defer to convention: Amparo, by accepting an unmarried state in payment for her past; and Caballero, by refusing to marry a woman who has been dishonored.

Federico Viera, Augusta's lover (*Realidad*), is the most complex example of stricken conscience among Galdós' characters, and yet his conflict is predominantly one of social maladjustment. His early background is recorded in *La Incógnita*. An undisciplined son of a wealthy aristocrat, he has acquired habits of shiftlessness, tastes for a life of vice, and irresponsibility. When his father, after a business failure, deserts his family for a life of roguish expediency, Viera is left to shift for himself, financially a peon with the tastes of a *bohemio* and the pride of a nobleman. His life now becomes a prolonged maladjustment as he shifts between his Bohemian haunts and the aristocratic circles of his family ties, attracted by both groups and unable to adjust to either. His sensitiveness, which is accentuated by his father's reputation, hardens into a rigid compensatory pride. It is manifest in his hostility to a plebeian marriage for his sister and in his resentfulness at accepting money from his aristocratic friends (though willingly taking it from a prostitute). The same feeling of inferiority that causes him to resent Orozco's and others' attempts to bring about his reform also leads him to rationalize that Augusta's love for him fails to satisfy his basic human need of being understood, and turns him toward the warm-hearted prostitute *la Peri.*

Actually, Viera feels strongly the need of belonging in some close personal relationship, but the bifurcation of his personality makes this impossible because his egoistic pride prevents him from adjusting in a practical way within his own social class, and his social values prevent him from identifying himself with a group socially below him. Meanwhile, unconsciously displeased with his own degeneracy, especially in the presence of the "saintly" Orozco, he develops in defense a strong moral sense of honor. This is revealed in his increasing feeling of guilt for betraying a friend (Orozco) and in his defense of a strict code of morality in reaction to the efforts of other men to win the love of his friend's wife (Augusta). The humiliation experienced from Orozco's repeated efforts to help, though mixed with resentment of his saintliness, stimulates the dignity and self-respect to which Viera has clung, in words if not in deeds.

This is the positive result developed out of his attempt to save his self-esteem in the face of the challenge laid down by a society which considers him a failure. The aristocratic sense of honor, which was at first really an abstraction, has materialized in the form of expiation for guilt. It is mixed, of course, with the evasiveness of one who cannot surmount harsh realities. Viera's guilt, his fear of discovery, and the poignancy of his misfit position in the world intensify into a physical and nervous weakness and end in suicide. In this way he pays homage to his only morally sustaining force: adherence to the lost cause of traditionalism. His suicide is thus the culmination of a maladjustment which has become focused in conscience. But the author's portraiture gives a much fuller analysis of the maladjustment than it does of conscience.

The preponderance of the motive of security over conscience in the novels is one element of Galdós' persistent realism. The novelist was intent upon observing representative people in society and recording the most probable modes of adjustment; and it must be admitted that the individual, when viewed as a member of society, manifests above all his capacity for arriving at a tolerable way of life. Shortcomings and violations of moral codes are commonly forgotten or subordinated through rationalization, more or less out of the necessity of survival.

Only in rare instances does a personality disintegrate completely because of a feeling of guilt, and Galdós concentrated on usual rather than extreme cases of adjustment. This is not to say that he failed to see in human nature man's ability to rise above the level of convenient adjustment. The reader needs only to recall Gloria, Fortunata, Nazarín, and numerous other characters to know that the author not only beheld intently the urge of human beings to realize their noblest potentiality, but that he saw a means of this realization in a social relationship where the independence of individual conscience meets in conciliation with the demands of society. Galdós was interested in conscience not so much as a complex that tears the individual apart, but as a co-ordinative and constructive force. Hence the predominance of problems of orientation and integration.

The psychological experience of one of the novelist's main characters, when observed over a long biographical span, is a veritable stream of expanding energy, but it should be noted that the stream is a fluctuating movement of advances, halts, retrogressions, and renewed advances rather than a uniform, uninterrupted flow. For Galdós is quite aware of the unevenness in psychological growth, and knows that the over-all development includes long periods of slow preparation punctuated by decisive moments when an almost imperceptible variation suddenly assumes well-defined contours. This is apparently what he has in mind when in *Lo prohibido* he says, "la facultad de asimilación varía según la edad y las circunstancias: en las épocas críticas y en las crisis de pasiones adquiere gran desarrollo" (IV, 1873). Comprehensively viewed, the characters present a picture of cyclical progression which includes defensive agitation in the face of threats to their sense of security, groping for decisive guides to action, and co-ordination of efforts toward well-defined objectives. The total picture is in a sense the re-enactment of individual maturational experience, with particular emphasis on the psychosocial reference. The groping for orientation, though always present, appears most prominently in the novels of the 1880's, and the emphasis on integration grows stronger thereafter, reaching its highest point in Benina (*Misericordia*), whose total psychical activity forcefully illustrates the co-ordinative process.

In observing Galdós' characters in some of their tensest moments, it is easy to think only of the immediate external activity and forget that specific dramatic scenes form together a continuity of psychological movement. Galdós often assumes the position of a reporter who is intent upon giving vivid surface pictures of people under stress; and yet, in the case of the principal characters, scenes of physical movement are but specific manifestations of a major psychological development. Consider, for example, the scene in which Fortunata, after her marriage to Maximiliano, awaits expectantly the arrival of Santa Cruz, half afraid and half hoping that he will knock on the door (II, vii, iv). The dominant impression is one of tense nervousness on the part of a person awaiting the outcome of a decisive turn of events. Fortunata's silence is broken at long intervals by a few remarks between her and her servant. She imagines that she hears sounds outside her room, feels the impulse to open the door, recovers her self-control, retreats, returns to the door as if hypnotized, recoils, and stands like a statue as she hears Santa Cruz muttering something outside. Then she hears him leave, runs to the balcony, watches him walk away, retires to Maxi's bedroom, where she sits in a chair and dreams of doors, locks, and men in her room.

Clearly, the author in his crisp dramatic reporting has produced a sensation of anxiety and fear; but the physical manifestations are inseparably linked with underlying motives. Mauricia *la Dura's* persuasive efforts to reunite Fortunata with Santa Cruz are still fresh in Fortunata's mind, inclining her to rejoin her lover. But her sense of loyalty and fair play is outraged by the presence and insinuating remarks of her servant, who has been bribed by Santa Cruz, and whose conversation and understanding air not only cause Fortunata to recoil from treachery and deception, which have always been foreign to her character, but also stimulate her sense of dignity in the presence of an inferior. This sense of dignity is a mark of social respectability which has gradually been seeping into her consciousness. She therefore tries first to avoid her servant's gaze, then looks at the servant, for a moment weakens as though agreeing that what is to happen must happen, and again recovers her dignity. She thus gives continuous evidence of moral conflict at a critical stage in her expanding sense of respectability.

Similarly, the meeting of Fortunata and Jacinta in the house of Guillermina (III, vii, iv) is a climactic display of pent emotions erupting suddenly in fierce nervous activity and ending in physical weakness and relaxation. The author writes with a dramatic use of the present tense, reporting, in a way that reminds one of Flaubert in *Madame Bovary,* on the small, trivial realities that loom large in the mind of one who is in a critical nervous state. Psychical activity is strong both in Fortunata's groping for sympathy and understanding prior to the explosive moment and in the intense loneliness and disillusionment which follow it. Anxiety, anger, fear, nervous hysteria, and the lethargic aftermath of frustration have probably never had a more competent painter than. Galdós. As far as his depiction of a specific situation is concerned, this is the kind of portrayal at which he is most effective. It must be remembered, however, that such scenes are held together psychologically in a chain of causes and effects.

It is easy to overlook this important aspect of Galdós' art because of a large amount of supplementary material in his novels, consisting of numerous secondary characters and incidental situations. Moreover, Galdós frequently adopts a leisurely narrative style that becomes rather lifeless summary and commentary. The reader, therefore, is obliged in some degree to take the role of novelist upon himself and weave together the scattered dramatic scenes. If he does so, he will discover a clarity and strength in the psychological design. The sequence of events may sometimes be terminated with no visible progression other than along a straight chronological line. But in almost every case there will be a progression in the characters themselves, and this will compensate in part for the lack of dramatic developments in the surface happenings. Even when the author leisurely summarizes and leaves until near the conclusion the presentation of decisive action, one can see a comprehensive, cumulative movement enveloped by the narrative whole. It is as though one were watching a stream that starts hesitantly, proceeds slowly, and finally assumes a definite direction and an accelerated speed.

La de Bringas (1884) is a good example of a cumulative psychological development amidst an inordinate amount of summary material. In ten introductory chapters the author presents a satirical, descriptive view of manners in a circle of indigent and spendthrift womenfolk of government employees. He then gradually directs his attention to Rosalía Bringas, whose worship of social fashion and appearances (symbolized by clothes) leads her into ever increasing financial difficulties. Specific scenes interspersed here and there make clear the conflict in Rosalía between a desire for fashionable appearance and rebellion against a staid, money-loving husband, on the one hand, and family responsibility, fear of her husband, and a sense of honor, on the other.

For the greater part of the narrative, however, the author wanders leisurely along, apparently without a specific objective. He begins as though interested in a tale of manners, but he becomes intent upon a biographical view of his main character. Hence his energy is transferred from descriptive to narrative technique. As a result, the reader is kept in a constant state of anticipation of some important event and becomes impatient when this is postponed in seemingly endless transitional passages. For he finds neither sufficient material to interest him in psychology alone nor a dramatic chain of happenings to satisfy his interest in a plot of action. Instead, he has to content himself with casual details about the comparatively trivial worries of a small social group.

Summary narration sets the dominant tempo until the last ten chapters (XLI-L), where Rosalía finally faces and resolves the crisis toward which she has been slowly drifting. Here the author redeems himself in part for his previous dilatoriness. Rosalía, now faced with an immediate need of money, is forced into decisive action and vividly reveals her agitated state of mind. In a typical Galdosian treatment, she passes through a state of uncertainty and emerges with a definite stabilization of personality. She wavers momentarily on the brink of selling her honor, rationalizing that she was not born to be a saint nor to be *cursi* like her husband; and is saved by chance, since Pez shies away from her approach. She swallows her pride as she appeals to Refugio (a woman of ill repute) for a loan; suffers a wounded ego still further on hearing of the disparaging remarks made by her "friend" Milagros; and having obtained the necessary money at the expense of nothing more than humiliation and wounded pride, emerges from her test with firm social self-assurance, a feeling of superiority over her erstwhile fickle and trivial associates, and a pronounced sense of responsibility for her family. The author's style in this part of the novel is one of rapid-fire relation of action, mixed with bits of dialogue and comment on his character's thoughts. In this way he achieves the effect of physical movement spurred on by psychological necessity. The portrait grows into a picture of tense co-ordinative efforts toward a single goal, with the complicating motives becoming merely a part of an onrushing stream.

Only after passing through the accelerated final section of the novel is the reader aware that he has witnessed an example of developing psychology, in which the protagonist reaches a stage of character unification. After wavering at the crossroad only to be saved by circumstances, Rosalía appears in the conclusion as a rapidly maturing dowager who henceforth will lead rather than follow women like Milagros, and who at the same time will assume a stabilizing, protective role in her own family. Her talents for management and manipulation may be overworked in the future, but she can be counted on to adhere firmly to conventional moral codes. For this decisive milestone in character development (to regard the novel as a psychological story), or for this decisive turn of events (to regard it as a comedy of marital adjustment), the slow-moving preparatory content was a necessity in the author's mind.

The reader of such a novel as *La de Bringas* might well wish that Galdós had been more concerned with a graphic presentation of events while preparing for psychological change; but if he has the patience which accompanies sympathy for the author's comprehensive objectives, he will himself take a part in defining the plot. Such participation on the part of the reader is in fact a necessity with respect to many of the novels. Clearly, the existence of this necessity is an indictment against the novelist's formal procedure. To be more precise, it is an indictment against his technique or the finer aspects of execution of plan, and not against his method, which pertains to the primary plan of composition.

The basic psychological structure of Galdós' novels, the consequence of his method, is in general solidly forged along a line representative of a rhythmical succession of moments of tension, rest, retardation, and advances. Whether we regard the personality change thus depicted as being sharply drawn or as an expansion of latent tendencies, the characters, seen in their ceaseless efforts to attain emotional stability, represent human nature in its restless, shifting movement, rather than in static form. This picture of restlessness is of major significance both as concerns the novelist's artistic accomplishment and his general perspective of life. For although the concept of change may literarily be of little consequence if it appears merely as an abstract principle in a writer's works, it can be extremely important as a basis of interpretation if it underlies the characterization, contributes toward producing a progressive narrative movement in conjunction with the sequence of events, and supplies a key to the author's vision of man's place in the world.

IV

THE PSYCHOLOGICAL STRUCTURE

I F it is true that Galdós' basic method is that of molding socio-psychological material into a story of developing personality, the essential
structural form of his novels should prove to be of psychological design,
having the oneness and finality usually expected in a work of art. The
happenings in the stories sometimes form a surface plot of dramatic
situation, but more typically they comprise a chronology of events which
seems to be simply the historical record of a person's experiences for a
given period of time. Even then, there are at least a few tense scenes or
episodes that provide dramatic interest.

No doubt the novelist felt a storyteller's responsibility for supplying
these episodes to enliven his slow-moving narratives. Like Pereda, he
makes a special effort at times to provide some kind of excitement, particularly in the concluding part of his stories. The big difference is that
Pereda depends largely upon external phenomena for a climactic development, after which he brings his narrative to a peaceful conclusion. A
notable feature is his dependence upon storms or other occurrences that
pit man against external nature (*Sotileza, El sabor de la tierruca, La
puchera*).[1] The behavior of Pereda's characters in such circumstances,
of course, has definite psychological aspects, and the climactic event
usually marks a decisive turn in the characters' lives; but the psychology
is primarily a reaction to the immediate situation, rather than the culmination of a slow progression consistently followed from the beginning. Galdós, on the other hand, is interested in external happenings
both as a means of supplying drama and as factors in clinching developments already psychologically prepared for. The situations which call
for decisive and accelerated activity therefore represent peaks along a
course of personality development. It will add greatly to an appreciation
of Galdós to regard these peaks not merely as dynamic spots in a narra-

tive chain of events, but as psychological peripetias linked together in deliberate design.

At first glance, the plots, visualized as centering around the characters that carry the burden of the narrative, would seem to be adequately illustrated by the following diagram:

It must be remembered, however, that before each of the high points, the central personages are in a state of psychical mobility which, with the turn of events, reaches a climactically tense moment and calls for tension discharge. In between these high points are found periods of relaxation, new orientation, renewed activity, and frustration. The diagram is thus more revealing if it is represented as follows, using wavy lines to indicate periods of marked psychological disturbance:

If the characters are observed still more closely, another feature appears in the design, pertaining to plateaus of personality development; thus:

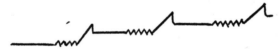

This advance of a personality from one plateau to another after recurring periods of tension accumulation and tension discharge characterizes the essential framework of Galdós' plots.

In order to explain more clearly the structural form here referred to, it will be necessary to demonstrate with specific examples—briefly with a few representative novels and in detail with one (*Angel Guerra*). *Doña Perfecta,* the most tersely wrought of Galdós' "dramatic" stories, is a logical choice to begin with.

The narrative problem of *Doña Perfecta* is clearly established in the first eight chapters. Pepe's vehement defense of science at the end of chapter eight arouses his aunt's worship of ecclesiastic formula, a major "axiom" of her behavior, which henceforth will dominate her treatment of her nephew. This occasion is the first conspicuous peripetia. In the minor incidents which follow, the major axiom, supported by provincial prejudice, guides doña Perfecta's efforts to block Pepe's marriage to her daughter Rosario, taking the form of feigned protective friendliness, petulance, frustration, and vengeful sadistic pleasure. When Pepe announces his determination to marry Rosario (XIX), despite all opposition, doña Perfecta is impelled into frenzied action, revealing an accumulating hatred for her nephew. This is the second decisive development. From this time on, doña Perfecta is like a warrior angel who will stop at nothing to enforce her will. The tension caused by the determined drive reaches the breaking point in a third peripetia (xxxi), when the protagonist discovers that Rosario has planned to elope with Pepe, and she orders Caballuco to kill her nephew.

That the three decisive steps which mark the course of an intensifying passion of hate together constitute one major episode, or plateau, in character development, becomes clear from a comparison of doña Perfecta's personality before and after the dramatic set of circumstances which provides the severe test of character. The change observable within the relatively brief space devoted to narrative action is essentially the solidification of a fixed value and the hard crystallization of dictatorial independence and aggressiveness. If, however, the brief exposition in reference to the protagonist's life prior to the beginning of the story and the epilogue which follows the catastrophe are considered as essential parts of the whole, two different levels of personality growth can be plainly seen. The author explains in chapter three that doña Perfecta's husband had been a reckless gambler and "algo mujeriego," and that she had taken over the administration of the family estate and returned to Orbajosa after her husband's death. This appears to be rather unimportant information, but it affords a plausible explanation for doña Perfecta's self-sufficiency and her recourse to formalistic religious activity as compensation for an unhappy married life. The epilogue, also brief in its reference to the central character, relates that she has proclaimed Pepe's death a suicide, that she is much upset and has lost weight, and that she passes most of her time in church and spends her money on resplendent religious functions. In short, the author seems to want to show how a person will continue along a challenged line of conduct as if to prove its justification by stubborn persistence. At the same time, the information plainly calls attention to a compensation for guilt by way of intensified religious activity, which is now oriented toward ascetic self-punishment and martyrdom.

From an all-inclusive viewpoint, then, the history of doña Perfecta may be illustrated as follows:

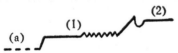

Section (a) represents that part of doña Perfecta's life referred to by the author but not included as a part of the narrative; (1) the plateau of her personality at the beginning of the story; and (2) the plateau of development at the conclusion. Regarded as a history of progressive adjustment, the personality story shows first a level at which the individual lives by worship of ecclesiastic formula and authoritarianism, and then advances, after a severe emotional experience which has challenged her established norm of conduct, to a level at which it is possible to live only by ascetic withdrawal from the world.[2]

The aesthetic quality of *Doña Perfecta*, of course, derives from a vivid and compact account of a single climactic episode in a life, and does not depend upon a comprehensive portrayal of personality growth over a long period of time. It is significant, however, that in Galdós' first important psychological novel there are indications of the plateau structure which becomes a basic part of his method. That the last of the plateaus in the narrative is but briefly denoted is not unusual. The novelist frequently terminates his stories at a point where his central characters have reached a new level of development.

La familia de León Roch best illustrates the transitional phase of the novelist's expanding method. For one thing, the history of León's personal struggle is extended over a longer time than that of doña Perfecta, though resembling it closely in that the change becomes evident in the conclusion of the story. For another, María Egipcíaca's personality shows a plateau development within the body of the narrative. León's ideal of an orderly, rationally controlled existence within a peaceful family life is subjected to a severe test. It triumphs, as the solidification of a value, at a level on which resignation to unhappiness enables the individual to preserve his integrity. Thus:

the ideal   the test   the triumph

María's portrait reveals a more sharply defined change than León's. The progressive development is from an initial plane of normal love to (1) a plateau of ascetic withdrawal and suppression of the flesh, and then (2) to a plateau of selfish egoistic hardening:

(1)   (2)

María's death terminates her conflict—a mixture of selfishness, suppressed sex, and mystic exaltation. If she had lived, she could have been expected to become another doña Perfecta, as the latter appears in the reader's final view of her martyr complex.

As concerns the identification of personality change with narrative form, the structural patterns discernible in *Doña Perfecta* and *La familia de León Roch* are found, with variations, in all of Galdós' *novelas contemporáneas*. The novels fall into three main chronological divisions: 1876-1878, 1881-1885, 1886-1897. (Omitted from the present consideration are the three novels written after 1900, since they represent a final stage of disintegration in a structural achievement that had long before reached its peak.)

In the first group, the decisive change in personality comes at the conclusion after a series of experiences which center around a dramatic situation or problem. Even *Marianela* may be placed in this category if the heroine's decline is regarded as a culmination of defeatism combined with physical change. In the second group, the shift in direction comes at the conclusion after a chronology of events recounted in biographical form. A gradual decline is observable in Isidora Rufete (*La desheredada*), though the most prominent phase of her development follows her final disillusionment. More typically, the reader becomes aware of change only in the closing part of the novels. Such is the case with *La de Bringas;* or with *El doctor Centeno,* where Felipe, in ambitious quest of a place in society, passes through a series of hardships which evoke his friendly concern for others and his deep-rooted practicality, and leave him at a level of sensible adjustment to a way of life commensurate with his capacities. In this group of the early 1880's, *Tormento* is something of an exception; for it resembles *Doña Perfecta* in its relatively compact treatment of a dramatic problem (the marriage of a woman who has been dishonored). Amparo begins on a level of timidity and retreat, and emerges, after a tense struggle with her ingrained defeatism, on a level of courage and self-assurance. Although the indication is that Galdós was not as consciously concerned with the fusion of plot and personality development in these early novels as he was later, there is no escaping the fact that he was interested almost as much in the question of what happens to the personalities as he was in the question of what happens to the persons.

From 1886 (*Fortunata y Jacinta*) on, the predominant pattern is that of an advance to a new level through two or more intermediate plateaus, after a series of experiences recounted in biographical form. The novels in this group represent scarcely more than an elaboration of the earlier method and are those in which Galdós merges plot and personality change most deliberately and with greatest effect. Structurally, *Nazarín* (1895), which has never attracted the attention that it deserves, is typical of Galdós' maturest period and is therefore an appropriate example to discuss here.

In Part I the author poses his problem. He is to study the curious case of a priest of vaguely known background, an orthodox believer but officially inactive and little interested in Church dogma, and a person who chooses to live apart from the world, indifferent to material needs and concerned only with his independent relationship with God. To the casual observer, Nazarín is a negative, if not abnormal, personality; but the author's imagination is stimulated to the extent of subjecting this seeming nonentity to a test. In this way he can decide whether Nazarín is madman, saint, or merely a harmless, insignificant person. The imaginary test, of course, will provide an opportunity for speculation—in a dreamlike world—upon religious ideals, and will reveal the author's own ideas even though the whole story is proffered as a fantasy for which no serious responsibility is assumed.

Part II brings Nazarín into sharp contact with his immediate surroundings; for he is unavoidably involved in caring for Andara, a prostitute who has taken refuge in his quarters while fleeing from the law (II, I-III). He has no intention of harboring a criminal, but he is definitely interested in correcting Andara's conscience. His capacity for sympathetic aid to others is thus activated as he finds himself for the first time in the role of helper and teacher, a role which will later become indispensable to his being. For some time, however, his reclusiveness remains ascendant and comes to be a veritable drive oriented toward living the life of a vagabond alone with nature. The occasion for this decisive turn is his forced departure from his friend's home (II, VI).

Part III presents the first really dynamic episode, in which two opposing forces vie with each other for ascendancy. Nazarín anticipates with pleasure a solitary life of hardships and self-suppression, but he is drawn involuntarily into an association with others; first with Andara, who attaches herself to him in search of sympathy and leadership; and then with Beatriz, a lonely person on the verge of embracing a life like that of Andara, who has led him to Beatriz with an ingenuity reminiscent of Sancho's clever management of Don Quijote. Nazarín's amenability and concessiveness allow him to drift into a group relationship in which his capacity for guidance and leadership is stimulated. This new stimulation acquires the force of another drive, now directed toward service to others, as he leads his two companions on a mission of mercy while attending the victims of a smallpox epidemic (III, ix).

Part IV recounts a further advance in Nazarín's personality. Though retaining his enthusiasm for service to the needy—as long as the opportunity lasts—and consistent always in his ideal of self-negation, he now manifests a vital pleasure in the companionship and affection of his two disciples, who lean on him for spiritual guidance, and whom he shepherds with paternal benevolence. This section of the novel marks the culmination of the idyllics of Nazarín's *cristianas aventuras.* It also marks the culmination of the author's "dream." For the novel is not pure fantasy, after all, but a realistic interpretation of human nature as observed in its confrontation with immediate social circumstances. Nazarín, therefore, is abruptly brought back to harsh reality, when he and Andara are arrested to be taken back to Madrid (IV, vi).

Part V now presents the test of Nazarín's character in the light of his warm personal relationships. The long-established habit of passivity and reclusion is revived almost instantaneously and becomes dominant again in Nazarín's adjustment. The hero passes nevertheless through a stage of emotional turmoil and indecision, in which rebelliousness and lonesomeness for his disciples are in evidence. This is the climax of the story and potentially the most dynamic part, though the author chooses to present the struggle in the form of a vision (V, v-vi), thus focusing attention more upon the subconscious mind and a feverish physical state than upon the operation of psychological causes. These, however, are discernible, and the final personality orientation is indicated despite the fact that Nazarín remains to the end of the novel in a stuporous state.

In the vision Andara and Beatriz appear as two beautiful angels, the one a righteous warrior fighting and conquering an army (*la Humanidad*); the other, a peaceful spectator who prays God to pardon evildoers. Though always impartial in his treatment of his two followers, Nazarín had given evidence of a warmer feeling for Beatriz, the more delicate and spiritual of the two. Her angelic passivity and Christlike forbearance in the vision thus indicate the path that her master will follow. That he had unconsciously been drifting into the danger of love for woman is apparent from his subconscious idealization of his disciples—of Beatriz in particular. His love for woman, which must necessarily be suppressed, is purged from his consciousness by way of the vision; or to put it more exactly, it is redirected to paternal affection and guidance. Now, more than ever, he is animated in this role, for he heartily welcomes to his retinue another disciple, the criminal *el Sacrílego*. In short, he returns to his former adjustment of passive submissiveness, but he has acquired and will not lose the vitalizing force of spiritual leadership.

The novel ends with Nazarín's hospitalization for illness and possible insanity. The author thus returns to his starting point, with a question as to his hero's sanity, and a second question as to whether those nearest to God are not in danger of being judged insane by the average citizen of this world. This is playful speculation on his part, in keeping with the mood of fantasy in which he has composed his story. That Nazarín now appears to be not entirely lucid is the physical result of an emotional reaction, for he has been perfectly normal throughout the story, and there can be no doubt that the author has related his hero's experiences with a definite objective of demonstrating reorientation and change in a person of fixed mystic ideals. Nazarín henceforth will remain chastened to the extent that he will be humbly obedient to his official superiors in the Church. This is the concession to established order which individual conscience is forced to make. His individuality, stamped with the ideal of spiritual leadership, eventually asserts itself clearly in *Halma,* which presents a view of his final stage of development.

The psychological story of *Nazarín,* then, may be summarized as follows: A negatively inclined personality, bent on withdrawing from the world, is reluctantly brought into human relationships in which positive service and personal affection become a source of pride and pleasure. With an abrupt blockage of the new-found values, the personality adjusts by renouncing individual affection in favor of self-abnegation, an underlying and constant trait. In the test, however, the personality has gained the values of fatherly, protective responsibility, an expansion of warmth toward humanity, a positive attitude regarding Christianity, and a Christlike forbearance tempered in the crucible of experience. In brief, an ascetic is changed into a teacher and leader. The following is a diagram of the psychological plot:

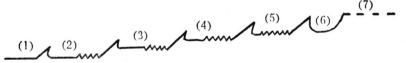

Section (1) represents the first rugged contact with the world; (2) the decision to seek solitude and privation; (3) the orientation toward positive service; (4) the plateau of personal affection and leadership;

(5) the test following a sudden blockage of the new-found values, and the resolution of the conflict; (6) the lethargic aftermath to the emotional climax; and (7) the plateau on which the personality eventually stabilizes (in *Halma*). Each of the psychological peripetias, while coinciding with an important turn of events in the surface plot, marks a decisive turn in personality development. Even more important is the fact that each step is psychologically dependent upon the preceding step. Consider the following simplified diagram:

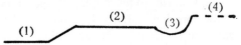

Section (1) represents the activation; (2) orientation and change; (3) the crisis; and (4) the stabilization. The level of personality seen in (4) could neither logically nor naturally have been reached without passing through (2) and (3).

Nazarín, especially in Parts III and IV, is a tale of *cristianas aventuras* which affords aesthetic pleasure simply as a story of adventure and personal relationships. If viewed as a whole, its progressive psychological movement must be visualized in order to appreciate its full aesthetic quality or to grasp the novel's moral and philosophic significance. As a story of events, *Nazarín* relates a series of experiences on the part of a priest who has the ideal of a life of poverty and Christian self-denial, and who as a result is finally arrested and tried for insanity (in *Halma*). This situational climax focuses attention on the question of the hero's sanity and the disillusioning fact that Christianity as a pure and simple ideal is impossible in this world of highly organized and unimaginative formalism—an idea undoubtedly prominent in the author's mind. The psychological story, however, makes clear the possibility of pure Christianity as an outgrowth of the opposition between individualism and conformity.

The number of plateau developments in the separate novels varies, but the comprehensive picture is always the same: an initial plane as a starting point, an intermediate ground of orientation and change, and a final plane of consolidation or anticipated consolidation. In *Fortunata y Jacinta* there are about twenty specific dynamic situations which may be considered as bearing decisively upon Fortunata's regenerative development in self-respect. These may be reduced to six different plateau advances: (1) a desire for social respectability; (2) a stimulated conscience in regard to honesty and aversion to treacherous action; (3) competitive incentive toward moral respectability; (4) competitive incentive toward physical superiority over her rival (especially as regards the capacity for bearing children); (5) magnanimity in competition and desire for mutuality of respect; (6) a drive for equality in saintliness with her rival. The fourth step, instead of the usual penultimate step, is the climactic one, because it assures Fortunata of the self-confidence which enables her to transcend the vengefulness of her inferiority and thus make a decided turn from negative to positive action. The novel also differs slightly from the norm in that the last step leaves the central character in the turbulent middle of a new advance (prematurely cut short by death), rather than at a point of relaxed transition. These different divisions, of course, merge in a more or less gradual ascent, which includes periods of frustration, relaxation, retrocession, and renewal of drives, and which produces an over-all impression of continuous rhythmical movement.

It seems fitting to examine in detail one of Galdós' most luxuriant creations, taking into account the novelist's handling of abundant collateral material in its relation to the dominant psychological plot. *Angel Guerra* (1890-1891) is a logical choice, since this novel is representative of the most vigorous period in Galdós' career. Like *Fortunata y Jacinta*, it is a vast tragicomic panorama with a wide range of human types and human experiences solidly grounded in a setting of rich local color. It is, however, a more subjective work, not only because it is freer of the attitude of social historian, but because it is more revelatory of the author's intimate personal aspirations. Also, its plot is more decidedly concentrated upon a single personage; for the psychological journey of Angel Guerra is the one dominating interest of the author. Summarized from the standpoint of situational progression, the story shows the following major divisions, each of which terminates with a decisive turn in events:

1. (I, i-iii)—Preparation for Angel's break with the proletariat and his return to a conventional life: his disillusionment with the life of a political and social revolutionist; an introduction to his paramour, the sincere and loyal Dulcenombre Babel, and her impoverished middle-class family, a curious mixture of upper-class aspirations, proletarian sympathies, and picaresque adjustment; his return home because of need of money and a desire to see his small daughter Ción; an introduction to the mystically inclined Leré, tutoress of his daughter; a glance back at his early youth and his relations with his despotic mother; his mother's death.

2. (I, iv-vii)—Angel's decisive reorientation to conventional living

and the transfer of his enthusiasm from Dulcenombre to Leré: his depression following his mother's death, giving way to a growing love for Leré; Leré's family background and her mystic aspirations; Angel's increasing indifference to his proletarian ties; Ción's sickness and death; Leré's departure for Toledo; Angel's definite withdrawal from Dulcenombre; her despair and the efforts of her uncle (don Pito Babel) to console her.

3. (II, i-iv)—The first stage of Angel's mystic orientation: his move to Toledo; introduction to the Toledan branches of his mother's family and to Leré's relatives, particularly the priest Mancebo, her talkative and money-minded uncle; the religious atmosphere of Toledo, with its cathedrals and its numerous priests; Angel's visits with Leré, and her preparation for entering an order of the strictest kind of self-abnegation; arrival of the Babel family in Toledo and Dulcenombre's temporary degeneration after her futile efforts to regain Angel's love; Angel's growing inclination to embrace a mystic goal; peaceful life on his country estate (the Cigarral de Guadalupe); his protective care of don Pito; his plans for a new religious order; his visit to Dulcenombre (at Leré's insistence that he either marry Dulcenombre or break with her decisively); his fight with Dulcenombre's brother Arístides, and his subsequent discouragement in his religious endeavors.

4. (II, v-vii)—Angel's decision to become a priest: renewal of courage, and preparation for becoming a priest; Dulcenombre's recovery from desperation and her peaceful withdrawal from Angel; the latter's indignation at the rumor that Leré must leave Toledo because of gossip about their relations; his excitement over the false report that Leré is going to give up her mystic calling; Leré's promise to govern his new order, on condition that he become a priest; Angel's mystic exaltation.

5. (III, i-v)—The high mark of Angel's "mysticism," in his ideals of *caballería cristiana:* serene life in the country and peaceful orientation to saintliness; benevolent protection of don Pito; association with the practically inclined priest Juan Casado; ecstatic visions; apotheosis of Leré; recurring struggle with carnal love for Leré; enthusiasm for his religious mission and plans for building a home for the new order; expansion of interest in helping those in need; protection of his former enemies, the brothers of Dulcenombre.

6. (III, vi)—Final test and dissolution of the mystic drive: Angel's continued goal of humbling self and helping others; resurgent anger and fight as Dulcenombre's brothers and don Pito's renegade son wound

and rob him; admission on his deathbed that his mystic drive was no more than love for Leré; bequest of his money to charity and friends; Leré's sorrow and stoical continuance of her religious work.

From the standpoint of surface happenings, then, the novel recounts the love story of a man who tries in vain to win his loved one away from her religious calling and then decides to follow her in a mystic journey, only to realize at last that his mystic enthusiasm was little more than the love of woman. The dramatization of this theme constitutes the body of the narrative action. Without searching far beneath the surface, it is possible to draw conclusions as to the novel's significance, looking especially to the subject of religion and love. Among the possible thematic interpretations may be included that of "por el amor, la fe,"[3] since Angel through love of woman is won back to his Christian faith. Or Angel's experience may be considered as representing a change in orientation from *lo politico* (Dulcenombre) to *lo absoluto* (Leré), at the same time picturing a particular case of mysticism as being a sublimation of sex.[4] A fuller understanding and appreciation of the novel will result from an examination of the psychological course of its plot, with attention to the major divisions listed above:

1. Although the author devotes comparatively little space to Angel's early history (Angel is thirty years old when the story begins), he makes clear a few facts that are basic to an understanding of his protagonist's personality. Most important of these is the relationship between Angel and his mother, one of the severe and dictatorial women so frequently seen in Galdós' novels and undoubtedly a remembrance of the author's own mother. An authoritarian who adhered rigidly to convention, demanding obedience always, and seldom responding with a show of affection, she had held her son in subjection during his early youth and had forced him to marry against his will. On the death of his wife, Angel had broken loose in rebellion against parental authority and the rigidity of convention, and had espoused a revolutionary cause, allying himself politically with the underdogs of society and embracing an anti-conventional ideal concerning love. In this way he had tried to satisfy his needs of self-assertion and affection. Both of these continue to be dominant forces throughout his life, the one manifest in his idealistic dreams of reform, and the other, in his love for Leré. The protagonist's delicate nervous temperament explains the recurring states of hypersensitivity and hyperanaesthesia which accompany the critical phases of his experiences. It also harmonizes with his idealism and in some degree explains his capacity for mystic exaltation, but the physical components

of his personality are of secondary significance in comparison with the effects of his family relationship.

Angel's political activity and his love for Dulcenombre were primarily an escape from his mother. The moment he experiences a serious setback in his revolutionary endeavors, the early conditioning of his personality begins to reassert itself, and his thoughts turn to the peace of home and family. The old attitudes acquired in a conventional atmosphere regain their hold when he is obliged to stay in his mother's house during her illness, and they triumph when, after his mother's death, he becomes his own master. The transitional stage of his return to conventional life is marked by two high points of psychological tension. The first, manifest in nervous excitability and frustration (I, i, *i-v*) follows the failure of an uprising against the government. The second is a stifled and confused conflict of opposition to and concern for his mother when he faces her just before her death (I, iii, *x-xii*). It is followed by a period of depression and stupor, from which he emerges with a definite reorientation.

2. After his mother's death, Angel rationalizes his desertion of Dulcenombre, using as an excuse the Babel family and the desire to comply with his mother's last request. He is plainly interested in Leré physically, but his opposition to her ascetic aspirations does not prevent his admiration of her mystic grandeur, and he turns to her like a docile child in search of comfort and consolation from one who is stronger than he. He thus finds in the strong-willed and orderly Leré what he did not find in Dulcenombre: a substitute for his mother; and he transfers to her both his ingrained submissiveness and his longing for sympathy and understanding.

At this stage, Angel is in reality a selfish and petulant child, whose dominant adjustive traits are nervous irritability and lack of self-control. Under Leré's sympathetic tutelage he begins to put into practice the main principles of her doctrine: self-domination, charity, and compassion for others. The evidences of anticipated change in this respect appear in a few easy steps, particularly in his charity with Dulcenombre and her family; but the main change continues to be the resumption of conventional attitudes, notably with reference to morality.

The one climactic episode in this section of the novel, Ción's illness and death (I, v, *i-iii*), is both a mechanical and a psychological development in the plot. For one thing, it leaves Leré to be the major focal point of Angel's close personal interest. It also represents an emotional preparation for his religious orientation. For although he responds under stress with his usual excitability and rebelliousness, he is forced to examine his conscience—more than he had on the occasion of his mother's death—and shows almost a willingness to enter the Church in exchange for his daughter's life. His religious inclination, like his examination of conscience, is superficial, to be sure; but his tense nervous state gives signs of the possibility of directing his capacity for exaltation into a religious channel. Most important of all is the definite turn in his conception of morality, arising from his comparing Dulcenombre and Leré. In his bargaining with God, he now thinks—selfishly—of Dulcenombre as a sinner who could gain pardon for her sinful life by dying in Ción's stead.

The peripetia of Ción's death, then, is marked by an intensification of influences and a decisive turn in Angel's thinking. What follows in Part I is largely an elaboration on the decision already made (the shift from Dulcenombre to Leré). The author departs for a time from his central personage to attend to the minor characters who have been drawn into the Angel-Dulcenombre relationship and who are to figure in the rest of the novel in this auxiliary way. The Babel family, including Dulcenombre herself, serves the primary purpose of testing Angel in his personality development. Don Pito, especially, is important in the story, not only because he later helps to shape the course of events, but also because he comes to be a primary means for testing Angel's growth in reference to compassion for others.

Having introduced these minor characters, the author takes delight in colorful descriptive delineation and presents both a picture of Spanish types and a view of the wretchedness of proletarian society. He thus goes further than is strictly necessary for his main narrative theme. Such is the case in chapter six, where members of the Babel clan swarm around Angel, taking advantage of his liberality. The material here, while forming a backdrop for Angel's desertion of his paramour, is unnecessarily drawn out, if not actually boring. The final episode in Part I, however, having to do with Dulcenombre's despair and don Pito's efforts to console her (I, vii), is a study in individual human misery viewed as being both tragic and comic, and artistically rises far above the level of descriptive sketching. This is one of the few places in the novel in which a situation stands out as an artistic unit independent of the main character. Incidentally, of course, it emphasizes Angel's cruelty at this stage of his development.

3. Beginning with Part II, the novel becomes a story of the modification of the hero's love for Leré and the resultant modification in him.

Entirely subservient to Leré and therefore co-operative, Angel shows an increasing susceptibility to her spiritual idealism, though he is never able to disregard her physical attraction. Also, by way of aesthetic appreciation, his mood finds easy harmony with the somnolent religious atmosphere of Toledo. His religious orientation thus has a peaceful and lyrical beginning, which is encouraged by his sympathetic companions among the priests and the idyllics of his life on his country estate. His earlier social idealism comes to the surface again in his association with humble people and combines with a renewed self-assertiveness as he begins to think of founding a new order. The new order, of course, is to be governed by Leré, and he himself is to be a *cofrade,* thus to remain close to his beloved in a kind of spiritual matrimony.

This peaceful reshaping of ideas is leisurely depicted amidst numerous scenes of personal relationships. The number of minor characters grows in an ever expanding circle of relatives and acquaintances centering around Leré and Dulcenombre. Galdós at times appears to be intent upon writing histories of families, for his novels are usually constructed around family groups which themselves form social units. This method is a convenient way of creating an impression of real life, since it keeps the same personages constantly before our eyes. In similar manner, the characters that reappear from one novel to another leave an impression of their realness as belonging to a family circle with which presumably the reader is already acquainted. They also afford a view of continuously related elements that knit Spanish society together in composite groups. The attention devoted to them slows down the main narrative movement but provides compensation in the enlarged perspective of human nature; for in some cases the minor portraits assume a psychological stature of their own. In *Angel Guerra* this is true with respect to don Pito and the priests Mancebo, Casado, and don Tomé, for example. Only in a few instances does the author become interested in scenic delineation for its own sake, either with regard to local types or physical surroundings. The interest lies predominantly in a picture of collective humanity as seen through individual problems of socio-psychological adjustment.

This seemingly dispersive material having to do with various personalities serves two main functions in *Angel Guerra*. For one thing, it is a means of depicting Spanish society from a comprehensive viewpoint. For another, it allows the main character to advance gradually in his psychological growth. This picture of slow advance is a very important feature of the novelist's structural method. Galdós prefers to let time run its course, instead of jumping from one dramatic episode to another, as in a theatrical composition; hence the slow transitions that work up gradually to climactic points in the story. Since the author is writing a novel of character, not a novel of customs, he sees in the minor personages an opportunity for portraying his protagonist's growth. Without the many associations with other people, Angel's self-enlargement would be impossible. In these associations he finds the medium for testing and observing his advance. Under Leré's direction, he deliberately tries to bring about change, constantly watching and analyzing his progress as he seeks to enforce a doctrine of service to others and suppression of the ego. His first setback comes when he gives in to anger and disgust, and fights Dulcenombre's brother Arístides (II, IV, *vi*). The psychological dynamics of this climactic scene consists chiefly of Angel's efforts at self-control while in a state of excitation, and is followed by lethargy and visions. The author thus dramatizes, in an intermediate peripetia, a test in self-domination, which is secondary to Angel's love for Leré.

4. In the latter half of Part II, however, the emphasis falls on the developing relation between the two principal characters, while the theme of self-improvement, manifest in self-control, indulgence, and compassion for others, remains in the background as a natural and spontaneous development. Although Angel renews his religious drive, thinking seriously of becoming a priest, he is altogether personal in his religion, associating piety and indulgence more easily with the "belleza ideal y lírica" of the Virgin than with male saints, and reaching quixotic exaltation in praise of Leré's saintliness. The fusion of religious lyricism and love for woman comes to a climactic peak when, after a renewed but short-lived hope of marrying Leré, he receives her promise to govern his new order, on condition that he become a priest (II, VII, *iv*). The dynamics of Angel's psychology at this point lies in his transference of worshipful rapture from a carnal to an imaginary spiritual realm. His childlike dependence on woman, his longing for sympathy, and his carnal desires all merge in a climax of complete abdication of self in mystic exaltation; and for the first time, Leré gives evidence of her love for Angel.

For Leré herself is undergoing change. In Part I she appears essentially as a frigidly fixed personality, supremely serene and self-satisfied with respect to her ideal of martyrdom. Though balanced by friendliness and tolerance, her mysticism points toward a severe and selfish kind of asceticism. Under the influence of Angel's company, she acquires a sense of responsibility in guiding him, takes pride in her directive mission, and develops a warm personal feeling for her ward which goes

beyond the limits of mere fraternal sympathy. This feeling is evident
not only in her request that Angel become a priest, thereby moving out
of the reach of another woman, but also in her happy contemplation
of the thought that the father of Ción is going to be associated with her
in a common undertaking. She thus pictures in her mind an intimate
family group. This is the same kind of mental image that Angel has
had in some of his visions and amounts to an unconscious acceptance
of a proposal of marriage. The scene here referred to (II, vii, *iv*)
presents, in fact, a subtle circumvention of the law against marriage on
the part of two persons who are about to become priest and nun, and
may appropriately be called a mystic betrothal.

5. Having reached this peaceful and satisfying height of requited
love, Angel takes a decided step forward in spiritual growth. He still
maintains a conscious struggle for mastery of self and a struggle with
the carnality of his love for Leré—sometimes portrayed, by way of
visions, as a subconscious conflict. His compassion for others is now
more spontaneous than ever before; and he now looks with repugnance
on his former life and finds serene pleasure in pursuing his saintly
goal, helping the needy, humbling himself before his former enemies,
and losing all sense of fear, which he defines as the subordination of
self to physical laws. His mysticism is still a form of lyrical exaltation,
which finds outlet at times in ecstatic visions, and is centered upon a
quixotic dream of establishing a religious order more liberal and humanitarian than any in existence. At the base of this ideal is the patriotic
desire to rejuvenate Catholicism in Spain. Angel's urge to assert his
individuality thus comes forcibly to the front again with the reappear-
ance of a revolutionary zeal directed toward constructive endeavor.

In this section of the novel, as in the first half of Part II, the author
deals leisurely with numerous personalities and situations. They include
the final dismissal of Dulcenombre, who has been all along scarcely
more than the victim of another's adjustive problem. Sincerely and
wholeheartedly in love with Angel, she had wavered momentarily on the
verge of disintegration, only to recover stoically and in conformity with
conventional respectability as she agrees unenthusiastically to marry a
distant relative. Angel's growing compassion has included her in its
radius, but he himself is wholly bound to Leré, the generative source of
his self-elevation. The major interest in Part III centers upon the new
plateau in his development, a direct result of the love of woman, without which—in his own words—all efforts to do good would be futile.

6. The author, however, must subject his hero—and his own

thesis—to a final test. Two questions must be answered: (1) to what degree has Angel succeeded in his religious goal of suppressing self, and (2) what has he gained from his emotional journey? The test comes in a climactic episode (III, VI, *ii-iii*), in which Dulcenombre's brothers and don Pito's son carry out their plan to rob Angel. At this point Angel believes that he has attained the ideal of self-annihilation: "anular la propia personalidad y no ver más que la del prójimo" (V, 1565). He is suddenly brought back to reality by Arístides' sarcastic remarks concerning Leré, and though struggling momentarily for self-control, he finally explodes with furious anger. He has been trying all the time to transfer his love to a substitute goal of self-annulment. In this he has failed, and he humbly returns to what seems to be his starting point: an admission that his mysticism is nothing more than love of woman.

What at first had been a purely egoistic desire, however, must now be judged on the basis of observable gains in self-improvement resulting from the love experience. Attention, therefore, as in Part II, is directed to a climactic scene of the love story, in relation to which the prior test in self-domination is only an accessory. The high point of the love story comes in the final chapters (III, VI, *v-vii*), where Angel on his deathbed speaks simply and earnestly of his love and calls Leré his wife. Here Leré again gives evidence of her love for Angel: in her plea to be forgiven for having hurt him, in her stifled emotions when he calls her wife, and in her assertion that she would like to die and go to heaven with him. This is the final dynamic experience and may be called the peripetia of mystic marriage.

The concluding paragraph directs attention to the saintliness attained by the main character and indicates how important a part of the story the author considers his hero's personal development to be. In an ascetic sense, Angel has failed to suppress his individuality, but he has advanced in the domination of his selfish and childish egoism. While having to admit, like Don Quijote, the illusoriness of his exalted dreams, he has developed a love for his neighbor, has become a champion of the unfortunate, and retains to the end an acquired magnanimity toward his enemies. The development in Leré harmonizes with that of the protagonist, for she has been saved from asceticism by her close association with another person. The love story, in fact, has confirmed what is undoubtedly the author's unifying idea (the expansion of love from a purely personal to a broad collective relationship), an idea embodied in the words of the hero shortly before he dies: "el amor, si iniciado como sentimiento exclusivo y personal, extendido luego a toda la humanidad" (V, 1573). The novel, therefore, ends in a peak development, with both love and personality transformation ascendant.

A diagram of the plot, when reduced to its essentials, shows three outstanding peaks with two major plateau evolvements between: (1) the death of Angel's mother, (2) the mystic betrothal, and (3) the mystic marriage:

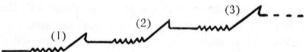

The first of these major steps marks Angel's release from the despotism of one woman and the beginning of his spiritual climb under the elevating influence of another. The second, which establishes a community of ideals, specifies the crystallization of generative power for renewed inspiration and spiritual activity. The third represents the triumph of human love and defines the results in spiritual growth.

The story of Angel Guerra depicts the sublimation of sex, but the emphasis rests upon the elevating effects rather than a detached analysis of the love experience. Leré becomes for the hero another Dulcinea—the priest Mancebo on one occasion (V, 1450) calls her doña Leré del Toboso—and personalizes a glorification of woman, an ideal necessary to the evocation of all that is good in man. Angel's dream of mystic achievement, which is motivated by his love for Leré, is a redirection of his drive for self-realization. His dream ends in seeming disillusionment, but the results are more important to him than attainment of the goal to which he first aspired. For the lyricism which envelops the love story does not obscure the practical, realistic core of the novel. The personality growth which accompanies the dream of self-realization carries with it a tangible reward in emotional maturity and spiritual self-enlargement. These parallel developments merge with the love story in a final point of harmony, which provides a logical terminus for the personal experience and invests the composition with artistic finality and oneness. The plot movement thus fuses lyricism and the portrayal of psychological growth in a deliberately organized structural form.

Angel Guerra is illustrative of the balance which Galdós maintains between character development and the sequence of events. To each he gives approximately equal importance in an interdependent relationship. Certain noteworthy happenings in Angel's history (failure of the uprising against the government, the death of his mother, the two fights with Dulcenombre's brothers) may be attributed in good part to chance, but they are inseparably linked with the protagonist's psychological problem. The novelist here and in general allows chance events and personality to interact, each with determinative force. An assertion of Sáinz de Robles is of interest in this connection:

> El no busca los problemas hondos y terriblemente humanos antes de crear los personajes que han de vivirlos. Galdós crea primero a sus criaturas . . . en cuanto ellas se lanzan al mundo a desarrollar y a desgastar sus energías se encuentran enredadas, aprisionadas, revoltijadas en la malla de los sucesos, de los actos y de las cosas reales.[5]

It would be well to modify this statement and say that Galdós places a particular personality in the midst of a series of *sucesos* and watches it develop as a natural growth out of the interaction with events.

This method is somewhat different from that of such writers as Stendhal (Julien Sorel), Flaubert (Emma Bovary), and Alas (Ana Ozores), who first visualize their personages as symbolic of a great human urge, and then conduct them through a succession of happenings that are presumably necessary to demonstrate a predetermined personality. For this reason the characters may seem to control the plot more closely than they do in the novels of Galdós. In *La desheredada,* the compulsion which propels Isidora relentlessly forward makes her seem like a personage from a novel of Flaubert or Alas, but even here the author is concerned with a personality development which depends upon the turn of events as much as it influences them. In the novels of Galdós, people, chance happenings, and environment are on an equal footing of cause and effect, and it can be said that every significant event involving his main characters is utilized as a means of presenting a logical progression in personality. Perhaps this is as close as characterization can be related to plot and still be consistent with probability.

Galdós visualizes his basic plot movement as being an interrelationship of environment, events, and individual growth, even when he resorts to the shortened form of the *novela dialogada.* In this form the novelist unfortunately gives free rein to the strong thematic purpose which is so characteristic of his late dramatic compositions. As a result, the characterizations are sometimes thinly sketched symbolical portraits—symbols of ideas rather than special aspects of individual human nature; but the method remains substantially the same. Galdós was unable to lay aside his long practice of tracing personality change amidst a set of relationships that can be expected to effect change.

This practice proved to be no handicap when the author developed his narrative as the resolution of a specific situational problem. *El abuelo* is a successful handling of the plateau development, primarily because, like some of the early works, it is concentrated around a situation having concise divisions that lend themselves easily to dramatic presentation: the Conde de Albrit's problem of confirming his ideal of family honor (nobleness of blood), the test and failure, and the substitution of a new source of strength. Merged with these steps is the psychological story of tension, changing orientation, climax which determines a shift from old to new values, and consolidation of change. The Conde's integrity, which he has sought to preserve by proving his ideal of honor, threatens to fall apart on the discovery of his granddaughter's identity. The new value (love), which had begun to effect a basic change and had thus initiated an intermediate plateau, now becomes the means of recovery and lifts the Conde to a firm level of development, at which love, and with it an acquired magnanimity and tolerance, assures the protagonist's regeneration. The author could have endued his conclusion with the momentum of tragedy by terminating the action at the point of breakdown and despair. Two motives apparently impelled him to add the *Escena última,* which, like the epilogue in *Doña Perfecta,* is a brief but important element of the whole: (1) a didactic intent and (2) a persistent inclination to produce stories of personality development. Both motives, of course, are grounded in his social and philosophical idealism.

Galdós' novels left much to be desired when he tried to compress an essentially biographical narrative into brief dramatic form. *La loca de la casa* (1892) is an example of this kind of *novela dialogada,* in which the design is precisely conceived and the story of character development severely abridged. Briefly summarized, the narrative traces the outcome of Victoria Moncada's decision to abandon her ascetic intentions and marry Cruz, a brutish kind of person, as a means of warding off her father's impending financial ruin. The marriage proves to be a contest between two strong wills. It passes through a period of threatening collapse and results finally in a firm and harmonious union, with both parties realizing their increasing need for each other. From one viewpoint, the story is that of the taming of a beast, and the author apparently did recall *La Belle et la bête* by Mme. Leprince de Beaumont, as well as La Fontaine's *Le Lion amoureux.*[6] This is a rather unimportant consideration, however, for as usual the real substance of the novel lies in the characters' behavior in the face of a given situation or set of circumstances.

In the case of Cruz, as is so frequently true in Galdós, the formative period of his personality must be seen in order to understand his actions.

The author supplies this information as fully as he can while using the dramatic form as a medium. In Act I, scene vii, especially, the causes of Cruz's warped personality are clearly seen. Feeling intensely the inferiority of his social position and the loneliness and lack of affection in his boyhood days on the Moncada estate, he had undertaken a determined campaign to prove his worth in society by calling on his natural strength and vitality. The drive thus initiated in his youth has become an inflexibly aggressive reaction by which he seeks to counterbalance the weight of class distinction. It has led him into the egocentric individualism of a self-made man who glorifies physical power, efficiency, mastery over others, the acquisition of money (as a symbol of power and accomplishment), and a defiant disregard of social niceties. His moral philosophy includes unswerving honesty and a brutal frankness, but it is heavily colored with antisentimental, anticharitable belief in the doctrine of the survival of the fittest, which reflects pride in his competitive power and a defensive compensation for his lonely youth.

This is the level of development which Cruz has reached when the story begins. At this time he is in the tense psychological state of a drive toward a goal: marriage with his former master's daughter. Tension relaxes after the satisfaction of this specific aim (II, xviii), itself a symbol of success and redress, and Cruz remains for some time in a calm state of mind, taking for granted the justification of his philosophy of life and following by habit his established norm of activity.

With Victoria's reversal of attitude from quiet submissiveness, however, Cruz is aroused to defend his role of master (III, xvi-xix). He responds with the angry, recriminatory frustration of one whose will to have his own way has been challenged, but the effects of his association with Victoria have initiated a change which he himself comes increasingly to realize. In this, his first test, he recognizes that his jealousy and suspicions are but evidence of a love which henceforth will be indispensable to his being, and this self-objectivation plainly shows a weakening in stubborn independence and self-sufficiency.

Thus begins a conflict between old and new values, which resolves itself in a compromise or "bargain" (IV, xvi), wherein Cruz relents in his selfishness and his antipathy to charity toward others, while retaining a strong pride in his personal accomplishment and the hope for a son to prove still further his place in society. He by no means makes an abrupt about-face. His concessions to charity have been wrung from him almost by force, but the imprint of his relations with Victoria is indelible, and he is on the threshold of a new personality plateau, where his staunch individualism finds new orientation and strength in his dependence upon the love of another. He himself affirms as much in the *Escena última*.

The developing psychological plot in Cruz's case may be diagramed as follows:

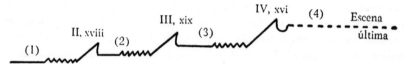

Section (1) represents the initial drive of a self-made man; (2) the beginning of change, which reaches a stage of test and suspended decision; (3) decisive confirmation of change; and (4) stabilization on a new plateau.

Victoria is a much more symbolic or abstract characterization than Cruz, but she too shows a definite development in accord with a deliberate design in plot structure. She appears first as a highly imaginative person with a strong aspiration for glorious self-realization. Her ideal is directed—misdirected, in the author's mind—toward ascetic withdrawal and self-punishment as a means of pleasing God. She is, however, a flexible individual, and without great difficulty diverts her impulsive idealism into self-sacrifice for her family (II, xviii), a natural and decisive transition to a new perspective of life. This is still a negative orientation much akin to martyrdom, but after a period of adjustment in which she becomes personally interested in her husband, she channels her urge to self-realization as if by inspiration into a positive direction (III, xii-xix).

With the resoluteness and zeal of a missionary, she now concentrates upon elevating Cruz spiritually. She assumes, in fact, the role of a *maestra* who is intent upon putting her ward in his proper place; and psychologically she exhibits a co-ordination of efforts in a drive toward a goal, until the successful outcome of her mission (IV, xvi). She has seemed to be a self-righteous authoritarian who imposes a one-and-only law of right on a person who is wrong *a priori;* but unconsciously she herself has been subjected to a natural law of change, in which she no longer holds a one-sided attitude. Her association with Cruz has broadened her range of values, even to include the business world; her missionary objective has brought out her practical capacities for management and manipulation; and she has come to realize finally (*Escena última*) that her own integrity depends upon the "evil" person whom she had despised. In brief, her urge to self-realization has been decisively channelled away from self-annihilation to a positive kind of self-assertion within a close personal relationship of mutual dependence.

The psychological plot in the case of Victoria is diagramed as follows:

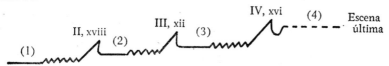

Section (1) represents the initial level of perspective, which assumes a new direction in the first psychological peripetia; (2) the second reorientation, in the role of *maestra,* which comes to its logical culmination in (3); and (4) the anticipated new plateau. The lines of development in Cruz and Victoria parallel each other closely, each having two ascending stages, and both merging on a level of concession to a law of mutuality or interdependence of personalities. The *Escena última* thus designates a central allegorical theme and at the same time gives finality to the plot development.

For the moment, the symbolism of *La loca de la casa* will not be discussed except to point out that the author's thematic intent overshadows the study of character and thus detracts from the novel's literary merit. The structural framework is clearly drawn, but the body of the narrative is insufficiently developed. This fact is substantially explained by a scarcity of material necessary to depict the process of personality growth. Hence the emphasis rests on the conclusions rather than the story on which the conclusions are based. The biographical nature of *La loca de la casa* calls for an elaboration of slow transitional stages. The author tries to fill the gaps by briefly calling attention to the effects of the association of Cruz and Victoria (III, viii-x; IV, vii-xii); but his sharp reduction in scenes which portray his characters' changing orientation results in an inevitable thinness, while making the ideological purpose even more conspicuous. The three steps in the biography of the central characters—four steps if the *Escena última* is included—underscore the author's ideas but leave barely more than a skeleton plot.

Instead of attempting a dramatic novel of precise formal proportions, Galdós would have done well to follow the technique which he occasionally tried in his earlier stories. The first chapter of *Tormento,* an example of sparkling fill-in material, illustrates how he could have written a *novela dialogada* without sacrificing the casual detail so appropriate to his talent, or without having to bother with the mechanics of stage production. The conversation between Felipe Centeno and the voluble Ido del Sagrario gives the author an opportunity to indulge his own volubility while laughing at the *novela por entregas* turned out in mass production. At the same time, the dialogue scene serves as exposition for the main plot while vividly portraying two minor personalities, both of them reappearing characters whose acquaintance the reader is glad to renew. Abundance in background scenes and situations may retard the narrative movement of Galdós' most representative and most substantial works, but it was indispensable to the full exercise of his novelistic ability.

Because of the retardative collateral material in the long novels of biographical design, the reader is in danger of overlooking their well-defined structure. For although the novelist was not painstaking in refining his compositions, he was deliberate in shaping his narrative plan. His most characteristic plot movement may be likened to a current that flows sometimes straight ahead, sometimes by circuitous routes, but always with sureness toward a definite destination. The amount of collateral material that is drawn into the stream varies with each novel and in varying degree retards the forward movement. The progression, however, is always clearly discernible in the form of a psychological development that binds multiple experiences to a central framework. The central characters themselves provide the chief plot development: a story of adjustment to a general social situation and the particular circumstances included therein. The narrative, adjustive problem amounts to a test of the individual in a natural conflict between his spontaneous self-assertiveness and the social whole, with which he must necessarily compromise. As in real life, the adjustive experience entails personality change, which is seen both in its transitional stages and in the decisive moments that crystallize developments gradually prepared for. It is especially important to note that the periods of new orientation are preceded by climactic scenes showing intense psychological dynamics. That this method was deliberate is indicated by the quotation from *Lo prohibido* cited earlier in this study: "La facultad de asimilación varía . . . en las épocas críticas y en las crisis de pasiones adquiere gran desarrollo" (IV, 1873). Change thus becomes a dramatic element of the plot and coincides with surface events along a line of peripetias and plateaus that mark recurring periods of tension and tension discharge. In Galdós' early novels, in which the test of the individual is treated within a single comprehensive situation more or less concentrated, the factor of change appears primarily as a terminal point that adds finality to the story. In the more elaborate biographical structure of the later novels, it is more deliberately incorporated in the developing plot. In either case, adjustment and change are dramatized as major steps in an organized progressive movement.

The very heart of Galdós' vitality is his view of individual personality and of life in general as a *continual becoming*. The story of Fortunata, which ends while she is still in a stage of foment and change, is the supreme example of this dynamic feature. The fact that the novelist was able to shape this conception of human nature into a dramatic consummation of organized movement constitutes a major portion of his aesthetic accomplishment. Whether or not readers of Galdós observe his fusion of psychological development and surface plot structure, they are conscious of his vigorous and broad treatment of life. Those who do observe the fusion, however, become aware of Galdós as an artist who molded socio-psychological material into well-defined artistic form.

V

THE SOCIAL PROCESS

THUS far in the present study the emphasis has rested on psychological processes and their integration with narrative form in Galdós' novels. It is now time to expand the frame of reference to encompass in broader perspective the novelist's vision of life. Interest centers first on the social picture, and in keeping with the general thesis, attention is directed more to the functional than to the descriptive view of society. That is, the aim is to observe what relationships are found in operation and how their operation produces change and growth both in the individual and in society itself. The portraiture of change in society as a whole will seem to be of secondary importance in comparison with that in the individual, but it is nonetheless demonstrable in some of the novels—as a process working itself out in the members of society, and not merely as an ideology which the author, especially in his later years, is known to have had.

No one can fail to be impressed by Galdós' marked attention to human associations. He is unmistakably a social novelist, and the primary significance of his mission as artist and intellectual leader lies in his understanding portrayal of man as a being who moves always within society, deeply affected, for better or for worse, by his social relationships. Merely to recall the prominent motives already discussed for several of the stories is to realize the heavy associational color of the novelist's works. Of the forty-four basic "biological drives" and "social motives" mentioned in an earlier connection (page 48), the following appear most frequently in Galdós' view of human nature: approval by others, devotion to others, sympathy for others, managing others, protection of others, gregariousness, competition, ambition (in social and intimate relations), social distinction, manipulation, respect for Deity, personal appearance, imitation.

These general characteristics may seem usual for any novel that deals with man in a social setting. That they have a special importance in the novels of Galdós is evident from the relatively scant attention given to other motives (pleasure, home comfort, economy, curiosity, amusement, domesticity, efficiency, and the like), to say nothing of "biological drives" (appetite-hunger, sex attraction, bodily comfort, physical activity, etc.). From his viewpoint man is indeed a gregarious animal, who not only wants to live with others but is unavoidably drawn into complicated relations with them. In his study of man and society, his emphasis falls always on the individual, who in the final analysis is the source of society's vitality. The reaction between the impulse to individualism and the impulse to form associations, which results in a continual formation of groups around individual interests and a continual exertion of reciprocal influence by means of group action, constitutes in fact the heart of the social process.[1] Such a picture of man's associational experiences unfolds itself in the novels of Galdós, who surely held the sociological opinion that individual values have little meaning apart from their reference to membership groups, whether of the simplest primary nature or of a supra-societal kind (such as man's relation to God), which itself is inevitably colored by societal factors.

Influences or causes of change may conveniently be regarded as belonging to the following categories: individual upon individual, group upon the individual, individual upon the group, group upon group. The first two categories have far greater importance in the novels than the last two; which is to say once more that the author focused his observation predominantly upon the individual as the central point of interest in the social complex.

One of the most noticeable features of the personal relationships portrayed by Galdós is the strong influence exerted by one person on another. In its sharpest light it is a transplanting of personality traits, and amounts to a spreading of social forces by individual carriers. In just such a way María Remedios, sister of don Inocencio, becomes possessed of doña Perfecta's ecclesiastic aggressiveness and acts in the concluding part of the novel like an apostle of fanaticism in her own right. In like manner, Gloria absorbs from her aunt Serafinita the adjustment of self-punishment, and María Egipcíaca (*La familia de León Roch*) becomes an extreme and prejudiced ascetic under the persistent and pernicious tutelage of the priest Paoletti. Similarly, doña Lupe, aunt of Maximiliano Rubín (*Fortunata y Jacinta*), has acquired the penurious habits of Torquemada; and Angel Guerra, though rebellious against his mother, doña Sales, shows the deep imprint of her rigid conventionalism.

Somewhat broader in scope are those associations in which the force of a dominating personality branches out in several directions, influencing the actions of various other persons, if not always creating change in them. Doña Perfecta exerts a tremendous force on those around her. She molds the will of her inferiors to suit her own objectives, enforces her authority with deadly results upon her daughter, and eventually dominates don Inocencio completely, repaying him, as it were, with the evil effects of the authoritarianism which he has helped to instill in her. In a much more favorable light, Guillermina (*Fortunata y Jacinta*) dominates her associates, especially Jacinta, whose ideals concerning religion, marriage, and morality she in some measure determines. In a role even more influential, Nazarín (*Nazarín* and *Halma*) shapes the lives of Beatriz and Halma, and through Halma, the lives of others. Benina (*Misericordia*) is the center of a large circle of dependents, on most of whom she exerts an elevating influence. Strong characters like these are forces capable in themselves of initiating and shaping movements in the social order. Although Galdós in some of his later works uses them deliberately to point the way to constructive social change, he treats them for the most part merely as the nuclei of personal relations, leaving the question of societal improvement to the reader's inference.

As a generalization it can be said that destructive forces are more noticeable in the novels before 1880, constructive forces more in the novels after 1890, and an approximate balance of both in the intervening decade. Friendship, love, sympathetic leadership are the major instruments of constructive influence. Examples are found in the bond of loyalty and respect that causes Felipe Centeno to adhere to Alejandro Miquis (*El doctor Centeno*) and serves in large measure to keep him from following the life of a *pícaro;* the elevating influence of Leré and a group of priests upon Angel Guerra; and the mutually constructive association of Cruz and Victoria in *La loca de la casa.*

Of the dominating personalities in Galdós' novels, the strong-willed woman is perhaps the most conspicuous. Outstanding examples are: doña Perfecta, Camila (*Lo prohibido*), Guillermina, doña Lupe, and doña Bárbara (*Fortunata y Jacinta*), doña Paca (*Miau*), doña Sales

(*Angel Guerra*), and Juliana (*Misericordia*). Undoubtedly a major explanation lies in the fact that the novelist's own mother, herself a tyrannical ruler of her family, had left an indelible and in large degree unfavorable impression upon him. There is ground for believing, however, that Galdós' mother was also representative of a rather prominent aspect of Spanish family life, which a studious social novelist could hardly fail to incorporate in his writings. In one place in *Tristana* (V, 1592), the servant Saturna declares that only three careers are open to Spanish women: marriage, the theater, and prostitution. It is justifiable to attribute a substantial element of truth to this severe statement and to assume that the Spanish woman asserted herself by ruling the family with an iron hand or by developing managerial and directive aptitudes in relation to small circles of friends and acquaintances.

For the major part of his career, Galdós portrays Spanish women as individuals fitting into a static social structure; he does not visualize them collectively as a force exerting pressure in the social process. This does not mean, however, that he thought of woman as being bound in servitude to man by a natural law of sex rather than by social law, or that his was the medieval view that woman is either man's salvation or his ruin.[2] Certainly he believed that man and woman are bound together in a law of common spiritual growth, but members of both sexes are treated by the novelist primarily as social beings. Although woman, as a generic class, is not allowed a prominent place in the picture of social movement, it must be remembered, from the examples of doña Paulitas (*La Fontana de Oro*), Rosario (*Doña Perfecta*), Tristana, and others, that Galdós did not ignore problems having to do with the restriction of Spanish women, even though he did not develop these problems as narrative themes. Moreover, he indicated the way for a constructive use of woman's self-assertion, apart from the duties of rearing a family, by having her take part in practical affairs of the business world (*La loca de la casa, Mariucha*), or by having her assume responsibilities of caring for the socially unfortunate (Guillermina, Halma).

What has been said about woman in general can be said about the mother or the mistress of a household. And with respect to other members of the family, Galdós shows the same tendency to regard people as individuals within sets of circumstances peculiar to themselves alone. The family receives a major share of attention in the novels. Mention has already been made of the novelist's liking for centering his narration around family groups, which sometimes branch out to include numerous relations incidental to the plot. The domestic relationships that encircle Juanito Santa Cruz, Jacinta, and Maximiliano in *Fortunata y Jacinta,* and Dulcenombre Babel in *Angel Guerra* are especially elaborated upon, though largely by descriptive rather than psychological treatment. Galdós' main characters, however, are usually closely bound to family backgrounds that help to explain their personalities and to shape their lives.

Yet, with all his interest in the household, the novelist takes the viewpoint of a psychologist and a recorder of social scenes rather than that of a sociologist. He is not directly concerned with the family as an institution, though indirectly he does make its importance clear by showing its stabilizing or its destructive influence. One of the best examples of the stabilizing influence is seen in *La de Bringas,* where Rosalía Bringas, after approaching a dissolution of marital bonds, recovers her equilibrium and gains strength through the responsibility that binds her to her home. Here the triumph of the household as a unit is seen, and this is about as close as Galdós comes to presenting the family generically as an institution.

There are other instances in which the family group exercises a constructive influence upon its members, notably in the case of Jacinta (*Fortunata y Jacinta*); or where individual members act as stabilizing —not necessarily constructive—forces upon the family (Victoria in *La loca de la casa;* Benina, as a servant member, in *Misericordia*). The unfortunate aspects, however, are much more noticeable. For one thing, religious and class prejudices, to say nothing of the tyrannical rule of the mother of the household, keep the individual in bondage to tradition. These factors explain in part the broken homes and the lack of cohesiveness in family groups, which are so conspicuous in Galdós. The need to belong in the intimate circle that characterizes a peaceful home appears prominently in the novels and goes hand in hand with the numerous situations involving orphans or other persons deprived of normal domestic associations. Similar in nature and slightly less prominent are the unhappy marriages and the number of unmarried people who would like to enjoy a peaceful matrimonial state. In *Fortunata y Jacinta,* for example, every character of consequence, with the exception of Juanito and Jacinta, is without a mate; or if married, as in the case of Fortunata and Maximiliano, is denied a normal relationship.

In view of this evidence, there is reason once more to place considerable weight upon the circumstances of the author's own life which pertain to his estrangement from his home in Las Palmas and to his bachelorhood.[3] Though the group influence is deadening at times, many of Galdós' characters, as he himself did, accept unfortunate circumstances as a challenge and develop strength in spite of or as a result of the handicaps imposed. The over-all picture which the novelist gives, of course, is not one-sided. Like his portrayal of life in general, it has balance; and yet it leaves an impression of constant turmoil in the family, which, while forming the foundation of society, stirs restlessly, ready always for adjustment of existing bonds. It is this ferment, rather than a clearly defined forward movement, that characterizes Galdós' view of the family as a part of the social process.

Aside from the circles of friends and acquaintances that gravitate around the family, congeniality groups receive relatively little attention in the novels. There are a few instances of small gatherings, in cafes for example, presented descriptively, but these are given little importance in their effect upon personality. The attraction which Miau feels toward the group of government employees with which he has lost his standing is an exception. The need for retaining a "membership" status is only a corollary to his unemployment, the chief source of his insecurity, but it is a noticeable factor in his futile efforts to regain his emotional stability. Federico Viera (*Realidad*) also shows a definite imprint of the Bohemian circles with which he has long associated, though what is clearest to the reader is the personal orientation toward the prostitute *la Peri*. Friendship is one of the values most stressed by Galdós, but to organized groups of friends he remains almost totally indifferent. He is a describer of social life as well as a literary social psychologist, and it is chiefly in the former role that he presents friendly gatherings in private homes. He followed the practices of an outright novelist of customs very little in general, and certainly to a negligible degree in regard to the various small social units.

Instead of compartmentalizing society, Galdós maintains a view of social experiences in general, including especially environmental influences that operate as a collective force upon the individual. In one of its broadest aspects, this influence assumes the form of convention. As is to be expected of a social novelist, subservience to convention appears rather prominently in Galdós' works, and it is sometimes presented purely from a descriptive and satirical viewpoint, especially as pertains to vain and hypocritical incidental personages. This satirical phase of the novelist's writings is indicative of his range of vision, but it is relatively unimportant to this discussion, which is primarily concerned with the effect of conventional values upon personality as a process. The author's position in regard to conventionalism and the question of right and wrong is a separate topic, discussed later under the heading of "Moral Perspective."

If Isidora Rufete (*La desheredada*) is regarded as a victim of the worship of a traditional social hierarchy rather than of custom, Rosalía Bringas is Galdós' first important character whose personality development shows a dominating influence of conventionality. Her worship of appearances and her urge to associate with the "proper" people lead her gradually toward moral disintegration, though conventionalism in the form of adherence to family respectability re-establishes her. Cruz del Aguila (the *Torquemada* series) is animated by a similar drive to "keep up with the Joneses," and this drive determines much of her essential behavior. The morally anticonventional conduct of Eloísa (*Lo prohibido*) is in large degree the result of overemphasis on certain conventional values, since she, too, is a slave to social appearances. Doña Paca (*Misericordia*) is hardly a developing character, but she is psychologically portrayed as subservient to conventional opinion in her effort to keep up appearances befitting her family background. Fashion, social correctness, the desire to maintain a respectable competitive standing in the social system are the motivations which exhibit in the novels one major aspect of conventionality.

On the other hand, the moral restraint of customs is no less noticeable. A strong sense of decorum born of the fear of public opinion in reference to marital honor is a primary factor in complicating María Juana's psychological behavior (*Lo prohibido*), though it does not operate with enough force to prevent her infidelity to her husband. Caballero and Amparo (*Tormento*), while unconventional in their decision to live together out of marriage, actually compromise with convention in bowing to the dictates of custom which frown upon marriage for a dishonored woman, and it is this compliancy that allows Amparo to remain emotionally adjusted. Confronted with the same collective attitude, Tristana accepts her social status with resignation. Conventional propriety and decorum operate with strong effect on Guillermina, Jacinta, and doña Lupe (*Fortunata y Jacinta*), contributing to, rather than weakening, their moral stamina; while a spineless acceptance of the average attitude toward dual standards of morality for man and woman has a deadening effect on Juanito Santa Cruz.

Although Galdós seems in principle somewhat more hostile to conventionalism in his early than in his later novels, there is no intention on his part to make it appear either predominantly destructive or constructive. Moreover, it is worthy of note that he never appears to be depressed by a heavy atmosphere of conventionalism, as some of the French realists are. Even in the novels of the decade 1880-1890, which, more than any of the others perhaps, record a mediocrity in social values, he does not overemphasize this aspect. He regards conventionalism merely as an inevitable part of the social picture and records it impartially for its important place in character formation.

Of the group influences that seriously affect the individual, there are two of an institutional nature that stand out conspicuously in the novels: the Church and the social hierarchy. The novelist's attitude toward the absolutism of the Church as a fixed system of beliefs and toward its executive arm, the clergy, is so well known that it seems unnecessary to enter into the subject in detail here. A few observations are in order, however, with regard to chronology of emphasis as seen in the role that the Church plays in its effect upon personality development. It is surely true that religious beliefs are among the most inflexible, and it is maintained by some that Catholicism exerts a more potent influence than Protestantism in molding personality to fixed rules of behavior. Certainly an inflexible Catholic attitude is prominent in the novels, but Galdós apparently had no intention of making a distinction between religious faiths as regards their relative influence upon the individual. It will be recalled that Catholic and Jewish intransigence are presented impartially in *Gloria*, but in this connection it must be remembered that racial pride is more potent than Church dogma in both Daniel Morton and his mother.

What Galdós was concerned with most of all was the destructive effect of intolerance, whatever its source. In three of his early social novels he concentrated his energy toward depicting the inflexibility which starts with belief in inviolable ecclesiastical rules, is enforced by the clergy, and grows like a cancer in the individual. With youthful, iconoclastic fervor, he initiated his campaign against traditionalism, attacking primarily ecclesiastical despotism. As a result, he gave a somewhat prejudiced picture of both the Church and religion, but he left in these novels his most vivid records (doña Perfecta, Gloria, María Egipcíaca) of the excruciating force with which institutional values can tyrannize the individual. His anticlerical and antidogmatic attitude crops up consistently throughout his works and in fact reappears with thematic vigor in the last stages of his career (*Electra, Casandra*); but the history of his treatment of the Church as an institution may be described as a shift from outright attack to a sympathetic presentation of religion within the Church.

For several novels after *La familia de León Roch*, religion is negligible as a factor in character portrayal. It comes to the surface again in *Fortunata y Jacinta*, where Guillermina's Christian sentiment, in the form of charity and sympathy, counterbalances her own religious formalism and the author's hostile delineation of the priest Nicolás, brother of Maximiliano Rubín. Religion is of some consequence in *Miau* as a consoling force in Abelarda and Luisito, daughter and grandson of the central character. It becomes a major part of the narrative theme in *Angel Guerra*, in which the Church exerts a definitely constructive influence on the hero. The influence, however, comes through close personal ties, principally through Angel's love for Leré, and secondarily through friendship with priests who are governed more by human interests than by dogma. Moreover, while submitting to the Church, Angel does so by way of compromise, for he is animated by a drive to modify religious traditionalism through the establishment of a new and liberal order, and it is this assertion of individuality in the face of fixed laws that enables him to make a healthy adjustment to authoritarian rule.

The subject is similarly visualized in *Nazarín*, the author's most concentrated treatment of religion, in which he shows above all his interest in the simple fundamentals of Christianity. Religion is the integrating force in Nazarín's personality, but he, too, retains his individuality within the confines of Church discipline. This vision of religion is characteristic of Galdós' maturer years. The individual compromises with unescapable formalism by observing surface rules while developing the spirit of Christianity as his source of personal strength. Though the author never ceased to oppose asceticism and dogmatism for their destructive effect on the individual, he tended gradually to observe the constructive side of religion. He perceived how it was possible for wholesome religious sentiments and theological doctrine to be harmoniously coexistent.

Religion permeates Galdós' novels as a powerful collective force whose influence, unconsciously absorbed through habit, is imposed by institutional action, or seeps into individual consciousness as a spiritual reality. Aside from its ideological aspects, its significance is seen as a part of the interrelationship between man and society. Strictly as a psychologist, the novelist recognized the sustaining force of religious faith, the beneficial effects of confession, and the hypnotic effect of the atmosphere found in cathedrals, in addition to the evil results of formalistic conditioning. Religion is depicted in his works probably to no greater extent than should be in a proportioned record of his age, for it was a very important part of Spanish society and could not be ignored by a conscientious social novelist. It may be observed, finally, that the current of influence runs almost wholly from the group (institution) to the individual. Nazarín, for example, though influencing a large circle of acquaintances, makes no impression on the established order.

Galdós devoted more time and space to a studious presentation of social class barriers and the problems which they raise than he did to religion. He occupied the position of one who observes society from a comprehensive viewpoint, though admittedly he was oriented toward the large city. His view of social classes is balanced in regard to the relative importance of the three general levels in Spanish society: the aristocracy, the middle class, and the proletariat or *pueblo*. Jasper W. Treat[4] has recorded as follows the number of Galdosian characters according to class: aristocracy, 249; middle class, 810; common people, 499. This count indicates that Galdós saw Spanish society as a whole of proportional parts. The number of middle-class characters is probably not out of proportion to their due share in the total scene.   73820

As early as 1870, the novelist recognized the importance of the *clase media* as fictional material that had long been neglected in the Spanish novel,[5] and he subsequently exploited this fresh store of subject matter. Seen as a generic whole, the large middle rank is not as succinctly etched as the other two divisions, probably because it is so multi-colored and inclusive. The author looks upon it with an impartial eye, recognizing both its heavy proportion of mediocrity and its solid values of work, industry, science, and leadership in practical affairs. In the role of social historian, and largely by comment and description, he points out also the inevitable breaking of barriers between the aristocracy and the well-to-do mercantile group (V, 65-66), or sizes up the basic quality of the *pueblo*, which "en nuestras sociedades, conserva las ideas y los sentimientos elementales en su tosca plenitud" (V, 423).

With all Galdós' manifest "objectivity," it is plain that his personal sympathies lay mainly with the lower strata of society and that he saw the advantages of an intermixture of classes. He beheld in the *pueblo* a simple and humble people too preoccupied with the hard necessity of survival to be seriously concerned with trivial social formalities. He also saw and admired a fundamental vitality that could contribute to the health of the upper classes. This is an auxiliary theme in *Fortunata y Jacinta*. The question is recognized clearly by Juanito Santa Cruz in connection with his relation to Fortunata, although he is too subservient to tradition to champion a new cause. It becomes a more important part of the Torquemada story, and a major theme in *La loca de la casa*. In Galdós' mind the aristocracy, especially, was in need of revitalization. Speaking of Fidela del Aguila (*Torquemada en la cruz*), he says,

> El tipo aristocrática presentaba en ella una variante harto común. Sus cabellos rubios, su color anémico, el delicado perfil, la nariz de caballete y un poco larga, la boca limpia, el pecho de escasísimo bulto, el talle sutil, denunciaban a la señorita de estirpe, pura sangre, sin cruzamientos que vivifican, enclenque de nacimiento y desmedrada luego por una educación de estufa. (V, 972)

And of Fidela's brother Rafael: "era una figura delicada y distinguidísima, cara hermosa, manos cinceladas, pies de mujer, de una forma intachable" (V, 974). Although Rafael's problem of adjusting to Fidela's marriage with Torquemada is complicated by his blindness and his having been spoiled by his sisters, he represents both the deterioration of the aristocracy and the tragic futility of an inflexible worship of noble blood. A similar attitude is found in Federico Viera (*Realidad*), to say nothing of various minor characters in other novels. On the other hand, don José Donoso, friend of "las Aguilas" (the *Torquemada* series), represents the practical and even sympathetic attitude of an aristocracy that accepts the surrender of caste to money as inevitable.

Galdós himself goes much further than José Donoso, for he felt the responsibility of pointing out to his countrymen the advantages of modifying the rigid observance of class distinctions. It was one phase of his mission of leadership, which became especially noticeable in his later works. His advocacy of a gradual modification of attitudes in this direction conforms with his long-held ideal of social change as a slow and natural process, rather than a sudden, revolutionary upheaval. José María Cruz (*La loca de la casa*) undoubtedly speaks for the author when he says, "Deseo que el pueblo se confunda con el señorío, porque así se hacen las revoluciones . . . sin revolución . . . quiero decir" (V, 1685).

It is much easier to advocate social change through the relaxation of class distinctions than it is to portray the process in operation. In his zeal as a writer with a mission to perform, Galdós tended more and more (in the latter part of his career) toward doctrinal demonstration. Even when his thesis was obvious, he assumed the viewpoint of a psychologist and centered his problem in personal relationships, by which changing ideals and conflicts between mixed loyalties work themselves out in the individual. He viewed the individual both as a victim of hierarchical attitudes and as a champion who could meet and rise above them, thus pointing the way to new values.

At first he was concerned primarily with the destructive effect of group influence. Susana (*El audaz*), carefully portrayed in the transitional stages of a changing outlook, is able to cross the barriers of class but is not able to face the denunciation of her social group after the debacle in which her lover's revolutionary endeavors end. Class prejudices in her case operate as a crushing external force. With Isidora Rufete (*La desheredada*), the worship of noble blood has become an obsession which destroys her inwardly, like a growing habit that creates other habits in its course and becomes psychologically independent of its source. It is, in fact, the same kind of cancerous growth as the religious bigotry of doña Perfecta and María Egipcíaca. In much the same way hierarchical servitude tortures Federico Viera (*Realidad*) and the Conde de Albrit (*El abuelo*), though the latter, in keeping with the author's constructive intent, acquires a stronger, regenerative interest in the form of love for the girl whom he had mistakenly declared to be his granddaughter.

In the examples just cited, the weight of class interests appears essentially as a one-way pressure exerted by an upper social stratum. In *Fortunata y Jacinta* the author's view of group values is much broader and embraces a wide expanse of irregular upward and downward movement. Although the social prejudices may seem to be of external significance only, they play an important part in character development. The upper middle class exerts a punishing effect on Fortunata, but the opposition with which she is confronted is also an incentive which helps to develop her personal dignity and moral stamina. Hers is the case of an individual caught in a complex cross pull of social, moral, and religious forces. In the thorough portrayal of natural adjustment between individual and group standards, a broad and agitated movement is produced, in which Fortunata rises to levels above her origin and pulls toward herself various people from higher levels. Thus, if no alteration in the total order results, at least a healthful disturbance is created. In this novel, Galdós, with no particular thesis to preach, gives perhaps his most vigorous depiction of social movement; and it must be emphasized that he does so by way of a study of personal adjustments more than he does by external description of the social system.

The reciprocal force in evidence in *Fortunata y Jacinta* (between the bourgeoisie and the *pueblo*), which is glimpsed even as early as *El audaz* (between the aristocracy and the bourgeoisie), becomes more deliberately defined in some of the works after 1889. The intermarriage of classes is hardly a theme in *Tristana,* but there is an example of changing orientation in an aristocrat (don Lope Garrido) who, through necessity of concessions in his personal relations, comes finally to accept the conditions of a bourgeois existence. (A similar idea forms the central theme of the drama *Mariucha,* in which two members of the aristocracy voluntarily step down from the exalted position of their class and embrace a life of work and business activity.) The intermixture of classes, however, is presented as a functioning process in the *Torquemada* series and especially in *La loca de la casa,* where the two extremes, the aristocracy and the *pueblo,* are brought together in a marriage that constitutes the basis of the personal drama. Galdós thus reached the point of recording a rather extraordinary evolutionary step. He saw, of course, that a natural way to bridge the gap between classes was through the surrender of noble titles to money, a fit subject for satire; but with his characteristic outlook he refused to be merely a satirist and sought to point out the advantages ensuing from the leveling of barriers, even when this was a forced concession to circumstances. In doing so, he combined ideas and art in an extensive picture of social locomotion, which includes a vertical, churning movement of evolution and change.

The family, the Church, and social classes are the organized portions of society that stand out most distinctly in the novels. Other collective forces are much more vaguely treated. The state or government, for example, is a rather shadowy part of the background. Galdós takes note of political events relating to the Revolution of 1868, the interim between monarchies, the Restoration, and various affairs of public interest; but neither political history nor political theory concerns him seriously in his contemporary novels. Politics sometimes forms the topic of conversation—usually among minor characters—but nowhere, after the semisocial novel *El audaz,* does it become a major force in the treatment of personality. The political ideals of Angel Guerra, as already explained, are purely secondary in his personal story, however much his disillusionment and his groping for a new life formula after the ill-fated coup against the government may reflect the author's state of mind around 1890.[6]

Certainly Galdós wished for reform that would improve the whole social order in Spain, and he experienced recurring states of disillusionment; but on the basis of his novels, it must be concluded that he placed little confidence in political measures and in fact remained almost wholly indifferent to politics. This conclusion is not in disagreement with his biography, for although he was persuaded late in his career to enter politics, hoping thus to champion some of the ideas he had consistently stood for, his enthusiasm cooled off after a few years.[7] His experiences apparently proved to him what he must have felt all along: that a change in government was in itself no assurance of a change in the nation's social philosophy, and that consequently political action was a rather hopeless means of bettering social conditions. The view of progress that he held was shaped by humanitarian ideals and would more logically precede than follow change in government. Perhaps for this reason he accorded politics an incidental place. His nearest approaches to portraying the government as a collective force entering seriously into the life of individual citizens are found in *La de Bringas,* where the atmosphere of governmental system hangs heavily over family units and is noticeably operative in the personality of Francisco de Bringas; and in *Miau,* where bureaucracy so conditions the individual as to destroy his ability to act for himself.

Economic conditions also appear in the background of several of the novels, but aside from the recurrent idea of industry and work as a healthy national ideal, they provide no particular theme for narrative development. Financial hardships sometimes form a part of the material settings and enter into the total set of circumstances in which characters are involved, but they constitute usually a minor part of the personal problems. In *Misericordia,* for example, the necessity of obtaining money is but an occasion for evoking the character of the heroine. The question of the distribution of wealth, which is perhaps most clearly observable in the *Torquemada* series, receives some attention also, but only as a corollary to the intermixture of social classes.

Galdós' depiction of group influence operating upon another group is very limited. *Doña Perfecta* is a vivid reminder not only that the novelist could describe regional life, but that he could portray group psychology as well. The feeling of provincial inferiority appears both in its strong effect upon individuals (doña Perfecta and don Inocencio, in particular) and in the behavior of the community as a unit, notably in the false pride of the townspeople and their hostility to outsiders. It is evident in the attitude of the community toward Pepe Rey and in the rebellion against the federal troops. Similarly, Church tradition is seen in *Gloria* as a collective force affecting the town as a whole. These are about the only instances, however, in which a collective influence leaves its formative effect upon an organized group. In various other novels, collective influences, such as conventionalism, moral standards, and class distinction, pervade the mass picture of characters that move in the background. Occasionally a definite local atmosphere crystallizes around the central personages: the mining region, in *Marianela;* the religious atmosphere of Toledo, in *Angel Guerra;* and the slums of Madrid, in *Misericordia.*

Galdós makes no effort to depict one section of society either as a personality in itself or in conflict with another section, nor does he purpose to leave a descriptive record of classifiable units in Spanish national life, such as the peasants, miners, laborers, tradesmen, business and professional groups. Even in his view of Madrid, his major field of operation, his perspective is comprehensive, but diffusive rather than categorical. He is concerned with human problems in general and seems to be little interested in the systematic procedure of a social historian like Balzac. He visualizes society, in all its ferment and movement, as a composite of particular forces revolving around individuals and assuming, in its constant tendency toward solidification of group interests, a dominant power over its separate members. Hence there is a predominance of psychological portraiture of one person in relation to another, and of group influences as affecting particular persons. Within this complex, where the organized whole is much more inflexible than its separate parts, change must necessarily be slow, but change is an inevitable natural law, and under the exemplary leadership of a few outstanding persons, it can be for the better.

The social process, as witnessed in Galdós' novels, is thus seen to operate specifically and almost entirely in the individual. In its most elevational aspects, it may be termed "socialization" or the blending of individualistic impulses with the interests of a social whole. To define the process in this manner is but another way of looking at the results of associational development which derive from an adjustment of reciprocal interests and which tend toward a gradual transformation of conflict into co-operation. For the individual, a growth takes place in which the socially important becomes personally important.

Such a development can plainly be seen in several of Galdós' characters. The first one significant in this respect is León Roch, who molds his will to the ideal of order in society. His guiding principle is a broad abstraction relating to the total social order, but it becomes indispensable to his integrity and sustains him in his personal misfortunes, in contrast to the narrow and destructive influence on María Egipcíaca. A somewhat similar though less potent development is seen in José María (*Lo prohibido*), who at least takes a step toward adopting the collective ideal of family integrity by recognizing in another (Camila) the moral value of marital fidelity. Also, Máximo Manso (*El amigo Manso*), in his descent from an intellectual, asocial realm, comes to recognize the values of a social existence.

The most important examples, however, are Fortunata, José María Cruz (*La loca de la casa*), and Torquemada. Fortunata's personal struggle forces her to develop gradually a social consciousness, wherein her individualistic impulses cede ground to standards of the organized whole. José María Cruz, though obviously presented in a thematic demonstration of the beneficial merging of classes, is a clearly defined case of brutal individualism turned in the direction of group values. The socializing process which takes place in Torquemada is perhaps less sharply indicated, but it is nonetheless significant. Torquemada is one of Galdós' most striking creations and deserves closer attention than has thus far been granted particular characters in the present chapter. An analysis of his personality will also serve as an elaboration on some of the points briefly referred to in the foregoing discussion.

Despite the fact that four years separate *Torquemada en la hoguera* (1889) and the second novel of the group (*Torquemada en la cruz*), which in turn was followed by *Torquemada en el purgatorio* and *Torquemada y San Pedro* in successive years, the series must be considered as a single four-volume novel; for the whole comprises a single story consisting of progressive steps in the life of the leading character. The first volume is an introduction which sets the stage for Torquemada's rise in society and the personal effect thereof. Taken as a whole, the story is concentrated more on the central personage and contains less collateral material and fewer climactic situations than is the case with the two massive works *Fortunata y Jacinta* and *Angel Guerra*. At the same time, it is very representative of the author's method, in that the narrative interest centers on the dual question of what happens to Torquemada's person and what happens to his personality.

As the story begins, Torquemada is the despised moneylender whom the reader has already glimpsed in some of the earlier novels. His portrait quickly broadens with the attention that goes with a special study of an individual, and it becomes an outstanding example of how Galdós avoids type portraiture, even when dealing with a person who might easily have been classified in the abstract category of "miser." Penuriousness is at the outset and always remains one of the protagonist's major traits. It is such a deep-rooted habit that it could not, within reason, have been discarded. But it is offset by devotion to his family, especially his son, by a desire for the approval of others, by pride in his managerial ability, and by protective and even generous impulses. The portrait grows to include friendliness, humility, ambition to contribute to the welfare of the government, and a certain magnanimity toward others, to say nothing of numerous variations of rebelliousness and submissiveness which are elicited by his entanglement in personal relationships.

The most noticeable development in *Torquemada en la hoguera* is Torquemada's turning from an obscure, asocial existence toward social expansiveness. Formerly, he has lived apart from society, moving around only to collect rent or interest on his loans, feeling indifferent to others except as they served his financial interests. Now, as if realizing for the first time that there are desirable things that money cannot buy, he begins to long for the respect of his fellow man. This new aspiration comes at first with the expansion of his business interests and is manifest for one thing in his desire to improve the appearances and comforts of his household. It is stronger than his sense of loss at the death of his wife and rises to a definite intensity with his growing pride in his young son Valentín, who shows promise of becoming a brilliant man. The feeling of inferiority in relation to his fellow man and the desire to belong with the social whole come forcefully to view as he builds his self-respect indirectly upon the respect which his son commands.

The impact of his son's illness, therefore, is doubled in force, involving not only his sincere affection but a threatened loss of prestige. Hence his desperate turning to God, of whom he is but vaguely conscious and with whom he bargains for his son's recovery. The charitable behavior by which he hopes to keep his part of the bargain is but a momentary impulse, of course, and he slips back toward miserly reclusiveness after his son's death; but he has been stimulated to the extent that henceforth he will be more susceptible to socialization. *Torquemada en la hoguera* is in itself an initial step and prepares for still another stage in the history—not of a miser, but of one who has been a miser; or better said, of one who has been imprisoned in himself. The main line of development promises to be an increasing expansiveness facing toward approval by the social whole.

This development quickly reappears in *Torquemada en la cruz.* In his role of moneylender, Torquemada becomes acquainted with the impoverished aristocratic Del Aguila family, is courteously though somewhat mockishly treated by the sisters Cruz and Fidela, and in their presence behaves like an awkward schoolboy who is anxious to please. His desire for others' approval causes him in this particular case to restrain his greed for money, even to the point of forgetting the interest on the loan that he makes. He finds satisfaction most of all in the friendly association within a family group, and under Cruz's coaching makes an effort to polish his manners and speech, taking as a model for imitation a friend of the family, don José Donoso. He willingly follows Donoso's advice in expanding his investments, moving to a more expensive home, and even in thinking of marriage into the Del Aguila family. In all humility he recognizes the social inequality between him and "las Aguilas," but with Donoso's encouragement he tries to convince himself that there is a certain aristocracy in his money that will compensate for his lack of noble blood. His desire to be a respectable member of society is confirmed in a further instance of rationalization when, in a vision, his deceased son indirectly approves the contemplated marriage by saying that he wants to be reborn and live again.[8] He is thus led willingly into his second marriage and an expanding social life.

In this volume Torquemada appears to be something of a "rube" who wants to make his way upward in society. With all his crudeness and his momentary rebellious anger at his socially superior relatives-to-be (Rafael in particular), he shows a consistent friendliness and a sincere desire to belong with others in a group relationship. His social experiences will prove to be much more rigorous than he has anticipated, largely because Cruz, while forcing her more docile sister to make the sacrifice of marriage, has engaged in a cold-blooded business proposition; but he is now on the threshold of an elevating, if forced, compromise between selfishness and concessions to the will of others.

Torquemada en el purgatorio carries the protagonist through the rather excruciating stages of his rise to social heights. For a while Torquemada continues to polish his manners and speech and to broaden his learning, favoring "scientific" knowledge, which he garners for the most part from newspapers. He is happy in his marriage to Fidela, who finds outlet for her emotional self in the playful attitude of a child, and he looks forward with magnanimous good will to the birth of a son. Cruz, however, comes gradually to dominate and antagonize him. In her relentless drive to re-establish her family socially she forces her brother-in-law to take an ever expanding part in public affairs, bringing about his election as senator, obtaining for him the title of marquis, and leading him to purchase a ducal palace. Torquemada fusses, rebels, and always submits. His standards of happiness are much more modest than those of Cruz, but even if his journey in the social world is involuntary, his personal interests become more and more identified with the interests of a widening circle of associations. His ambition to utilize his financial talents to improve the state of the national treasury is an outstanding example of the socially important becoming personally important, and marks the culmination of a development in which the integrity of his personality comes to be dependent upon the identification of individualistic drives with the interests of society at large.

Torquemada y San Pedro is essentially a volume in which stock is taken of the previous happenings. It is in effect a settling of accounts, under two headings: physical and spiritual. Now that Cruz has attained her social goals, she turns her interests to religion, first for herself and then for her brother-in-law, calling to her aid the rough and sympathetic priest Gamborena, former chaplain in the Del Aguila household. Since the death of her brother Rafael, she has become desirous of Torquemada's good will, but her despotic rule has taken its toll. Torquemada, now completely estranged from her, feels the need of breaking out of the prison that his palatial home has come to be. Under a constant nervous and emotional strain, he has developed an ulcerous stomach. His unhappiness and poor health are aggravated first by the fact that his newborn son is an idiot, and secondly, by his wife's death. Between periods of illness and angry resentment against Cruz, he listens willingly to Gamborena and contemplates for the first time his chances of entering Heaven. Though agreeing to a *modus vivendi* with Cruz, he turns for affection and friendship to his daughter by his first wife.

Finally, because of nostalgia for his old associations, Torquemada returns to the haunts of his former life. Here, in a grand fraternal impulse, he indulges in an orgy of conversation, eating, and drink, with a resulting physical crisis from which he never recovers. He is not afraid of Hell, for like Fortunata he is too primitive and naïve to be bothered seriously with formalities of conscience; but since others have raised the question of eternal salvation, he is willing to consider it as he would a business proposition. He therefore submits peacefully to Gamborena's urging that he leave part of his wealth to charity, thinking in terms of the priest's personal handling of the money, for he is still indifferent to charity as a general and abstract principle.

Before his death Torquemada's interest in Heaven intensifies somewhat, and he reasons that his contributions to the welfare of his country are worthy of God's approval. He is happy that under the priest's direction he has purged his heart of evil, and in a moment of culminating need to belong with others, he feels an impulse of gentleness and good will toward all people, including his sister-in-law. The warmth of this benevolent attitude is the immediate result of a momentary physical state in which his hopes revive for recovering and carrying out his ambitious projects. He is withal a far different person from the selfish and self-sufficient moneylender whom the reader had first met. His social rise has resulted in a physical breakdown, but the compromise with others' wishes has converted him not only into a social being, but perhaps—as the author humorously insinuates—into one who has earned his salvation, despite the fact that personal ambition may have been mixed with the prescribed formula of words imprecisely pronounced in his dying breath.

Far from being the characterization of a grotesque miser, the *Torquemada* series is the story of a person's socialization, in which the necessity of adjusting to social circumstances forces a reshaping of ideals and habits and results in moral improvement. Aside from the superficial change in manners and speech, the quest for knowledge, which arises from the challenge to meet social needs, leads Torquemada to develop a set of values that conform to the interests of others. Even his stinginess undergoes a remodeling, because he is forced to defend his penurious habits, and as a consequence develops through rationalization the ideal of the *justo medio*. Anyone will recognize that in doing so he is making excuses for his stinginess, but few will deny that the resulting principle is sound, whether applied to the home, to big business, or to national affairs. Similarly developed is the pride in his financial ability, which expands into a veritable drive to help the government.

Torquemada also crystallizes for himself a moral philosophy, which is summed up in the following words from his picturesque banquet speech: "el trabajo, la honradez, el amor al prójimo y las buenas costumbres" (*Torquemada en el purgatorio:* V, 1130). Even if his speech is a medley of borrowed phrases and trite concepts, it contains a few fundamental ideas that the protagonist sincerely believed in and in reasonable degree lived up to. Galdós himself, though presenting the speech in burlesque manner, is nevertheless sympathetic with his hero—a kind of Sancho Panza of the Madrid business world—and with characteristic irony imparts his own beliefs. For Torquemada, after all, is a man of action and a champion of industrial progress; and if his "amor al prójimo," when involving money, is laboriously wrested from him as in the pulling of a tooth, he at least has some justification in the explanation that he does not want to encourage laziness.

Actually, Torquemada expands in the direction of love for his fellow man. Beginning with the solid foundation of sincerity and devotion to his immediate family, and led on by the strong desire to belong with others in group relationships, he extends his friendliness to acquaintances of the Del Aguila family, to people in public life, and finally to a representative of the Church. Meanwhile he gradually subdues his selfishness and becomes conciliatory to the interests of others. In this process of shaping personal ideals to the demands of social living, he arrives finally at an enlarged standard of personal dignity based on the doctrine of being true to himself and living free in accord with nature as long as his individualistic pursuits bring no harm to his neighbor.

The crystallization of this ideal comes in a rebellion against restrictions imposed upon Torquemada as the result of a social life that has got out of hand, but it contains the lessons absorbed in the crucible of experience. His lesson has been hard and in large part involuntarily absorbed, but the result has been beneficial to his "spirit," if at the same time detrimental to his body. He has unconsciously made a profitable exchange, of which he as a businessman would have been proud, and the bargain which in the end he tries to effect may—in Galdós' mind—have had a good chance of meeting with God's approval. The story of Torquemada, in short, is that of a man who *has been* a "miser," *becoming* a socialized individual through *imperative adjustments* to living amidst group relations, and developing moral values in the process. From one viewpoint, it is a story of the moral redemption of a miser, just as *Fortunata y Jacinta* relates the moral redemption of a fallen woman. With respect to either novel, the emphasis should be placed on the personality development as a whole; for this, a condensed representation of a life process, constitutes the wholeness of the narrative.

In the case of Torquemada, collective influences spring from various sources and combine with individualistic aims. The novel, therefore, cannot be considered a thematic demonstration of a precise group effect, such as that found in a relationship between the Church and an individual or between the aristocracy and an individual. The organized social system in its structural form, however, does appear plainly in the background, and Galdós shows his interest in a sociological subject: the *nivelación* of classes and of subgroups within a class. In one place he comments on the changing social topography of Madrid, where old aristocratic homes are being taken over by the moneyed bourgeoisie (*Torquemada y San Pedro*, I, vi). In another place he calls attention to the fact that there are no longer any clear-cut types, such as a pedant, a Don Juan, or a miser (*Torquemada en el purgatorio*, I, xi). He is consciously dealing with an aspect of the leveling process, but he has deliberately taken a difficult case in order to show how opposing extremes tend to meet on a common middle ground through a natural adjustive development.

It would have been an easy instructional task to depict the intermixture of the aristocracy and the upper middle class, for this was a development already accepted in Spain. The incorporation of someone like Torquemada into aristocratic or any other respectable society presented a much greater problem and was therefore more challenging. The aristocracy was not so much opposed to Torquemada's humble origin as to his vulgarity and the fact that he was a usurer. Galdós was not unsympathetic with this justifiable hostility, and when Rafael cynically ponders the necessity of accepting Torquemada into the family, the author seems to agree that there is a certain grotesqueness in the reversals in social ideals brought about by changing times (*Torquemada en el purgatorio*, I, IV-V). Unlike Rafael, he refuses to accept the reversal as a tragedy. Agreeing with more practical persons like Cruz and Donoso, he proceeds to show how the drawing together of extremes can be freed of potentially grotesque elements. He thus adopts a positive attitude based on unescapable facts. The facts begin with the broad question of receding class and group distinctions, become concentrated around individual psychology in contact with social forces, and assume definitive form in the portrayal, through the individual, of the life process of change.

If, therefore, Galdós be regarded as a social historian of nineteenth-century Spain, he must be regarded as a historian of society in movement. The descriptive or static view of society admittedly is large in his novels, but in so far as its contribution to artistic wholeness is concerned, it is mainly supplementary. Judged solely on the basis of this phase of his writings, Galdós appears to be primarily a novelist of customs, or a satirist. He is both of these in some degree, but his picture of society in its fixed structural form is (in the novels of noticeable sociological color) but the shell in which social locomotion provides the base for the main narrative movement. The reason is that his perspective encompasses underlying causes of ferment and change.

In this respect Galdós takes a distinctly modern view of society, well abreast if not actually in advance of systematized sociological thought prior to the 1880's. Both Comte and Spencer, despite their visualization of society's growth in terms of a broad historical or evolutionary process, were concerned primarily with questions pertaining to social structure in a state of equilibrium. Employing the methodology of a classifying sociologist, Comte sought to explain the parts in terms of the whole, seeing in the individual a recapitulation of society at large. His was essentially a mechanical system of concepts aimed at explaining social structure as it currently is.[9] Spencer, whose influence was at its height around 1880, also focused his study upon social organization or the static "side-by-sideness" of categories. These approaches tend to obscure psychic elements and present the picture of society as a fixed order to be described but not to be analyzed as a growing organism.

When Lester F. Ward published his *Dynamic Sociology* in 1883, he presented a new viewpoint in his insistence that society is not the passive result of unconscious forces, but something that can be shaped by human intelligence. With a similar socio-psychological view, Galdós believed that the social field structure, which is basic in the study of the individual, can be controlled as an environmental factor. His conception of structural change, in so far as it is manifest in his novels, did not crystallize until the middle 1880's (*Fortunata y Jacinta*), though it is evident that as early as *La Fontana de Oro* and *El audaz* he was thinking of change in the social system. Clearly, he was more concerned with psychology than with sociological generalizations, but in his attention to the reciprocal influence of individual and organized interests, he became in effect a leader in a new school of sociology. He did so, of course, incidentally and not as a sociologist; but a number of his novels could easily be utilized to demonstrate the developing sociological thought in the last two decades of the nineteenth century. His view of dynamic society appears at its best in the novels from 1886 to 1895. Later it tends to degenerate into propaganda. In *Fortunata y Jacinta* and the *Torquemada* series especially, it surges forth in a vigorous presentation of conflicting loyalties, reciprocal reinforcing of individual and group interests, transformation of conflict into co-operation, and the permeability of fixed barriers.

Galdós was not a theorist and in a strict sense, therefore, not a social philosopher; but he was a reformer, interested in improving the social system in Spain for the common benefit of the individual and the nation. Though somewhat iconoclastic, especially in his youth, he was more of a practical leader than a revolutionist. He recognized not only the power but the inevitability and the necessity of fixed order, and he apparently felt that the stabilizing influence of an institution, which is based on long cumulative growth, is in itself compensation for the slowness with which tradition changes. He nevertheless regarded institutions as existing not for their own sake but as a means of serving the individual, who himself becomes a part of the consciousness of the social whole. Though realizing that the lack of traditional and conventional norms would lead to personal disintegration, he saw and depicted with sharp decisiveness the effect which rigid formalism has in starving the individual's higher life. When, in his Academy address (1897), he asserted that the main concern of art has to do with human rather than social values (by which he meant abstract formulas), he voiced the fundamental principle that led him throughout his literary career to study the particular human being in relation to society, and not society as an abstract synthesis of classifiable parts. His "sociological" approach, therefore, was from the particular to the whole. As early as his first two novels, he realized that reform must be brought about by revitalization of individual consciousness.[10] He hoped that institutional reform would follow as a natural result, but his works reveal his recognition of the imperceptible impression that even the strongest character makes upon long-established tradition.

In his anxiety to accelerate the unusually slow social locomotion in his own country, Galdós deliberately depicted the conciliation between extremes, leaving relatively untouched for dynamic portrayal the easier shifting of barriers such as the intermixture of the aristocracy and the moneyed bourgeoisie. Perhaps, too, because of impatience in the face of an impregnable Church tradition, he returned in some of his later works (*Casandra, Electra*) to bitter attacks upon clericalism, and in his disillusionment gave in to idealistic dreaming of social change which he could not detect in reality. Despite recurring periods of impatience and disillusionment, however, he remained hopeful, knowing that prejudice against minority groups derives more from contact with thought about these groups than it does from contact with their separate representatives; hence his continuous efforts to bring conflicting group interests into touch with each other by way of personal association between individuals. By just such means in real life the most wholesome kind of innovation comes about through the assertion of fresh personality against mechanical system. Though the novelist fell short of his goal, his method was sound, for he turned to life itself for the illustration of his ideals.

The social philosophy of Galdós may be described as that of an idealist who sees in the past and the present a preparation for the future, and who believes that what is good for society is that stage which fits it for advance in a natural process of change.[11] However, he was not one to remain passive and watch change take place. He would have wanted to co-operate with the process and try to direct it toward the general dignification of human nature, toward freedom from formalistic worship and freedom of the individual to develop morally but naturally. To such ends he made use of the novel and drama. At his best his social and ethical purpose lies deep in the representation of a life process in which advance from one stage to another takes place in the individual.

VI

THE MORAL PERSPECTIVE

THE subject of morality is so deeply ingrained in the works of Galdós that it must be regarded as having fundamental significance for the comprehension of his stories. In his preoccupation with the relationship between self and society, the novelist gave constant thought to the question of conformity. Undoubtedly because of the severe restrictive influence of his mother, he was hostilely inclined toward authority from the time of his early youth and his will to self-assertion received added impetus during his student years in Madrid, where he participated in the liberal movement of Julián Sanz del Río and his followers. He embraced enthusiastically the ideals of freedom of conscience and freedom to determine one's own place in the world, and he maintained always a certain attitude of defiance toward the rigid enforcement of institutional orders—those of the Church in particular. At the same time, he sought to give positive direction to his individualism. Out of an intellectual background that placed a great deal of weight upon philosophical idealism, a moral concept of major importance gradually took form in his thinking. This concept centered upon the idea of mental unification and the duty of the individual to realize the fullest potential of his intelligence while developing his resources in harmony with natural and purposeful growth. It calls to mind, incidentally, Pestalozzi's plea for the harmonious development of all the faculties of the child.

The subject of morality in Galdós' novels, therefore, can best be appreciated by keeping in mind the idea that obligation calls not only for limitation but for expansion in the direction of a fuller understanding of one's relationships within the universal order. The two most important specific considerations in this connection are integrity or wholeness, and mobility or growth. Duty to self, duty to society, and duty to a higher order can be seen to harmonize in a maturational process in which individual freedom becomes one with integrity.

Comprehensively speaking, Galdós begins with rebellious assertion in the face of obstacles to freedom, makes a transition in which an imperfect understanding of freedom is depicted, and advances gradually to a perfected view of personality wholeness. The rebellious spirit which comes to view in his portrayal of Susana and Muriel in their confrontation with social prejudices (*El audaz*) is the source of strength in the portraits of doña Perfecta, Gloria, and María Egipcíaca, where the author's artistic energy is used to paint the destructive effect of enslavement to the dictates of society (including religion, in the sense of custom). The same spirit, toned down considerably, appears intermittently in the novels of the middle period. It surges forth again with renewed vehemence in *Casandra* (1905), whose main theme is morality and religion, presented more through scenic sketching than through psychological analysis. In this hybrid work, Casandra is clearly the champion of the belief that "Cada uno, dentro del castillo de sus pensamientos y de su conciencia, es rey" (VI, 137). She is the "fuerza expulsora, la razón," that exorcises the evil spirit of doña Juana (Jornada V, escena x), herself a reincarnation of doña Perfecta and a slave to rigid formalism.

When Galdós wrote *Casandra*, of course, he had already passed through a long period of creative thinking, and he includes in the novel some of his often repeated constructive ideas: that religion is found in living the essentials of Christianity (symbolized by Rosaura); and that unbridled freedom to live in accord with nature (Rogelio) is subject to a higher law of love and devotion to others (Casandra). Under the influence of this force, Rogelio bows before convention and submits to marriage with Casandra. The author's enthusiasm, however, is concentrated on the theme of ecclesiolatry and formality as opposed to true religion and morality—the same kind of thinking that permeates *Doña Perfecta, Gloria,* and *La familia de León Roch.* It is concretely expressed in the heroine's words "Demasiado ruido hace en el mundo la devoción para que sea de ley" (VI, 223). Thus in this novel the author completes a cycle by returning to his youthful rebelliousness.

Aside from the general idea that the individual should be free to follow his conscience in regard to religion, a constant belief with Galdós, the meaning of freedom gradually takes form after several experimental approaches to the subject. It appears first as the right to self-realization, understood to be the development of one's natural potentialities. This thought is expressed indirectly by the author in *El doctor Centeno* through the bizarre Jesús Delgado, who champions (IV, 1395) Pestalozzi's theory of complete education for a complete life, and Froebel's belief that education is essentially a participation in life. Delgado is a kind of Don Quijote, whose translations of liberal works from the German had brought upon him the displeasure of the Archbishop of Toledo, and the author is apparently enjoying the discomfiture of his orthodox countrymen with respect to the influx of progressive ideas from abroad. It matters little that the novelist's mouthpiece is slightly less than mad, for Galdós characteristically presents favorite ideas through persons who are considered mad by society.

There is no doubt that as early as *El audaz* (Susana), and especially in the case of Gloria, he was thinking of what a superior personality might be, were it not shackled by prejudices. In the early works the problem of harmonizing individual rights and conformity with social and religious tradition is seen in its negative, unsolved form. Later a positive solution is indicated, but meanwhile, save for the characterization of León Roch, self-realization is presented from a somewhat different viewpoint: the individual's desire to find his own place in the world. Thus arises the theme of self-esteem.

This theme comes to light faintly in *Marianela*, but Galdós is still concerned chiefly with the handicaps besetting the individual, and in keeping with his youthful tendency to see the negative side of his problems, he shows how not to use freedom. Thus in *La desheredada* he presents a fundamentally sincere and kind person whose inability to exercise self-control in regard to ideals of social caste and luxury is as immoral as false religion or unrestrained sensual pleasure. A similar lack of stamina to earn one's reward appears in *Lo prohibido*, and again in *Miau* and *Tristana*, in combination with the effects of a social system that encourages a rationalization of weakness and a tendency to drift with the current of mediocrity. From the standpoint of individual morality, the weaknesses in these characters can be summed up as an inability to direct self courageously and intelligently. José María's taste for *lo prohibido* is immoral in one important sense by reason of a lack of self-mastery, and hence a lack of wholeness. Similarly, Eloísa (in the same novel) is immoral more for her enslavement of self to superficial values than for her unconventional love affairs. These are the lessons embodied in the personality stories themselves. The characters from the novels of Galdós' so-called naturalistic period long for a place of respect in the world, but some of them are too weak to take hold of themselves and develop stamina from within. They are not the victims of an all-powerful force of heredity and environment that precludes healthy growth. In this same period the positive, creative view of personality growth also makes its appearance.

The development of stamina from within first comes to view in León Roch, in the form of rational control that places the ideal of orderliness above rebellious impulses. In this case, however, the conflict between self and society evokes an individual response of stoical forbearance. It is essentially a negative solution as compared to the renovating adjustment observable in Máximo Manso (*El amigo Manso,* 1882), who acquires through rational self-discipline the new values of service and leadership. Here, then, is the first view of self-realization interpreted as the constructive use of freedom within the demands of social living.[1] A still fuller view is found in the person of Felipe Centeno (*El doctor Centeno,* 1883), a humble, almost insignificant particle in the universe, who sets out to find his place in society. Although potentially a *pícaro,* Felipe acquires the dignity that develops from friendship, loyalty, work, and perseverance. With his developing sense of responsibility to others, he undergoes a maturation of personality that adds breadth and balance to the meaning of self-realization. In contrast to Felipe, Alejandro Miquis, his friend and "master," lacks the wholeness that combines with kindness a sense of responsibility in practical affairs.

With *El doctor Centeno,* Galdós is definitely in the period of mobile or dynamic morality. The puzzling and seemingly insoluble question of love versus religious prejudices is put aside temporarily while the study of personality is approached by trying to find in the individual himself the means of surmounting the impasse of static situations fixed by the dictates of closed minds. By shifting the emphasis from social laws to the duty to self, the novelist presents the individual not so much in rebellion against conformity as independent of it. To put it another way, dignity and self-respect come increasingly to depend upon personal rather than social worth. Amparo (*Tormento*) achieves through self-determination a regenerative independence with respect to convention. As noted in an earlier analysis, Amparo's main struggle is to overcome a fear of what people think and say; and her eventual confession to Caballero, which satisfies her conscience with regard to her sin and her sense of fairness, enables her to regain her equilibrium—and her morality—through a triumph over cowardice. She is now no longer a slave to social law because she has triumphed over self. Caballero and Amparo together represent victory of the individual over convention, but it is not a triumph of hollow defiance, for they both have found values (pardon, courage, loyalty) greater than the standards of conventional morality and are therefore able to live independent of these. This novel, clearly a study of morality, raises a problem similar to that of Gloria (love versus tradition) and solves it by defying tradition, not blindly, but with a substitution of values that supersede it. Máximo Manso had said, "La conciencia es creadora, atemperante y reparadora" (IV, 1273), and had in some degree demonstrated his assertion. In *Tormento*, conscience is even more clearly seen as a creative force which leads the individual to follow loyalty to an order higher than the law of society while receiving challenge and stimulation from the very law which he succeeds in transcending.

In *Fortunata y Jacinta*, Galdós reaches a high mark in his treatment of morality from the standpoint of combining conventional demands with the creative force which these demands give rise to. By such a combination he presents, in Fortunata particularly, a picture of mobile morality. The change in values begins with the challenge of convention, which in turn stimulates a feeling of rebellious independence and a subsequent elevation of self toward a law higher than society or self. Aroused from passivity by her rivalry with Jacinta, Fortunata attaches great value to the ideal of being *honrada,* which she understands at first purely in the conventional sense of rules governing the relationship between man and woman. Once her self-esteem is revived, she stands up to assert her rights as an individual and a woman, including especially the right to love the father of her child. In her moments of confusion and frustration, she appeals to a higher law, which she vaguely associates with Nature; and yet, through her longing for the approval of her social superiors, she is more and more inclined to conformity.

From a moral viewpoint, the story of Fortunata is fundamentally one of regeneration, but the regenerative process carries with it, in addition to the reactivated virtues of courage, loyalty to friends, sincerity, and selflessness in love, a new movement of values. For the concept of *honrada* broadens in Fortunata's mind, even though she is scarcely aware of it, and her self-respect comes eventually to entail self-sacrifice and the pardon of her enemies. The personality is thus expanded by the addition and strengthening of virtues which are independent of social regulation without being contrary to social law. Neither the "angel of society" (Jacinta) nor the "angel of Nature" (Fortunata) is supreme unto herself. They meet sympathetically on a level superior to either of them.

Fortunata, of course, achieves only a partial harmony of freedom and conformity, for she remains always intensely insecure in a social sense and to the very end experiences a certain savage delight in triumphing over her opponents. Moreover, she discounts the importance of fidelity to her husband, Maximiliano, albeit with some degree of extenuation because of her initial indifference to the marriage and her honest defense of the right to be loyal to her first and only love. She has advanced as far as she might logically be expected to, in view of her background and the time allotted to her recorded struggle. The important point is that she is learning to determine self and is progressing in sympathetic understanding of her relationships. Galdós does not overtly pass judgment on his heroine, but it may be inferred that he would judge her on the basis of her capacity for absorbing the lessons of organized social order without sacrificing her rights as an individual human being. Clearly, he would not subject her to static formulas, either social or religious. Torquemada must be judged in a similar manner, and though he fails to reach the level attained by others of Galdós' characters, it must be remembered that he started at a lower level of hard incrustation in self and therefore had further to go.

In the 1880's Galdós is expanding his treatment of questions raised in earlier novels: the right to disregard religious barriers in marrying (*Gloria*), the right to live with a woman outside of matrimony (*Tormento*), and indirectly, the right to obtain a divorce (*La familia de León Roch*). He never comes nearer to reviving these questions than in *Fortunata y Jacinta*. Although the problems are not exactly the same, it seems almost certain that his solution would be, for all of them, the defiance of tradition, provided always that the individual adheres to values that are above controversy. In other words, the conflict between love and society can be solved by way of transformation from within.

In short, the novelist demonstrates that morality is not merely the observance of social rules, but a natural product generated by the demands of one's duty to self, which necessarily involves a broadening of responsibility to embrace the highest relationship to which man is capable of aspiring. This is, in fact, the doctrine which Orozco (*Realidad*) subscribes to, for he voices the dynamic principle that conscience calls for constant growth and for rising above conventional morality. In practice, however, he tends to contradict his doctrine through his overemphasis on self-effacement. Guillermina (*Fortunata y Jacinta*), in spite of her worship of formal rules, is a much better example of a moral person than Orozco, because her charitableness is the natural outcome of her need for activity and accomplishment, which has been channeled into a direction determined largely by her training and her spinsterhood. What makes her a virtuous person is not her interest in charity, but the fact that her charitable activity is spontaneous and therefore creative in her own personality. It is simply the case of one good deed calling for another until the doing of good deeds becomes a necessity.

With *Fortunata y Jacinta* Galdós approaches the point in his thinking at which morality merges with religion.[2] His religion is one that seems to have grown out of a desire to bridge the gap between the demands of individuality and those of society. Never losing his aversion to the worship of ritual and dogma, he develops, particularly in *Angel Guerra*, *Nazarín*, and *Halma*, a philosophy that emphasizes what he had felt all along: that true religion must conform with a "ley que es divina a fuerza de ser humana" (*La familia de León Roch*: IV, 909).

Galdós' constant preoccupation with the subject of love between man and woman no doubt accounts in large part for his giving this theme a religious interpretation. It underlies his first clearly developed presentation of constructive religious experience. The assertion of León Roch that love of God is a sublimation of the love between man and woman (IV, 943) is revived to form the basis of plot and psychological portrayal in *Angel Guerra*. The hero of this novel tries to acquire religion by renouncing earthly love in favor of divine love. His efforts to separate the two end in failure, but the lesson that he learns, one which directly contradicts his earlier assumption and which the author demonstrates through psychological change in both Angel and Leré, is that spiritual growth and religious fervor come as natural complements to love between man and woman. This stimulative force is charged with generous impulses that fructify in love of fellow man and of God. In brief, Angel Guerra and Leré—the latter less prominently studied—undergo the mystic experience of an approach to God through the demands of human nature.

With his analysis of Nazarín, Galdós takes a further step in the study of mysticism. Love of woman is not altogether absent from Nazarín's experience, and it reappears clearly in the relationship between Halma and José Antonio in *Halma*. In *Nazarín*, however, the emphasis rests upon the individual-fellowman-God relationship. The author is concerned as always with the kind of practical religious living that leads to close association with God, as opposed to religious contemplation in isolation from society. The novel, in combination with

Halma, may be regarded as a demonstration of false mysticism becoming true mysticism.

Nazarín at first wishes to withdraw from the world and nurture his closeness to God with complete self-denial. In a sympathetic way Galdós is attacking an error in thinking which he recognized to be a prominent feature of religion in Spain: salvation through abstinence, a belief that frequently develops into self-punishment as an end in itself. Nazarín follows his creator's own ideal in so far as he considers religion to be strictly a matter between the individual and God. But in trying to simplify Christianity, he has reached the point of excluding his fellow man. Abnegation is close to becoming a goal that excludes all other goals, and extremism, in the author's mind, is as much a false guide to conduct as formalism.

The course by which Nazarín learns that the love of God is love of man manifest in personal associations underlies his mystic experience. This reaches its climax with the vision (V, vi) in which Beatriz and Andara, the one transformed into a celestial angel and the other into a beautiful warrior of God, together symbolize harmony between peaceful forbearance and an active assertiveness against evil. An abnormal state from an everyday viewpoint, the vision nevertheless represents the hero's passage to a new understanding. It can appropriately be described by Henri Bergson's statement that a vision, though it be pure hallucination, "may express the fact that the disturbance is a systematic readjustment with a view to equilibrium on a higher level: the image then becomes symbolic of what is about to happen, and the emotion is the concentration of the soul awaiting transformation."[3] Having felt an intimate association with God, Nazarín is prepared for the advance in which he becomes sure of his mission as leader and teacher, the positive religious action to which he has been converted and which henceforth will be combined with his humility and submissiveness.

The most dynamic phase of the life of Galdós' mystic hero, and the one most poetically portrayed, is found in *Nazarín,* the first of the two novels in which he appears. The author was interested, perhaps secondarily, in mysticism as emotional exaltation, but he was above all concerned with the practical necessity of living in society. After he allows his hero to return to the crass reality of the world around him, in a natural recessive step following an ecstatic experience, he has him pass through the ordeal of mockery and punishment at the hands of the civil order and also has him submit to correction by the Church.

Nazarín's docility toward authority represents a compromise with organized society, but it does not mean that he has sacrificed his freedom of conscience. It means simply that he has been able to adjust to environment, and since his environment is Catholic, he conforms with Catholic rules. In other words, he learns to render unto Caesar—and this includes Church authorities—the things which are Caesar's and yet to reserve loyalty to a higher law. It is precisely in his ability to determine self through conformity with social order and loyalty to a higher order that his freedom lies.

Nazarín thus undergoes a forced reinterpretation of individual freedom, learning that the approach to God lies not in isolation, a form of whimsical self-gratification, but in the co-ordination of self and society. Such a co-ordination necessitates conformity with rules as a means of performing service to others in close personal relationships. When Galdós wrote *Nazarín*, he was undoubtedly intrigued by the thought of what would happen if a man were to try to imitate the life of Jesus. In a sense Nazarín, living and suffering among men, feels his kinship to God as Jesus did. Since he is more a subject of the earth than Jesus was, he suffers more from the problem of harmonizing human nature and divine nature. He nevertheless attains the quality of wholeness that frees individuality from the tyranny of material and social laws, and he does so through a process of renovation from within.

It is obvious that one cannot properly understand Galdós' conception of religion or of morality without thinking of two distinct kinds: the formal and the personal. It must be clear by now also that the personal kind meant more to the novelist than merely following one's own convictions, free of dogmatic demands. For him, both morality and religion were fundamentals of life itself, and marked the natural course of man's progress in this world, in the sense of movement from a lower to a higher state of completeness. The contrast between static and dynamic, which stands out in the novels, is therefore basic in a consideration of the subject. What Bergson has to say in *The Two Sources of Morality and Religion* is suggestive of Galdós in several respects, though it must be kept in mind that the novelist probably was not thinking of static and dynamic exactly as these terms are used by the French philosopher, and that he did not attempt to reduce his thoughts to systematic theory.

Bergson draws a sharp distinction between morality as social obligation (static) and morality as obligation to humanity at large (dynamic). The one is pressure or custom within a closed society, which arises as a natural law whereby society preserves itself; and religion of the static kind is society's enforcing agent that keeps the individual from sudden revolt and wards off the dangers to which individual intelligence might expose collective man. Human or dynamic morality, on the other hand, derives its strength from appeal and aspiration, not pressure, and is the more powerful the more it is aroused in specific human beings. In its leaders, force takes the form of aspiration and enthusiasm for forward movement. The morality of the Gospels, for example, is essentially that of the forward-moving, open soul that spreads Christianity through love. Both kinds are necessary complements in nature's biological process, which is normally intent upon preserving society and yet capable of transfiguring it. Strict obligation tends to absorb aspiration, just as aspiration tends to materialize by assuming forms of obligation, but the two kinds of attachments to life remain entirely distinct. An individual may make a transition from static to dynamic, but he does so by bounding over the former, not by expanding its circumference. (Herein lies the essential difference between Galdós and Bergson.) For dynamic morality is the manifestation of an innate force that links man intuitively to the transcendent cause of all things. The plunge forward in evolution is represented always by the vital impetus, the creative impulse of dynamic religion or true mysticism; while current morality and religion continue always to be necessary halts in mobility, absorbing at the same time some portion of vitality from those exceptional individuals whose morality seeps into aggregate man.

Galdós clearly understands both the pressure and the stabilizing value of social (static) morality, as he does the irresistible impetus of human (dynamic) morality. Moreover, he recognizes man's urge to embrace passionately the love of God, not as a commandment, but in answer to his own nature. Such a manifestation of vital impetus, he realizes, comes not from dignitaries of the Church, champions of static rules, nor from the leaders of society as it currently is, nor from mass consciousness. It comes from rare individuals who, as Bergson says,[4] feel an enthusiasm of liberation, who visualize as possible what is impossible in a given society, imagining what would be its effect on society and then inducing a state of receptivity by propaganda and example.

Nazarín is just such an exceptional individual who represents the religion of the Gospels, both as it uplifts self and as it spreads creatively to others. The priest don Manuel Flórez (*Halma*, III, v) realizes this when he contrasts himself, a conventional priest of society, with Halma and Nazarín, though he does not at the time mention the latter by name. The author deliberately makes a question of his hero's nationality, allowing him to call himself Castilian while describing him as an Arab. Of similar intent is the assertion that spirituality knows no national boundaries (*Halma*, III, II), which is obviously the author's denial of Russian influence, but at the same time a declaration that true religion is free of national limitations. Nazarín, having been brought into an active attachment to life and yet pervaded with a spirit that unites him with a Being immeasurably larger than himself, spreads a simple religion of service and love by teaching and example. The creative results are observable in a few individuals: Andara, Beatriz, *el Sacrílego* (*Nazarín*); and Halma, José Antonio, and even the "social" priest don Manuel (*Halma*), though he does not live to effect a change in practice. Society as a whole, meanwhile, goes its way stolidly, thinking Nazarín a madman and confirming what the author himself felt: "la verdad de Diós . . . sinrazón de los hombres" (*Halma:* V, 1918).

Galdós thus recognizes that change in organized religion, if not impossible, will be at the best almost imperceptible. This recognition does not keep him from dreaming of the "impossible," and he himself takes the role of a leader who reaches imaginatively toward seemingly unrealizable goals. He does this in *Angel Guerra* as well as in *Nazarín*. Angel aspires to making changes in the Catholic Church, the most prominent one being to permit "la comunión de los sexos." The humorous treatment of don Pito's suggestions (III, I, *ii*) with reference to establishing a new religion that would allow priests to marry—a practice which in his opinion would raise no conflict between nature and God— may be considered an expression of the author's own ideas. The same idea is more subtly presented in the love and imaginary, or mystic, marriage of Angel and Leré. Another important consideration is the protagonist's insistence on retaining his own initiative within the Church, manifest in his unwillingness to become a Jesuit (III, I, *iii*).

During the period of his religious fervor, Angel's dreams also include ideas which indicate a new consciousness of the potentialities of religion in practice—notably, the thought that fear is nothing but the subordination of self to physical laws. For this reason he would banish fear of disease from his new order (III, III, *i*). Similarly, Nazarín preaches freedom from fear of sickness and danger (*Nazarín*, III, IV, IV, IV), saying that sickness is in the mind and that belief in one's wellness, combined with prayer and trust in God, will make one well. These may have been ideas which Galdós took from the common fund of thought because of their poetic appeal to the imagination, but they could be the author's interpretation of what Jesus himself demonstrated. They bear, incidentally, some slight resemblance to the teachings of Mary Baker Eddy. The essential point, however, is that such thinking represents a positive approach to man's relation to God, which far transcends formalities and puts religion on a basis where God is immediate in man's life. It envisages the religious experience as a vital and close association with divinity, as contrasted with habit, which easily becomes nothing more than the "fossilized residue of a spiritual activity."[5]

To reach this understanding of religion, the characters of Galdós pass through the urgencies of social obligation. This is not to say that moral self-enlargement, which is especially noticeable in the novels after 1885, is merely an expanding circle of current morality. It means, rather, that the higher conception of duty comes after contact with the strict demands of current authority, which itself acts as challenge and stimulant. The passage from closed to open morality bridges a gap between social and human demands. The transition, then, is a separation from static regulation in that it is a transference of allegiance. This is hardly a leap beyond that phase of nature which holds man subject to society. Perhaps it would be more accurate to say that the leap of which Bergson speaks—and the reference is made not so much to note the difference or similarity between the two writers as to contribute to an understanding of Galdós—is with the novelist a gradual rising above the level of static morality. For with Galdós, dynamic moral and religious consciousness is a slow accumulation which is fundamentally an adjustive process of maturation and renovation carried forward to fruition within social living.

The novelist's point of view can be illustrated by reference to compassion, one of the salient character traits in his novels. The difference between courtesy and compassion may be likened to the difference between social obligation and brotherly love. The one functions primarily as habit, and however sincere it may be, it is acquired essentially from the pressure of society. The other is basically impulsive. It cannot be imposed by commandment, nor can it be attained merely by expanding one's obligations to include formal charity; for it is an emotional experience as spontaneous as love. Yet it can be aroused in an individual through association with other people. Nazarín, at the outset of his journey, is ostensibly little more than a courteous person who does harm to no one and acts kindly toward others when forced into their company. His association with Andara and Beatriz stimulates compassion in him, and only then is his love of God alive and creative. Angel Guerra, starting with love for a woman, undergoes a similar experience. And

Benina (*Misericordia*), beginning with dutiful acceptance of a servant's responsibilities, becomes a living example of increasing compassion, through which she transfers her allegiance from social to human obligation.

Galdós thought much about love of God as being equivalent to love of one's fellow man. But he knew that such a great ideal as "the love of humanity" has in itself only an intellectual appeal; that it can become truly effective only if it has an emotional appeal; and that for the average person, this emotional quality can be experienced only in close personal relationships. If "the love of humanity" were reduced to some kind of concrete manifestation, one of its clearest earmarks would be magnanimity. Whether magnanimity is innate or acquired is of little importance to this discussion. The important thing is that it is in the truest sense emotional and is spontaneously bestowed. It may come as the result of one's gaining confidence in self. It is then clearly an accompaniment to a practical kind of self-realization. Fortunata, for example, becomes more magnanimous the more she satisfies the demands of self-esteem as measured in terms of approval by others. In this respect she is simply demonstrating what a general observation of human behavior confirms: that a person becomes more generous in his attitude toward others as he overcomes a feeling of inferiority.

One might go so far as to say that at the lowest levels magnanimity is closely restricted by a law of physical survival. At the higher levels, however, it is more and more removed from the material and even the social world, because the source of security is now understood to lie in an affinity with a supra-real power. Through a natural transition in valuation, the individual gains liberation from the restrictions of society. The broadening of the capacity for generous action is one result of this liberation. The larger kind of love, whether it is called magnanimity, sympathy, compassion, or charity, is thus activated by contact with people and rules that serve either as a challenge to assertive activity or as a stimulus to the development of the "better self." In either case, love of humanity is a cumulative force that begins within narrow limits and is later freely expended in wider circles of associations. Among the fundamentals of Galdós' moral and religious philosophy is the thought that man's capacity for sympathy and magnanimity toward a widening circle of humanity is a natural development within the restrictions of a static society.

In the three novels (*Angel Guerra, Nazarín, Halma*) that deal most openly with a positive kind of religion, Galdós is attracted to the contemplation of mysticism as a poetic theme. Even so, he does not forget his moral purpose, for his conception of true mysticism as being the active and creative energy of love is an interpretation of the higher levels of morality. It is but an extension of his persistent idea of "la conciencia creadora" which is found in most of his novels after 1880 and repeated finally in *La razón de la sinrazón* (1915), where it is aimed openly at the Spanish nation. In this fantasy the author's ideas are personified in the heroine, Atenaida, who declares that virtue consists not merely in complying with social duties, but in diligence, activity, and the spreading of energy to others (VI, 395), and who exemplifies, in her reclamation of Alejandro, the creative force of love.

It seems quite obvious that Galdós for the whole of his career was possessed with a determination to combat what he apparently considered the two most pernicious maladies of Spain: asceticism and *el picarismo*. There is ample evidence to indicate that he understood these to be products of a society steeped in the worship of authoritarianism and the *status quo,* where healthy individualism finds itself blocked by dogma and hierarchy and reacts in one extreme manner by accepting self-punishment as a virtue in itself, and in another, by circumvention and a *laissez-faire* attitude that leads to degeneration in moral stamina. The antidote which Galdós proposes and illustrates with living examples is a dynamic, renovating morality that makes dignity and self-respect dependent on individual worth rather than social and religious tradition. His preoccupation with this ideal no doubt explains why he is less interested in subtle analyses of problems of conscience than he is in general guides for wholesome living.

Described in broad terms, the novelist's moral philosophy can be reduced to what seems to be a very simple rule of two interdependent parts: be true to self, and love thy neighbor. The first demand stresses freedom of individual conscience and the right to develop one's own capacities. The second receives impetus from the first but makes freedom harmonize with a law higher than self. Only when both demands are met can one have realized self fully. The culmination of such a morality is a new religious consciousness.

If Galdós' contemporary novels are visualized as a whole, the merging of morality and religion referred to in the foregoing statement can be seen as an integration of qualities which support the demands of self (initiative, courage, industry: in a word, intelligent self-direction in constructive activity); which conform with the demands of society (respect for order, co-operation, tolerance, self-objectivation or humility in regard to one's own importance); and which affirm loyalty to ideals independent of social regulation (sympathy, charitableness, self-sacrifice for the benefit of others—the various qualities associated with "love"). The last category is essentially a spontaneous acknowledgment of harmony with a law of humanity at large and is free of the dictates of any closed society. When the integration is seen as development within an individual, it constitutes an advance toward wholeness, which includes duty to self, duty to society, and a combination of these in duty to a higher order. This higher duty, consciously recognized, may be called religion; but it is a religion of liberation, by which a person in the very turmoil of social experience becomes less fettered by it. In short, it is the goal of self-determination, in which subjection to external control is no longer needed because of transformation from within.

This comprehensive picture of morality-religion is nowhere better presented in a particular novel of Galdós than in *Misericordia*. If the self-discipline of León Roch, the courage of Fortunata, the efficiency and charitableness of Guillermina, the humility and selflessness of Nazarín were combined in one person, Benina would surely be that person. From the standpoint of wholeness, Benina represents the culmination of Galdós' portrayal of individual personality. From a practical psychological viewpoint, also, she is the author's maturest personality; and her maturity consists precisely in her ability to conform with the demands of material and social laws without being a slave to them, for these laws become submerged in a law that transcends material and social exigencies.

Benina's independence, as it develops, may be defined as an increasing freedom from insecurity, resulting from a transference of the need of security in the social realm to confidence in a human realm, which merges finally with the security that comes from harmony with a supra-human power. Although she has never had time to think seriously about religion beyond certain surface formalities akin to superstition, her ultimate self-assurance takes on a definite religious color; for she is conscious that pardon, long-suffering, and magnanimity are in harmony with God's will. With no ostensible purpose of promulgating moral or religious beliefs, the author lets morality and religion of the highest kind unfold in an exceptional individual, who is very much of the earth and yet free of it. For a person who has entered into this religious understanding, the rules of a static religion are something that can be worn or laid aside like a cloak, with little consequence to personal integrity.

If Galdós had been asked to state his conception of religion, he probably would have been satisfied to point to Benina as a living illustration of his belief that practice of the simple fundamentals of Christianity makes unimportant the Church to which one "belongs." His bitter attacks on the excesses of Catholicism may give the impression that he would have preferred some version of Protestantism. There are indications, however, that he felt no enthusiasm for the Protestant faith. The brief attention given to the renegade priest José Bailón and his relations with the English Protestant couple don Horacio and doña Malvina, in *Torquemada en la hoguera* (ch. III), reveals a rather cool indifference to their religious faith. This indifference may be a manifestation of the patriotic fervor that causes Galdós generally to try to improve what is definitely Spanish. Such patriotism with respect to religion is clearly seen in *Angel Guerra*. Perhaps, too, the novelist felt that there would be little profit in exchanging one variety of formalistic practice for another. This explanation is confirmed by the fact that he makes a sharp distinction between "church" and true religion; which is another way of saying that he distinguishes between static and dynamic. His interest lies decidedly with the dynamic, which, it may be repeated in conclusion, means, for one thing, the creative effectiveness of love; and for another, moral integration in an advance toward a personality wholeness in which the individual is relatively free of the superficial realities of society.

Whether or not Galdós regards this dynamics of personality as being illustrative of an evolutionary process that accomplishes divine law involves a consideration of the novelist's philosophic perspective.

VII

THE PHILOSOPHIC PERSPECTIVE

To portray developing personality solely from the viewpoint of a competent observer is one thing. To purpose that such a character development represent a fundamental law of the universe is quite another, which definitely places an author in the realm of philosophy. Can it be said that Galdós went so far as to formulate a specific philosophy based on his observation of human nature, or is it more accurate to say that he was intrigued by certain philosophical doctrines current in his day and reflected them incidentally in his works? A close study of his novels indicates a middle ground between affirmative answers to these questions. Galdós was opposed to hard and fast theory, just as he was to dogmatism, and with the possible exception of *Realidad*, he attempted no exclusively philosophical demonstration. Yet there is no question that he had a philosophical mind, and that he respected the search for truth which transcends empirical and scientific knowledge. He was certainly interested in metaphysical (ontological) aspects of life, and for the greater part of his career was actually seeking a philosophy in which human experience is seen as purposeful activity in harmony with an ultimate cause or Being. His novels cannot be fully appreciated without relating this phase of his thinking, which closely parallels his preoccupation with the subject of morality, to the fundamentals of character and plot development.

In some of Galdós' later novels especially, the philosophical theme forms a basic element of the psychological plot; but his interest in philosophy is also evident from various specific remarks scattered here and there in his works. For example, in an article (May 15, 1872) written for the column which he conducted under the title *Crónica de la quincena,* he welcomes a Spanish translation of Hegel's *Logic,* and expresses the belief that positivism must be balanced by metaphysics:

> ... porque los estragos que en entendimientos muy ilustrados hace la escuela positivista, exigen grandes esfuerzos para devolver a la metafísica el puesto que le corresponde entre los acontecimientos humanos.[1]

Don Buenaventura, in *Gloria,* shows a similiar desire to include philosophy among the guides for living when he declares: "Creo que la conciliación entre la filosofía y la fe es posible, que si no es posible, vendrá el caos" (IV, 620). Many years later the emphasis has shifted toward religion. If judged from the following remarks of Nazarín, the author is plainly disillusioned with philosophy:

> ... la filosofía es, en suma, un juego de conceptos y palabras, tras el cual es el vacío, y los filósofos son el aire seco que sofoca y desalienta a la Humanidad en su áspero camino. (V, 1772)

In reality, the disillusionment has resulted from expecting too much. The novelist's youthful approbation of the rational and scientific outlook has been tempered, primarily by the realization that science and philosophy cannot answer the question of man's origin and destiny. Nazarín also says of science, "La ciencia no resuelve ninguna cuestión de trascendencia en los problemas de nuestro origen y destino" (V, 1772). This modification of youthful enthusiasm does not keep Galdós from speculating on the mysteries of the universe, and even in his last novel (*La razón de la sinrazón*) he is thinking of "el ritmo Universal . . . la sublime armonía de los mundos lejanos" (VI, 387). Atenaida, in fact, senses that this *armonía* is somehow operative in her faith in conscience, love, and creative energy. In the long interval between the terminals here referred to (1872-1915), the novels reveal a development that assumes the proportions of a philosophical creed.

The initial step, the foundation for the development, is a rebellious assertion of the right to think for oneself and to correlate science, philosophy, and religion; in short, a defense of the right to be a philosopher. This first stage is represented most pointedly by *Doña Perfecta, Gloria,* and *La familia de León Roch.* Curiously enough, however, the sentimental story of Marianela is the most "philosophical" of Galdós' early novels. Its philosophical subject matter is contained not so much in the development of the central personalities as in the contrasts inherent in the situation, most prominent of which is the difference between a reality of the senses and a reality of the imagination. Just as the earth, in contrast to the heavens, appears ugly to some (to the doctor, Teodoro Golfín, for example), so Nela is ugly; but she is beautiful to Pablo until he is brought into the bondage imposed by the senses.

Professor Casalduero interprets *Marianela* as a symbolic demonstration of Comte's theory (*Philosophie positive*) of the "three states" in human progress, and believes that Galdós is championing science, the positive stage, as a necessary replacement of the preceding stages of theology and metaphysics.[2] To stress Comte's influence seems unwise. Is the novelist not thinking that perhaps nature, by making Pablo blind, has given him the key to the reality of mind, and that by a trick of science, also inherent in nature, has blinded him to a higher reality? The irony of nature is that it allows human beings to believe in an ideal world and yet place visual, physical standards above the reality of spirit, which is manifest especially in kindness. Golfín admits finally the insignificance of science in the presence of the mysteries of passion. The author makes it clear that the heroine is capable of expanding spiritually when treated with love. Nela is physically a victim of nature, but she is also a victim of man's inability to see beyond his tangible, formal surroundings, and the science of Golfín can do nothing to help her.

For this reason, the story's reference to Comte's three stages of civilization seems to be more a refutation than an indorsement—in any case, an unhappy contemplation—of the positivistic outlook. It is true that the author compares Nela to primitive peoples, who are dominated by superstition, the senses, and passions; but if he is making his heroine symbolic of a stage of civilization that must be replaced by a new Age of Science, he is cruelly identifying her dominant motives with slavery to the senses. Actually he shows that her basic motive is the need for love and friendliness, the very things that science cannot provide. Pablo is ruled by the senses and a cult of form much more than Nela is. It would seem, therefore, that the novel is representative of Galdós' desire to harmonize reason (including science) and humanness. Such a conclusion seems all the more valid in view of the quotation just cited from *Crónica de la quincena* (1872), in which a plea is made for a balance between positivism and metaphysics. Largely by suggestion, *Marianela* raises the question, "What is reality?"; to which the author with maturer thought returns later in his career. It reveals no particular philosophy, but it shows an interest in philosophical ideas and thus communicates a more positive attitude than the other novels before 1880, in which the emphasis, from a philosophical viewpoint, rests upon the evils resulting from a lack of rational thinking.

In the early years of his residence in Madrid, Galdós absorbed much from the teachings of Julián Sanz del Río. This famous *krausista* wielded great influence on the young liberals of the 1860's. In accord with the doctrine of K. C. F. Krause, he espoused a "racionalismo armónico," whose chief aim may be described as a desire to maintain balance between reason, science, and religion, rather than an effort to promulgate a particular system. He championed freedom of conscience guided by rational understanding, but he refused to draw absolute conclusions or to formulate any specific theory other than that of "la razón moderadora" or "la razón conciliadora," which he maintained was necessary for the sake of common peace and equity while man seeks ultimate truth.[3] His main contribution to the generation that followed him, therefore, was that of a moral leader who, while instilling respect for the rational discipline of philosophy, stood for tolerance and the humanization of both philosophy and religion.[4] The plea for tolerance, for reason leavened with humanness, for a vital, practical religion that can stand up in the face of philosophy, and for balance between scientific knowledge and a reality of the spirit are marks which Galdós bears for the whole of his career. The most noticeable influence before 1880 was a respect for rational thinking as a general discipline and guide for conduct. The following remarks of Francisco Giner de los Ríos, disciple of Sanz del Río and friend of Galdós, is applicable to the novelist's early emphasis on the individual's right to think like a philosopher, as compared to his interest in any particular theory: "En mi cátedra no enseño filosofía, sino a filosofar."[5]

With *El amigo Manso* (1882) Galdós expands his thinking in regard to the mission of a philosopher and demonstrates his idea by character development. His primary orientation is still the *krausismo* of Sanz del Río, and his emphasis rests on the humanization of philosophy. Máximo Manso has been conditioned by early training and long habit to an asocial life, in which his main enjoyment derives from the contemplation of abstract values, and in which he has developed his basic adjustive pattern of rational self-discipline. His temperament and intellect fit him for such a life, and he has been encouraged in it by a sober unsentimental mother. Basically, he craves the affection and warm human ties that have been suppressed in a passive kind of existence, in which he has maintained his equilibrium by a rather unenthusiastic faith in rational ideals. When he is brought into contact with earthy living and begins to fall in love with Irene, he makes a transition from the theoretical to the practical by seeing the real as a reflection of his ideas.

As the emotion of love becomes stronger, Manso's philosophical supports weaken; for he wants to be just an ordinary social man. When he realizes that Irene loves Manuel, his own pupil, he is forced to make a readjustment, which turns out to be a combination of an old and a new set of values. His habitual self-control and self-effacement harmonize with a new pride in the directive activity of a teacher, manifest in his generous, protective attitude toward Manuel and Irene. He thus returns to the heights of philosophical equanimity, broadened by the effects of warm personal relationships in which he has acquired new stature by way of pride in the kindly role of master. In a word, his mission has been imbued with life.

This symbolical tale is plainly an interpretive demonstration of certain aspects of Sanz del Río's teachings. Several of Manso's statements are echoes of the professor's lectures.[6] For example: "Existe alianza perfecta entre la sociedad y la Filosofía"; "Se halla colocado [el filósofo] entre dos esferas igualmente grandes: el mundo exterior y su conciencia" (IV, 1273).[7] And there is a further resemblance between the novel and the philosophical dissertations with respect to the relation of the particular to the whole, including the idea that even though total truth is superior to any particular truth, the particular is the starting point for rational thinking in its gradual ascent to broad generalities.[8]

This general aspect of idealism seems to have challenged Galdós' thinking most. For in *El amigo Manso*—and in later novels also—he wants to emphasize the meaning of the following assertion, made by Manso while in the early phases of his readjustment, and which, incidentally, embodies a fundamental of the novelist's literary realism:

> A veces el hecho aislado, corriente, ofrece, bien analizado, un reflejo de la síntesis universal, como cualquier espejillo retrata toda la grandeza del cielo . . . El hombre de pensamiento descubre la verdad; pero quien goza de ella y utiliza sus celestiales dones es el hombre de acción, el hombre de mundo, que vive en las particularidades, en las contingencias y en el ajetreo de los hechos comunes. (IV, 1273)

The philosopher, by constantly generalizing, is likely to ignore the particular, but the particular is the very thing on which the generalization depends. Manso's view of Irene as the *mujer-razón* represents the generalization. When he later thinks of her as the *mujer-mujer,* he is seeing the particular, which gives life to his abstract ideas. The idea here is that in order to make philosophy a part of life, the "man of thought" must become also the "man of action" or "of the world," just as later in *Nazarín* the point is that the religious ideal must be effectuated in particular relationships within society. The philosopher is thus obliged to descend from the realm of the absolute to reveal his truth in active living, just as Christ descended to the earth:

El Cristo es la imagen augusta y eterna de la Filosofía, que sufre persecución y muere, aunque sólo por tres días, para resucitar luego y seguir consagrada al gobierno del mundo. (IV, 1273)

Manso ascends again, but through his contact with the earth, he not only has fulfilled his mission; he has broadened his conception of philosophy, and in fact has saved himself from sterile passivity by acquiring (again like Nazarín) enthusiasm for the role of beneficent master. This is the practical, realistic idea that interests Galdós most, and it is worthy of note that in this, the first novel that presents a definite constructive theme, an ascending line of personality development is traceable in the central character.

With all the obvious attention to the mission of a philosopher, Galdós is indicating, by his suggestion that a philosophy which is lived unconsciously is superior to any kind of abstract discussion of life, the direction that his artistic endeavor takes thereafter. Though he soon plunges into the portrayal of life so thoroughly that the reader almost loses sight of any philosophical purpose, such a purpose gradually assumes form as if it were growing inevitably out of life itself. It is a philosophy grounded upon an interpretation of the "self and others" relationship, which is the subject of greatest magnitude in Galdós, whether regarded from a psychological, moral, or metaphysical viewpoint.

Taken as a whole, the novels present a broad and balanced picture of human nature comprising the basic needs of security, activity, and response or belongingness. The last of these needs, which includes affection, sympathy, and dependence, comes to overshadow the other two and in fact becomes the answer to them. Although this development is suggested in *Marianela* and again in *El amigo Manso*, its first definite manifestation is found in *El doctor Centeno* (1883). Here the comfort and moral strength to be had from friendly associations appear especially in the Alejandro Miquis-Felipe Centeno relationship, a picture of mutuality that suggests the alliance between Don Quijote and Sancho Panza.[9] The main profit falls to the Sancho of the partnership, who, while smiling sympathetically at the illusions of his master, finds in the friendship a wholesome goal of self-realization. Miquis, however, is the one who voices a philosophy based on personal ties, for he discounts his own importance except as it is manifest in others: "Mi yo es un yo ajeno" (IV, 1415).

The author is pondering here the possibilities of a "self and others" concept which comes to the fore with much greater force and breadth in *Fortunata y Jacinta*. In this novel almost every character of consequence shows an intense longing for the identification of self with others, and this theme forms the basis of the Fortunata-Jacinta plot. Subsequently, with the exception of *Miau* and *Tristana,* where the author concentrates on a negative side of personality adjustment, the psychological theme most consistently followed is that of self-enlargement in vital personal relations. Even in the mystic aspirations of Angel Guerra and Nazarín, it is clearly shown that self can not advance by itself alone. The idea is not so much that selfishness, in the usual sense of the word, is a deterrent to healthy growth; it is, rather, that self depends upon other selves, that it must emerge from the stricture of self-sufficiency and partake of other personalities in order to expand morally and spiritually—or to make a sane adjustment to environment.

Galdós' treatment of this particular subject can best be understood by inquiring into its philosophical background. Along with the nineteenth-century discussion of the natural and social sciences, a top layer of metaphysical thought is present in the belief that the individual, while being a social organism that develops in a natural, maturational process through community of experience, is bound to that selfhood which includes all individuality. This thinking is pervaded with a good portion of post-Kantian idealism, manifest in the "self and others" concept. The subject receives wide attention in the second half of the century, with emphasis resting on conciliation of the two components, and with a tendency to see in organisms a purposeful activity of reciprocal influence.

It seems unquestionable that the philosophical ideas of the age in which Galdós grew to his intellectual maturity—from 1862 to 1885— played an important part in his formulation of metaphysical beliefs based upon the observation of personal relations. The marked intellectual activity in Spain during the years immediately preceding and following the Revolution of 1868 carried with it an influx of philosophical and scientific ideas from abroad. That Galdós was abreast of this intellectual movement is clear, if from nothing more than the frequent references to scientists, psychologists, and philosophers found in his novels. The mere fact that he mentions a writer's name, of course, is no proof that he had read a given work, though some of his allusions show a clear understanding of the material referred to. He was hardly more than average in originality, but he was unusually alert and quick to grasp the significance of a new idea, whether from hasty reading or discussions with friends. It is certain, from the content of his novels, that he exercised independent thinking in selecting and shaping the ideas of others to fit his own idealistic inclinations. With all his enthusiasm for science, his idealism is dominant, even in his early works, where it is seeking a definite direction to give it meaning. The idealism of Galdós reveals a general similarity to the Krausism of Sanz del Río in the belief in the unity of God with all things in a relationship where the parts, though they may be in opposition to each other, form a harmonious whole whose totality is superior to any particular being or to any particular relationship; and also as regards the notion of continuity or gradual evolutionary movement in the universal order, including the concept of society as an organism. The diluted Kantianism and Hegelianism of Krause, however, were too soft and vague for Galdós to apply to the roughness of everyday living. Perhaps this attitude is rightly to be inferred from the remarks of one of the characters in *El doctor Centeno* (IV, 1443): Federico Ruiz, who has written a treatise on Hegel and is also studying Spencer and Hartmann, laments that all intellectualism in Spain is *krausista*. (The date of the novel's setting, 1863, should be remembered in this connection.) Worthy of mention also are Torquemada's ludicrous efforts to conceive of God as being the equivalent of "la Humanidad" (*Torquemada en la hoguera*). The phrase suggests Sanz del Río's collective human being, "la humanidad universal," though it is more probably a derisive allusion to the "Humanity" which Comte substitutes for a divine Being (*Politique positive*). In any case, Galdós sought a metaphysics that had more backbone to it than Krausism, and there is considerable evidence that he found it in Hegel's theory of self-consciousness.

The question of Hegelian influence on the novelist is of enough importance to justify a rather detailed examination. The similarity between the two thinkers is to be found primarily in the concept of spiritual evolution, which is set forth in detail in Hegel's *Phenomenology of Mind* (1807).[10] The practical implications of this theory that must have appealed to Galdós pertain especially to the process of self-realization, by which individual consciousness passes laboriously from materiality to spirituality, slipping back upon its lower self in the process, but ever acquiring new awareness that leads to a realization of unity with the Absolute Spirit. Through successive stages of opposition to and fusion with the otherness which underlies it, individuality progresses upward to a point at which consciousness is not hampered by but wholly in harmony with what is seemingly foreign to it. Perhaps the most fundamental elements of Hegel's system are: dependence of self upon an otherness which holds a key to self's own reality; the neces-

sity of conflict and of reciprocal absorption therefrom; and self-enlargement by way of a transcending movement in which present states,
though partially retained, are ever being superseded.

The novels of Galdós contain a rich representation of competition,
co-operation, interdependence of the individual with his social environment, and human association seen as a process of change and growth.
From one viewpoint, this aspect of the novelist's writing is but a general
reflection of psychological and sociological thought in the latter part of
the nineteenth century. Since, moreover, there was in the same period
a pronounced metaphysical interest in the unity of man with God in
a harmonious world order, it is difficult to separate from Galdós' presentation of maturing personality that part which shows a direct Hegelian
influence. In certain of the novels, however, Hegelian ideas are rather
sharply defined, and there is also a broad similarity between the thinking of the philosopher and the novelist that cannot be lightly dismissed.

It is hardly necessary here to review examples of the constructive
influence exerted by one person upon another that characterizes most
of Galdós' novels after 1880; nor to demonstrate again the psychological
structure which takes the form of an ascending staircase in character
development. From *El amigo Manso* (1882) on, plot movement and
moral improvement generally coincide on an ascending line. The moral
advance comes as the result of natural adjustment in personal relations
that are sometimes harmonious but more often frictional. In broad
terms, it can be said that mutuality of dependence, conflict, and transcending movement are fundamentals of Galdosian portrayal. The
novelist's most outstanding ideal is harmonious progress through the
medium of love, but the picture of life found in his novels gives prominence to opposing forces, struggle, and conciliatory endeavor. The
Hegelian conception of antithesis and synthesis thus suggests itself and
has, in fact, been mentioned by scholars in reference to the general view
of contradictions in Galdós' depiction of life and of Spanish society.[11]

The idea assumes much more importance if it is associated with
specific instances of personal relations. In *El doctor Centeno* (1883)
Galdós apparently was pondering the Hegelian notion that one finds
one's essential reality in an "other." At least the previously cited statement of Miquis ("Mi yo es un yo ajeno") suggests this, and the picture
of mutual esteem between Miquis and Felipe supports the assumption.
The first major application of the philosophical idea, however, comes
in *Fortunata y Jacinta* (1886-1887), particularly in the relationship
between the two principal feminine characters, with the emphasis now

shifted to a study of conflict. Here is a clear-cut example of two persons in direct opposition, engaged in a life-and-death struggle and yet drawing more closely together with an increasing realization of their need for each other. Unmistakably the author means to show that the two personalities are complementary; for after Fortunata has revealed her longing for Jacinta's friendship and has finally made the magnanimous gesture of giving her child to her rival, the latter admits that she, in turn, admires Fortunata, some of whose qualities she would like to possess.

The story brings out incidentally the thought that the social classes represented by the two rivals are also subject to mutually beneficial results by way of intermixture, but the emphasis rests upon the individual's struggle and growth. Since Jacinta remains in the background most of the time, Fortunata is the chief exemplification of the results of bitter opposition becoming constructive competition. It is exact to say that in her case the needs of self (notably approval by others) bring an increasing subordination to an otherness which is indispensable to its integrity and from which self draws and adds to its own being. So it is that Fortunata develops strength in a communion of spirit with both friend and enemy, losing in the social struggle to establish herself as an acceptable member of the Santa Cruz family, but growing morally in the development of sympathy and magnanimity. In other words, she rises above her former state, and though still on a primitive level of understanding, is approaching the point at which an affinity with Spirit (or God's approval, as she perceives it) and self-realization dawn upon her consciousness as being one and the same thing. All of this is the result of an invigorating warfare, in which the mastery of conflicts contributes to spiritual advance, that is, to an expanding consciousness of one's active part in a divine, if also earthly, community. Even the abnormal Maximiliano Rubín, who is forced more and more into himself, fights and wins battles caused by external relations and rises, in his own mind at least, to a closer kinship with Spirit.[12]

In *Angel Guerra* (1890-1891) the theme of antithesis and resultant spiritual growth centers primarily on the internal struggles of an individual. Since Angel's love for Leré is the basic cause of his elevation, his self-enlargement comes essentially from a spontaneous subordination of self to another. The love experience, however, far from being a peaceful development, is enveloped in the antagonistic circumstances of social and human religion, and complicated further by the wilfulness of the central character, whose struggle thus becomes an effort to dominate his impulses and co-ordinate them with the demands of a world hostile to unruly individualism. Angel's mastery of self, fundamentally a unification of the opposing forces that are essential to his integrity, is his major accomplishment and his major reward. Whether or not Galdós was thinking of Hegel in this case, such a view of opposition, integration, and consequent expansion of self's horizon is in harmony with the Hegelian thesis, which envisages not only conflict between people and collective forces, but between ideas and emotions within an individual as well.[13] This inner conflict, too, represents the endless contention of good with evil. From the contest the strong of heart emerge with proof of their spirituality, satisfying the demands of the universal by such results as the triumph of courage over cowardice or the suppression of selfishness and base impulses in favor of consideration for others.

Perhaps it is too much to propose that Torquemada is another example of the Hegelian interpretation of spiritual advance. Yet Torquemada advances morally by widening his vision of self in its relation to others, and this improvement derives to an important degree from his association with the person (Cruz del Aguila) who most bitterly antagonizes him. It must be remembered also that the author is depicting here an integration of opposing social classes.

If the *Torquemada* series offers questionable evidence of Hegelian influence, the same can hardly be said of *La loca de la casa* (1892). In this too obviously ideological novel, Galdós combines the themes of class fusion, ascetic versus positive religion, and the interdependence of one person and another.[14] The last of these themes is the backbone of the plot and provides the major element of human interest, for the solution of the situational conflict grows out of the psychological interaction between the stubbornly egocentric Cruz and the militantly evangelistic Victoria. These two are mutually antagonistic and yet are gradually forced to recognize that each possesses qualities which are indispensable to the other, and that this fact necessitates concessions, if for no other reason than self-interest.

Victoria, whose mystic aspirations have been redirected to an active participation in the hard realities of life, does not understand the mysteries of consciousness (*conciencia*) that draw her to Cruz, but she feels that the struggle inherent in the association with her husband somehow represents the demands of a supreme plan (Act IV, scene vii). That the author means this experience of his heroine to have philosophical significance is made plain in the *Escena última*. Here, the dominant psychological-philosophical theme is underscored with two Hegelian ideas: self-realization through surrender of self to another self, and conflict between good and evil as being necessary to the existence of good. These ideas are expressed in the words of Cruz, "Mientras más la quiero, más me afirmo en ser lo que soy"; and of Victoria, "Eres el mal, y si el mal no existiera, los buenos no sabríamos qué hacer . . . ni podríamos vivir."

There is yet another important instance of similarity between Hegel and Galdós, which has to do with the question of what is reality, the underlying theme of *La Incógnita* (1888-1889) and *Realidad* (1889). In these two novels the author assumes the role of an experimenter who inquires into man's sedulous efforts to comprehend life's true meaning. The subject is localized in the framework of a dramatic triangle of husband (Orozco), wife (Augusta), and wife's lover (Viera). The main psychological interest centers on Viera's unhappy entanglement in the webs of environment, and attention to this environmental problem constitutes in effect an independent part of the story's hybrid structure. The author, however, is especially intent upon a philosophical consideration of values, which he treats under the name of truth and reality, regarded as being the same, and of morality, an inseparable corollary of the other two.[15] To this end he subordinates dramatic action, showing a greater interest in the viewpoints of his various characters.

The experiment begins, in *La Incógnita*, with an examination of the domestic issue from the standpoint of outsiders, personified in the main by Manolo Infante, a self-styled detective and would-be Don Juan. What slight literary merit this novel has—if it is judged as an independent work—lies in its satire of superficialities. Its primary function, of course, is to introduce the problem by establishing the idea of contrast between apparent and essential reality. In the two novels together, the principal deliberate interpretations of truth or reality are exemplified by Infante (*La Incógnita* and *Realidad*), Augusta (*Realidad*), and Orozco (*Realidad*), each of whom represents a different level of enlightment.

Infante visualizes reality simply as factual, tangible truth. His curiosity about the nature of Orozco's mysticism and Augusta's love affair impels him into an assiduous investigation weighted with a desire to supplant Viera as Augusta's lover. He is interested to some extent in knowing whether Orozco is a sublime conscience or a vulgar misanthrope, but for his purposes "la verdad, la santa verdad," in whose name he justifies his fatuous tactics, is adequately determined by finding answers to the following questions: Does Augusta have a lover? Is Viera the lover? Did Viera commit suicide? Together with other parasitical hangers-on, he recognizes the superficiality and immorality of upper-class society, but he accepts conditions as they are because their existence makes them true. From this viewpoint, both truth and morality are entirely subject to the whims of adventitious circumstances.

Augusta is a woman of unusual vitality, alert imagination, and exalted, if misdirected, idealism, who turns impulsively away from the ordinary and the conventional. Married to a man who commands her respect but not her love, she has developed a philosophy of obedience to nature, in whose name she justifies her earthy, sensuous tastes and her love for Viera.[16] To her way of thinking, truth or reality, whatever it may be, is rich, varied, unfathomable, and not subject to formulation. She therefore argues against trying to reduce life to a set of rules (V, 823). Viera—and Galdós, it may be assumed—reminds her of the danger of fleeing one *amaneramiento* only to fall into another through worshiping what is exciting and novelesque.

It is Augusta's weakness to place too much emphasis on sensual pleasures, but she has the imagination to see beyond the surface appearances of reality, and with the exception of Orozco, is the person most capable of rising above a factual interpretation of truth. Had it not been for the cold otherworldliness of her husband, she might have corrected her waywardness; for she is conscience-stricken at times and inclined to doubt the validity of her doctrine of sinful humanness. After her lover's death, she is motivated above all by the necessity of preserving appearances and retreats into a conventional domain. Even so, she draws near the decision of confessing her guilt to her husband and thus undergoing the purification which he has hoped for; and although his intellectual "saintliness" repels her, she promises herself that she will make amends for her sin. (This promise she apparently kept, to judge from her upright and charitable conduct briefly glimpsed in *Torquemada y San Pedro*, I, vii-xi.) Augusta, then, is an example of insubordinate individualism bowing inevitably before social law, and her initial interpretation of reality, stressing the senses as it does, is stamped with error because of its moral unreliability.

Orozco undertakes a more exalted approach in his quest of truth than any of the other characters of *Realidad*. Dominated by the ideal of spiritual self-elevation, he proposes to discover ultimate reality by himself and within himself, working on the principle of self-subordination, which takes the form of charity, forbearance, and the suppression of egoistic desires. He easily achieves his aim of self-discipline in all the tests with which he is faced, but with his constant introspection he becomes something of an abstraction, deliberately trying to demonstrate a theory in himself and stand off and observe his reactions at the same time. Moreover, he develops an almost fanatic zeal, both with respect to his goal of self-annihilation and his drive to impose his doctrine of spirituality on his wife and Viera. He acquires unconsciously a "holier than thou" attitude, which alienates him more and more from the social world, the only medium, according to his own assertion, in which good can be effected.

In the end, Orozco realizes that he has been following an illusion, for he decides that obedience to one's conscience, illustrated by Viera's suicide, points the way to ultimate truth. His efforts to grasp the Absolute thus seem to be redirected to a simple human standard of conduct, but even as he embraces this new discovery, he retains a pride which is still colored with self-satisfied holiness. This trait stands out even more clearly in the stage version of *Realidad* (1892), where Orozco declares to Viera's apparition, "Tú y yo nos elevamos sobre toda esta miseria de las pasiones, del odio y del vano juicio del vulgo" (VI, 576). The story of Orozco is that of a person who tries to solve the enigma of ultimate truth by deliberate, intellectual experimentation with self, shifting to a new interpretation (obedience to conscience) after disillusionment with an old one (self-effacement).

Can it now be said that the author meant to propose a specific answer to the question "What is reality?" Berkowitz assumes as much, for he asserts that the way to absolute truth is revealed in *Realidad* by the individual's search of his conscience.[17] Such a conclusion would be logical if the plot were essentially the biographical study of a leading character whose final decision grew out of his own search of conscience; or if Orozco's final experience represented a solution of the complication inherent in the dramatic situation. To place the major thematic content in the story of Orozco is to disregard the novel's basic structure, which combines around an abstract idea a plurality of personal standards. The various answers to the philosophical question must be viewed simultaneously with Orozco's solution, the best perhaps, but still an imperfect one, because in its broad generalization it is an answer to nothing.

Galdós certainly believes that obedience to conscience is a desirable moral guide, but he also knows that such a guide can lead one to error as well as to truth. The author surveys the whole intellectual and emotional network of personal relationships, seemingly agreeing with Augusta as regards both the richness of truth and the futility of trying to reduce it to a simple formula. Even dreams and visions are real—he would remind us—in so far as they reveal psychological needs and the ideals which are possible of attainment. What is presented, then, is a multisectional view of consciousness rather than a study of conscience, and the unifying thematic movement revolves around Reality, itself the central character, which, like a will-o'-the-wisp, escapes all the other characters. The explanation for this elusiveness is the individual's inability to see beyond the particular aspects of Truth that encompass him in his own narrow, personal world, and to behold it in broad perspective. Hegel's theory of the totality of Truth and Reality thus comes to mind as being pertinent to an elucidation of *Realidad*.

From an Hegelian viewpoint, Truth and Reality are the functioning of the world process in its unified allness. In its finite forms, Truth is elastic, restless, experimental, changing with new experience and following a progressive course whose many steps are merely approximations, tainted always with falsehood in so far as the Absolute is concerned.[18] But since these finite moments, these abstractions of Spirit, are the indispensable substance of the total process, they are together—not separately—the truth. Any given moment of experience, when viewed in isolation, is only partially true, since its real meaning can be understood only in relation to a pattern of multiple parts. By implication, knowledge of the universal scheme of relationships is always partial, since finite mind, though capable of visualizing a general pattern of the universal principle, fails continuously to comprehend the complete details of such a pattern.

In this view of reality and truth, morality assumes a secondary but fundamental position with respect to expanding intelligence. Conscience is consciousness with reference to all activity, not merely to acts whose goodness or badness is determined by fixed social laws or by personal convictions, which are subject to the capriciousness of circumstances. For fixed concepts of either morality or truth are but pauses in the mobility that underlies all reality. Moral consciousness, in short, is an increasing understanding and is one with growth toward realization of the essential reality that binds individuals together. It necessarily passes through stages of greater and lesser imperfection.

The characters in *Realidad* stand for various imperfect conceptions of reality. The lowest level of understanding is found in Manolo Infante, who judges truth by what he can see and touch, and who adjusts his morality to a code based on appearances. His interpretation corresponds essentially to what Hegel calls the stage of sense-certainty, the most remote semblance of truth. Augusta, whose aspiration to grasp the full meaning of life definitely stamps her with more than average spiritual potentiality, is nonetheless an independent seeker of pleasure, negatively disposed in her relationship to social order. In the end she submits to order by way of conventional adjustment and thus prepares for a more advanced step in the direction of self-discipline. Her major part in the novel makes her an outstanding example of one who, in Hegel's words, worships the law of the heart, seeking the realization of immediate, undisciplined nature, ignoring the law of the universal heart, and ending in unreality rather than reality.

Orozco's portrait so closely resembles Hegel's description of the "virtuous consciousness" that there can be little doubt as to Galdós' source of inspiration in this case. The stage of consciousness here referred to is that of a person who tries to achieve virtue as an end in itself, as "good" to be realized in opposition to world order, and who becomes vain in the pursuit of his exalted goal, not yet having learned that essential reality is the process and not the "good" *per se*.[19] Orozco is convinced at last that he has followed a false doctrine and transfers his enthusiasm to an interpretation that places emphasis upon conscience— a step which in the author's mind no doubt represents a directional improvement, but not the final answer. Orozco is simply entering a new phase in his quest of the Absolute. Even this change of direction—the reader feels certain—will not prove to be the necessary correction if he continues to hold himself aloof from society, which alone makes possible the functioning of conscience.

In addition to these major examples of conscious philosophers, there are numerous personages who in their living reveal various aspects of reality without serious thought of philosophical theory. Clotilde, Viera's sister, in her acceptance of a plebeian's love, represents the principle of practical adjustment to circumstances. Her action is approved by her father, rogue though he is, and even by Infante, who departs from his cynicism long enough to give Viera some sound advice. For an habitual parasite like Villalonga, this principle is a cruel one and evokes the complaint that those who have plenty can look at reality as they please, while those who have to work must adapt themselves to whatever reality has to offer. Villalonga is thinking of reality primarily in terms of fortuitous events, but he also raises indirectly the question of relative truth, albeit on the superficial level of selfish comfort.

Cisneros, Augusta's father, presents a somewhat higher interpretation of relativity. Under the persistent hammering of Infante (in *La Incógnita*), he declares in defense of his daughter—and of himself, incidentally—that Absolute Truth can not be grasped, and that truth as man comprehends it is always relative, depending upon the dictates of individual honor and the exigencies of social circumstances. He thus accords theoretically a high place to individual conscience as a measurement for both truth and morality. His interpretation of conscience, however, is flexible enough to rest solely on the term "honor," however superficial one's concept of honor may be. Viera demonstrates a higher conception of conscience, for although he is a hopeless victim of his social environment, his aristocratic sense of honor is turned finally to an expiation for the guilt that comes from violating loyalty to a friend.

The viewpoints just recorded have no special Hegelian complexion, but they add to the impression of a comprehensive process of trial and error, in which the characters participate without comprehending their roles. The theory of relative truth posed by Cisneros, for example, is a venture in the direction of Hegelian relativity on the part of one who is unable to give substantial meaning to his theory because of his failure to integrate self-interest in a broad pattern of relationships. *La Incógnita* and *Realidad,* then, jointly depict man's confused strivings, conscious and unconscious, to satisfy the seemingly unknowable law of truth and reality. The emphasis is upon the imperfection of man's understanding, but the possibility, if not the certainty, of an orderly advance is seen in the gradation of categories represented by Infante, Augusta, and Orozco, which exhibit a succession of steps whereby the individual, through a process of disintegration and integration, gradually moves toward a unified wholeness.

Galdós thus presents a descriptive and partial view of Hegelian theory without carrying his demonstration to a confident conclusion. He senses that the totality of relations constitutes absolute reality, but with less assurance than Hegel, he stops short of the latter's absolutism. He is, instead, content to wonder at the magnitude of the philosophical problem and to remain on comparatively safe ground, where he can observe the parts without attempting to visualize the systematic, abstract whole. Hence the question "What is reality?" is left unanswered. In his own uncertainty, the author falls back upon a simple doctrine, which holds in effect that the world process is perhaps most clearly seen when spirituality develops unconsciously in the individual through selfless devotion to others. He sees, too, that truth or goodness, while always incomplete in so far as particular instances are concerned, comes in different guise to people of widely different circumstances; and that, paradoxically enough, it is manifested by rank sinners like *la Peri* (in the form of warm human sympathy), or by a person like Augusta (in her selfless love for another).

Thus, as Galdós tastes imaginatively of an esoteric Hegelian concept, he shows his inclination to follow the simpler thesis that the universal principle reveals itself in individuals who, seeking their own interest, spontaneously prove their affinity with Spirit by effecting their essential reality in a law of mutual dependence. This idea, still Hegelian and probably the philosopher's most enduring contribution, is the one that Galdós embraced most wholeheartedly and the one that stands out as the dominant philosophical theme in his novels after *La desheredada*. The novelist is tempted intermittently to speculate upon the complexities of truth and reality, but he prefers as a general objective to trace the individual's self-enlargement amidst the hard circumstances of social living, in which self-realization follows a moral course of expanding respect for others and of liberation from the tyranny of a self-centered existence. The highest station in this advance may appropriately be called the Hegelian stage of religious consciousness, at which self is in harmony with the idea that it is Spirit operative.

Three of Galdós' characters in particular call to mind stages in the spiritual life analyzed by Hegel. The successive levels of advance which they represent follow a chronological sequence in the novels from *Fortunata y Jacinta* to *Misericordia*. Fortunata is a person in the early stages of maturation, with self aware above all of its opposition to an otherness, on which it nevertheless depends for its own reality. Orozco represents the more advanced state of one who is awakening to his relationship with Spirit but who, still fettered by a self-centered pursuit of abstract virtue, is only a half-virtuous, half-opening soul. Benina moves in the higher reaches of harmonious and spontaneous co-operation with a law of mutuality, where self-interest and interest in others are one.

Galdós does not venture a decisive opinion as to the individual's destiny after death. At this point in his speculation, he seems to lean with some uncertainty toward a traditional conception of Heaven—and with little thought of Hell—apparently unwilling to believe in the ultimate absorption of individuality in the total activity of Spirit, an extreme consequence of Hegelian theory. But he and Hegel alike are preoccupied most of all with man's temporal existence, and the comprehensive sum of their similar beliefs is an optimistic combination of empirical knowledge and faith in a divine Being. The common core of their beliefs is, in fact, a rational interpretation of Christianity, in which Christ is not the Christ crucified in atonement for the sins of man, but one who has demonstrated man's unity with God.

The comparison could probably be carried further after an analysis of Galdós' plays and his *Episodios Nacionales*. The question arises, for example, as to the novelist's philosophy of history. On the basis of his social novels, there is little opportunity to draw conclusions on this subject. It seems clear, however, that Galdós agrees with some of the generalities of Hegel's philosophy of history in reference to the thought that underlying the restless mutation of peoples is change at large, but change of a transcending kind, in which progressive reintegration insures the continuity of national groups. From the Hegelian viewpoint, national self-realization is moral and vigorous only if it advances to the adoption of some new purpose, thus gaining a new understanding of itself. Such a course of activity is the pulsating rhythm of a universal law, whereby newness is added to oldness in gradual passage.

It is not amiss to think in this light of *El caballero encantado* (1909). In this fantasy, La Madre, the soul of the Spanish nation, seeks to teach her children that they can recover their former vitality by reversing the tradition of a nonproductive aristocracy and adopting a new, decisive course of action. She offers as concrete remedies a return to the simple ideal of hard work and pride in earning one's own bread, improvement of the peasant's status in Spanish national life, and education of the common people. With all its idyllic haziness, the story stresses what was unquestionably one of the author's most consistent ideals: that his country should turn to new goals and rise to new challenges, thus triumphing over calamities and insuring its life by purposeful action. For a nation, as for an individual, he felt this to be a necessity and perhaps a demand of universal law; and he personifies his belief in La Madre, "la que al mismo tiempo es tradición inmutable y revolución continua" (VI, 329).

Aside from specific examples of affinity between Hegel and Galdós, there is, in their comprehensive perspective of life, a general similarity that deserves at least passing mention. J. Loewenberg regards Hegel's dialectical analysis as expressive of a comic vision of the world, which emanates from the realistic conception that human delusion (narrowness of perspective) and folly (exaggerated particularity) are today and always the great repetitive beats of a universal rhythm.[20] In the universal urge to wholeness, Loewenberg observes, the whole becomes a bacchanalian revel, in which each part, while struggling to be more than a part, is incited and yet defeated by the whole. Since the whole

depends upon all its parts, the doctrine can be construed to justify anything that is, as being necessary to the total motion. Such a comic
portrayal of everything human, however, is far from being an apology
for the established order, for Hegel's analysis is actually a merciless
criticism of whatever is prized as fixed and invincible. Above all, the
total picture is raised above absurdity by the underlying idea of the
individual's capacity for lifting himself upward through spiritual warfare in harmony with a purposeful, forward movement.

Galdós, too, has a fundamentally comic vision of life. It comes
to the surface in a humorous, ironical style that reveals a skeptical attitude with respect to all manifestations of inflated particularity. It is
further evident in his general picture of human extravagance and delusion, in his contraposition of fixed beliefs with antagonistic hypotheses,
and in his depiction of the human being's constant tendency to mistake
for absolute what is merely relative. It is a vast comic scene permeated
with tragedy, but the tragic happenings are but moments in a spiritual
world in which the great mass of delusions and contradictions comprises
a grandiose pulsating stream that leads to God. The comedy—to use
Loewenberg's description of Hegel's view—may be called divine comedy,
because the whole is spiritual. If the chronological relation of the two
thinkers were reversed, it would be appropriate to say that Hegel could
have found no better source material for the formulation of his theory
than the novels of Galdós.

The foregoing discussion has not been intended as an attempt to
prove that the novelist was an outright disciple of the philosopher. It
is important, however, to know that while Galdós drew upon nineteenth-
century thought in general, he found in Hegel, especially in the idea
that "being in self" is "being in another," a directive stimulant for his
metaphysical inclinations. Among the most significant intellectual
movements of the century are the exaltation of positivistic science, the
theories of biological and psychological evolution, the notion that man
is fashioned by his environment, an emphasis on the reality of mind,
the doctrine of individual freedom to direct self in accord with a law of
reason, the belief that an individual develops his full potentiality through
a community of experience, and the spiritual evolutionism of Hegel.
German idealism, predominantly Hegelian, was first the starting point
for a reaction in the direction of empiricism, and later a support for a
weakening structure which theoretically depended solely on physical
facts.

In very broad terms, perhaps the two most outstanding developments of nineteenth-century thought were the concept of flow and growth as being a fundamental feature of the universe, and a reintegration of rationalism with ancient mysticism, underlying which is the belief that one comes closest to God within one's own true self. With these lines of thought Galdós soon found himself in full accord; which is to say that he insisted upon and succeeded in harmonizing science, philosophy, and religion. That he did so in an age of marked conflict between science and religion—particularly in his own country—is a tribute to his broad perspective and his intellectual equilibrium.

Perhaps the most interesting way to look at Galdós in relation to his age is to think of him as the product of a century that witnessed an expanding comprehension of the theory of evolution. He professes no special interest in the theory as such, but he definitely reflects the results of its impact upon modern thought, and he belongs intellectually to the more recent stages of interpretation, which extend from the late nineteenth century to the present day. He believes that change and growth are just as demonstrable on a psychological as on a biological level, that a similar process obtains in society, even though it be much more gradual, and that, individually at least, man is subject to a spiritual law of evolvement which is just as natural as physical growth. He shows little concern with the question of man's development from a subhuman species, and he apparently had little sympathy for the emphasis of early evolutionists on man's passive relation to his environment and the survival of the physically fit. Let Darwin's theory of natural selection, however, be elevated to a moral plane on which the survival of intrinsic human values and the discarding of disproved values coincide with the survival of man, and a conception of life emerges—still an evolutionary one—which conforms fundamentally with Galdós' view.

It is not too much to say that the novelist subscribed to the belief that love of one's fellow man is a directive force as imperative as biological law, and that the Golden Rule, more than a command imposed upon all in the name of Christianity, is a universal principle, indispensable to man's existence. The justification for such a statement lies in Galdós' harmonization of the knowledge which is explicit in nature with his faith in divine order. At the lower limits of his perspective he sees man as a biological and psychological organism. If the function of an organism's parts is thought to be merely that of keeping it alive in movement without direction, the result is a nihilistic view of life. If the viewpoint is that the organism, while seeking a goal of self-determination, assimilates its environment and transforms itself, the process, on a psychological and even on a biological plane, can be interpreted as one of self-expansion.[21] At this point psychology gives way to philosophy, and Galdós, who takes over the role of philosopher, visualizes the activity as one of spiritual self-expansion. His view of the life process, therefore, is one of dynamic, evolutionary movement upward. He may not have realized that he was an exponent of evolution as a theory, but he embodies an enlightened version of the evolutionary conception of human experience as probably few men of his century did.

Without being a systematic theorist, Galdós demonstrates in his novels the mission of philosophy, in that he shows not how reason, religion, and empirical knowledge differ, but how they belong to each other. The combination is one of practicality, imaginativeness, and optimism, capped with the belief that man fulfills his destiny by way of his social experiences. Herein lies the fundamental difference between the most philosophical of nineteenth-century novelists in Spain and certain representatives of the generation that followed his own. As Angel del Río aptly comments, Galdós sees the social, historical man, in contrast to Unamuno, for example, who tries to penetrate the mysteries of the world by divorcing the "self" from and destroying the "other."[22] Unamuno, finding in Kierkegaard a tonic for his melancholy existentialism, would aspire to Heaven by leaping over society. Galdós professes the belief that Heaven is to be reached by climbing upward through society, which is both unescapable and an indispensable medium for the spiritual ascent.

The incorporation of this vision of man and society into novelistic form is an artistic as well as a moral accomplishment. Philosophical systems theorize on the enthusiasm for living which precedes them,[23] and they can draw humanity after them only if they are proved in the experience of living. Galdós performs the role of popularizing morality and philosophy by blending them in a portrayal of the dynamic life process. He is at his best when his ideas are submerged in his plots. *Fortunata y Jacinta* and *Misericordia* are not only more deeply philosophical but more artistic than *Realidad* and *La loca de la casa*, because they are richer in the study of character and situation, the substance of which philosophy is made; and they utilize creative energy more for the portrayal of human beings than for the communication of ideas. From an artistic viewpoint, the moral-philosophic quality of Galdós' novels does not make them either good or bad. It is of particular significance, however, because it is a solidifying substance that holds the stories together, merging characterization and plot, and thus determining the basic, psychological structure. It is the author's "subject," and the form, especially the structural framework, is the means by which the author tries to make the most of his subject.[24] Despite some unevenness of craftsmanship, including variation in balance as regards integration of plot and ideas, the novels of Galdós leave a general impression of purposeful progressive development. From 1882 (*El amigo Manso*) to 1897 (*El abuelo* and *Misericordia*), at least, philosophic perspective and novelistic form blend in one meaningful design.

VIII

THE PERSONALITY OF GALDÓS

IN a discussion that has stressed the portrayal of personality growth, it is appropriate, if not obligatory, to focus attention finally upon the novelist's own personality as reflected in his works. Like all novelists and to a greater degree than many, Galdós put himself into his stories, and it is profitable to visualize his entire career as one long course of personal development, beginning with the decisive conditioning of his childhood and youth. The picture of interaction between personality and environment in his own life is one that he would have delighted in transposing to novelistic form, and in a very significant degree his novels are, separately and as a whole, a fictional record of his growth from youth to maturity and old age.

In broad outline, Galdós' life may be divided into two major periods: one which determines his goals and his general adjustive pattern; and the other, an extension and gradual modification of these in the face of experience and increasing understanding.[1] The first period falls naturally into two parts: childhood and youth in Las Palmas up to his departure for Madrid in 1862 at the age of nineteen; and experiences in Madrid up to 1867, when, after a trip to France, he began *La Fontana de Oro*. Following the completion of this novel in 1868 there is a period of transition or orientation, of some four years' duration. The novelist then launches forth toward definite objectives and passes through three significant stages, which—with reference to the social novels—are: (1) youthful rebelliousness, colored heavily by iconoclastic fervor (1876-1878, *Doña Perfecta* to *La familia de León Roch*, inclusive); (2) response to moral challenge, and growth to moral maturity (1881-1888, *La desheredada* to *Miau*); and (3) growth to philosophical maturity (1889-1897, *Realidad* to *Misericordia*). The social novels which follow

Misericordia (Casandra, 1905, *El caballero encantado,* 1909, *La razón de la sinrazón,* 1915) are characterized by a mellowness of old age and a diminution in creative energy. The divisional dates listed here, of course, represent a convenient means of visualizing essential stages and must not be regarded as abrupt turning points in the novelist's life.

Unquestionably, the most determinative period in Galdós' life was that of his early years in Las Palmas, where he was held in almost complete subjection by his austere and dogmatic mother. *Mamá* Dolores, who is remembered in several of the author's women characters, had experienced a stern family training, had married for practical reasons rather than love, and had assumed a dictatorship over her family, directing her energies into channels of rigid formalism as if determined to make others pay for her own unhappiness. From the moment of his birth, Benito was doomed to a severe authoritarianism that sought to decide his private and his public life. A sickly and ungainly boy who was subject to stern masters at home and at school, he not only became timid and inhibited, withdrawing into himself and cultivating his artistic imagination as an outlet for self-assertion, but also kept alive like a smoldering fire more than a usual amount of childhood rebelliousness.

Maternal domination also had the effect of making Galdós dependent upon woman. After he had established himself in Madrid, his widowed sister-in-law Magdalena joined him and virtually took over the role of mother. Remaining estranged from his home in Las Palmas, the young writer transferred his submissiveness to Magdalena, and late in life he apparently depended heavily upon his sister Carmen. Like José María Bueno (*Lo prohibido*) and Angel Guerra, he was something of a "bad boy" who must have a woman to rule and lead him. Galdós, of course, turned out to be more like Angel Guerra, for he succeeded in taking charge of his life and creating his own destiny; but the marks of his relationship with his mother are heavily stamped on his whole career and represent the strongest single environmental factor in his personality formation.

Related to this maternal influence but still distinct from it is the novelist's youthful experience in love. His love for Sisita, natural daughter of his uncle José María and an American woman (Adriana Tate), which was frustrated by his mother, undoubtedly left a lasting impression. It accounts in part for a persistent opposition to conventional formalities and a preoccupation with the idea that sincere, spontaneous love is its own justification. The youth's fondness for his uncle José María, the black sheep of his mother's family, probably encouraged him in his hostility to convention; but more than anything else it must have been his mother's handling of the Sisita affair, together with her despotism in general, that turned him toward a private life of defiance. Unconventionalism in intimate affairs seems to have become a stubborn fixation, similar to the adamant anticlericalism manifest in his refusal on his deathbed to accept the services of a priest. This rebellious attitude and fear of an inharmonious home life may explain why he never married.

There is plainly some rationalization on Galdós' part in his sympathetic attitude toward certain irregularities of his characters. Viera (*Realidad*), for example, probably speaks for the author when, in reference to his friendship with the prostitute *la Peri*, he says, "¡Qué misterio en los afectos humanos! Y hay tontos que quieren reducirlos a reglas y encasillarlos como las muestras de una tienda" (V, 844). This is an expression of filial revolt carried forward in maturity to the affirmation of a conviction confirmed by experience—that social dogma cannot substitute for love and sympathy. Denied affection and sympathetic companionship at home, the novelist had as a youth paid secret visits to *Mamá* Tate, and he continued throughout his life to seek intimate associations outside the formal circles of the family.

Berkowitz, apparently on the basis of evidence which by reason of discretion he but modestly reveals, attributes the novelist's irregularities primarily to a sexual enslavement that was pathological in nature. A biographer can at best merely approximate a full explanation of a writer's personality, and the task is especially difficult in the case of a shy, reticent person like Galdós, who disclosed few of his innermost thoughts to his acquaintances. Nor can a writer's works be depended upon for a complete picture; but they must be taken into consideration, for they inevitably bear the stamp of the writer's deep-rooted motives. What is seen in Galdós' novels is not the overpowering force of sexual instinct, but the stronger needs of sympathy, devotion, and confidence in the love and protection of close companions. Love of woman is indispensable in Galdós' world, but its course, with all its conflict and frustration, is one that gradually becomes a sublimated conversion of the erotic instinct into spiritual creation. The novelist's treatment of love, in fact, parallels his own development from an unhappy youth at home to a mature man pursuing a journey of constructive self-affirmation.

The seeds of rebellion fostered in Las Palmas were ready to break forth when Galdós went to Madrid in 1862. He acceded to his family's wishes that he study law, but the long-distance control of his mother gradually grew weaker as he now began to live his own life. There was, no doubt, a certain rebellious release in the form of night revels and irregular attendance of classes in the University, but more important was the intellectual atmosphere of the time. For Madrid in the years preceding the Revolution of 1868 was the center of a great intellectual activity that included the discussion of liberal and scientific ideas from abroad. These were also the fruitful years of the Krausist movement, which must be given much credit for its liberal and yet stabilizing moral influence in Spain. With the enthusiasm of a youth who for the first time is allowed to think for himself, Galdós entered wholeheartedly into the current of liberalism, absorbing moral and philosophical ideas that he was later to utilize in his own way. His primary concern at first, however, was to choose a career and accomplish something in his own right. His choice of a literary career was foreshadowed by his youthful compositions in Las Palmas. It became more conclusive with his journalistic activity in Madrid and, after his disappointing efforts at writing plays, narrowed down to the novel with *La Fontana de Oro* (1867-1868).

At this time, Galdós' mind was fermenting with ideas which he was struggling to shape into definitive form. His communion with leading minds of the nineteenth century had broadened his vision of human values, and his journalistic apprenticeship had contributed further to serious thinking about Spanish problems. With a mixture of patriotism, ambition for personal accomplishment, and the revolutionary zeal of a reformer, he faced the question of what was wrong with his country, and determined to do something about it. In substantial degree he was reacting to his experiences at home, and like a boy who had been held in check, he was straining to break his leashes and show his mettle, at the same time feeling the joy of creation and the pleasure that goes with doing something useful but something different. After his groping efforts (*El audaz,* 1871) to settle upon a decisive method, he finds himself literarily when he chooses to follow separately two distinct kinds of novelistic writing: the historical and the social novel.

As Galdós launches forth in the social novel, the pent-up resentment of his early years is released in the portrayal of doña Perfecta, a symbol of all women of strong will who, like his mother, are victims of unfortunate circumstances in combination with the formalism of a closed society, and who in turn victimize their own families. For some four years the novelist evinces both the enthusiasm attendant upon the choice of a life's work and the hot-headed rebelliousness of a youth who is antagonized by obvious flaws in the social system of his country. His writing is a continuation in concentrated form of the negative attitude of dissatisfaction noticeable in his earliest known compositions. Even so, the seeds of constructive development are present, for he is thinking of the individual's freedom to determine his own life, of the importance of love as a guide for conduct, of moral orderliness, and even of the reality that transcends the visible world. These are ideas that have already taken root in his thinking, especially during his intellectual preparation of the 1860's. They will need to be molded and channeled into positive directions, but it is important to remember always that Galdós' literary and personal development is a continuous transition, in which the author expands on an idea previously touched upon or undertakes a new approach, showing in his constant movement back and forth a broadening intellectual and moral horizon.

The most clear-cut division in the novelist's career comes after *La familia de León Roch*. *La desheredada* represents a new orientation, marked by a change in temper, perspective, and method. As if purged of his most virulent resentment, he settles down to a more businesslike treatment of his subject matter, studying his sources in the urban life that he knew best, following the "biographical" method as the most suitable means of exploring the interrelationship between the individual and society, and adopting wholeheartedly the realistic technique in the use of background detail, the relation between personality and environment, and attention to ordinary circumstances of everyday living. His enthusiasm, now more professional, is concentrated on his medium, and this accounts for his heavy emphasis on the social milieu. But it does not mean that he is oppressed by the material world or that he has adopted a positivistic philosophy. It means simply that he is eagerly exploring a new field, where he can make use of his interest in the sciences, particularly in psychology. He has reached a definite plateau of maturity as a novelist and he embarks with self-assurance toward new goals.

With all his attention to the human being as an organism reacting to and acted upon by environment, Galdós continues to be a moralist at heart. The question of morality and religion had been too deeply impressed upon him ever to take an incidental position in his writings. The rectitude of *Mamá* Dolores left its imprint on her son, who, while fearing and avoiding his mother, admired and in some ways imitated her. The novelist's unconventional love affairs were, it may be assumed, more the result of revolt against dictatorship than of a tendency toward dissoluteness. Certainly, if the writer is judged by his literary works, moral stamina is one of his outstanding traits. The novels of the 1880's are fundamentally moral in quality, and the author becomes progressively the exponent of an enlightened morality.

After his early belligerence, which is directed against evils in Spanish society as a whole, Galdós realizes that he is called upon to offer something better than that which he would destroy. His acceptance of the challenge forces him into a studious examination of the individual in his relationship with society. This step becomes in turn a course in self-education, in which the effort to satisfy a need brings with it the discovery of new interpretations. By living imaginatively the experiences of his characters, he learns by "experience," not by theory, that the removal of external restraint raises the necessity of internal control. Preoccupied with the subject of conscience imprisoned by tradition, he ponders the question of what role conscience should play and advances to the demonstration of "la conciencia creadora," underlying which are the ideals of active, creative living, the development of one's full potentialities, the necessity of proving one's own worth by means of accepting responsibilities, of making courageous adjustments to circumstances, and of triumphing over the handicaps imposed by social and physical forces.

At the same time, while studying the individual entangled in the webs of social environment, Galdós is concerned with the idea that love between one individual and another is so fundamental in human nature as to have a transcendental explanation. Hence his search for a philosophy that will reinforce rationally what he is emotionally sure of. His observation of the transference of character traits from one person to another and the beneficial effects of intimate personal associations makes it easy for him to accept the idea that one self is inevitably dependent upon another self, and that competitive individualism must be subordinated to an over-all law of consideration for others. The morality of individual freedom, of creative conflict, of dignity apart from social dogma, of growth through association, and of self-mastery are crystallized at a high point of development in *Fortunata y Jacinta,* which also reveals the foundations for further expansion in the direction of philosophy and religion. By the necessity of his self-imposed mission, the novelist reaches a level of maturity at which rebellious independence assumes the predominant mark of individualism disciplined from within.

With *Miau* (1888) and again with *Tristana* (1892), Galdós retraces his steps to some extent, in that he notes especially the oppressive effects of social forces. Both novels, of course, underscore the fact that the author continues to think in terms of social environment. The general direction of the 1890's, however, is clearly that of a broadening conception of life. Pondering always man's place in society, the novelist gradually expands his horizon with reference to man's place in the world order. In doing so, he develops ideas that have been present all along, even though not fully utilized. *Realidad* (1889) is something of an experimental introduction to the question of ultimate values. It stresses the impossibility of limiting such a complexity as truth to fixed boundaries but holds that whatever truth is, it is inseparable from morality and includes the emotions of love and sympathy.

In none of his subsequent novels does Galdós attempt to define morality in absolute terms, but he emphasizes more and more that love, compassion, creative activity, and self-discipline constitute the foundation of whatever may have ultimate value. His growth, therefore, is toward religion, or to be more exact, toward the combination of religion and philosophy. It is an intellectual growth, but it is also an emotional maturing characterized by an increasing tendency to tolerance and compromise. While proving to his own satisfaction how to infuse individual freedom with positive meaning, he passes to a level of conciliation, as if pride in his accomplishment allowed him to assume with confidence and magnanimity the role of master and leader. This attitude combines with a deepening patriotic sentiment and an increasing sense of belongingness with the Spanish people. In the novelist's mind, the individual continues to be the master of his own destiny, but self-discipline becomes more important than ever as a means of harmonizing the conflicting forces of static order and dynamic human drives. The novels of the 1890's represent the full fructification of psychological, moral, religious, and philosophical ideas that have been fermenting for more than two decades.

With *Misericordia* Galdós virtually exhausts the vein of his long and fruitful exploration. Without passing full judgment on his dramas, it is probably safe to say that after 1897 there is no important forward development in his creative course. Some of his plays, *El abuelo* for example, are constructed with enough dramatic intensity to insure their fame. Yet in its content even *El abuelo,* considered either as a novel (1897) or as a drama (1904), is but the repetition of an idea already fully exploited in earlier works. In this respect, it is representative of the novelist's late period, which is marked by the reworking of old themes, a nostalgic return to former haunts, and a preoccupation with his mission as a teacher. Several of the works of this period are saved from sentimentality only because they are clothed in fantasy and symbolism. From a moral or philosophical viewpoint, the last stage of Galdós' personality development is characterized by a prominent show of benevolence, and therefore may be regarded as a further spiritual advance. From a literary viewpoint, it must be observed, a long period of sustained creative activity comes to an end with a marked relaxation and a retreat into a dreamworld in which ideals long fought for can now be realized.[2]

The influence of literary movements cannot be disregarded in an appraisal of Galdós' literary personality. The stages of his own growth, in fact, harmonize with movements which explain in part the changing direction of his novelistic endeavor. Thus, curiously enough, his youthful belligerence and his novels of thesis are in keeping with the controversial atmosphere of the 1870's and the emphasis on "ideas" in literature. The mild penetration of naturalism into Spain in the 1880's comes at the same time that Galdós plunges into a studious examination of the individual and his environment. The general "spiritual" reaction of the 1890's is contemporaneous with his own intensified interest in values that transcend the material world. Far more important than these minor developments is the fact that Galdós is a product of the age of realism. This was the world to which by historical chance he belonged, and its marks were early and indelibly impressed, both as pertains to literary technique and to the attitude of practical confrontation with contemporary social conditions.

The literary background, together with the nonliterary intellectual environment, helped the novelist to chart his course once he decided on his career. Within this broad framework, that which is peculiar to him was of his own making and can best be understood as the personal development of one who lives the full span of an individual life, formulating on the way a sound personal philosophy. The maturational growth may be summarized briefly as follows: A subdued and sensitive youth breaks away from the dogmatic severity of his home life, allies himself imaginatively with revolutionists and the underdogs of society, finds in the liberal thought of his day not only encouragement for his rebelliousness but also a source of moral equilibrium, adopts the novel as the means of a stout-hearted self-assertion that has social and moral reform as its goal, experiments with novelistic method while releasing much of his pent-up resentfulness, settles down to a calm study of his medium, and gradually matures through the crystallization of a broad and positive outlook on life. The underlying motivating forces are love and aversion to authority, and the outstanding adjustive feature is courageous response to challenge. On his belief that love is the most important force in life, Galdós builds a religious philosophy, expanding his ideal of love for woman to include compassion for one's fellow man. On his belief in the necessity of adjusting to whatever life has to offer, he builds a philosophy of self-creation and transformation from within.

The three outstanding phases of his literary and personal growth are characterized by peak developments, which follow each other at intervals of approximately ten years. *Doña Perfecta* is the foremost peak of his youthful rebelliousness; *Fortunata y Jacinta,* his novel of greatest magnitude in the handling of social and personal relations, is the high mark of his treatment of the conflict between static and human morality; and *Misericordia* is the highest point of his religious-philosophical equanimity. The development is marked by periods of tension, tension discharge, relaxation, retracing of steps, consolidation of gains, renewed drives, and continued advance. The comprehensive picture is one of gradual self-enlightenment and emotional stabilization, which in diagram form would resemble some of the novels analyzed in the discussion of psychological structure.

It has been said that a novelist never has more than one story to tell, and that its essential pattern is determined in the writer's childhood.[3] Intrinsically, this observation applies to Galdós. His story is that of a moral revolt brought under control and made to justify itself by producing something better than the static set of values that prompted it. His novels, therefore, become—especially after 1880—a record of self-extension and integration. Aware that man in his longing for ultimate values jumps easily to hasty conclusions or accepts authority without bothering to think for himself, he turns to the particularities of experience as the ground on which to build his generalizations, and uses himself frequently as a source of psychological knowledge. His material thus independently studied becomes a source of insight—not of sudden illumination, but of gradual enlightenment.

The healthy skepticism which caused Galdós to reject the superficialities of social morality and religion was a necessary preliminary to his initiation of a positive course of action, just as his exploration of moral and social values was indispensable to his formulation of a philosophy that combines the most fundamental truths of religion with knowledge of the biological and rational human being. Certain facts of his private life (petty jealousies and animosities, agitated concern over financial matters and public applause, extreme sexual drives) may seem out of harmony with the personality that shows through his novels. Such a state of incongruity is by no means strange; for the writer must be rare indeed who achieves in practical living what he achieves in his art, the one place he can most closely approximate what he would like to be. The novel was for Galdós not only the medium through which he acquired an understanding of personality; it was also the means by which he himself developed in the direction of personality wholeness.

At the heart of this development, impelling it forward in pulsating movement, is the author's spiritual restlessness, which began as dissatisfaction with things as they are and led to a quest of the individual spirit seeking its ultimate end. Concerning this aspect of his character, Galdós remarks, on the occasion of Pereda's reception into the Spanish Academy in 1897:

> Pereda no duda; yo sí. Siempre he visto mis convicciones oscurecidas en alguna parte por sombras que venían no sé de dónde. El es un espíritu sereno, yo un espíritu turbado, inquieto . . . [El] se recrea en su tesoro de ideas, mientras nosotros [los que dudamos], siempre descontentos de las que poseemos, y ambicionándolas mejores, corremos tras otras, y otras, que, una vez alcanzadas, tampoco nos satisfacen.[4]

With a healthy combination of skepticism and faith, he grasped continuously for greater insight, exhibiting in this respect the marks of a philosophic mind. Such an attitude can, as Bertrand Russell remarks,[5] free men's thoughts from the tyranny of custom and the obvious world around them, and though unable to define absolute truth, can increase men's knowledge of what things may be by diminishing their certainty as to what things are. No one can read Galdós' maturest works without recognizing the wholesome objectivity that prevents him from giving undue importance to his own or anyone else's opinions. His uncertainty about absolute values led him at times into moments of disillusionment, when he felt, much like Angel Guerra, that love is perhaps the only verity that man can cling to in the "juego de la vida" (V, 1571). He was, withal, an incurable optimist who—in contrast to a number of twentieth-century writers—never gave the slightest indication of a desire to resign from the human race, and whose longing for an orderly conception of the universe was irrepressible. Herein lies his close affinity with Hegel.

It is not surprising, then, that one of the most prominent features of Galdós' novels, and one that accounts for much of their dynamic quality, is the characters' striving to attain goals. In large degree, this is the author's projection of himself into his art. Some of his characters, principally among the minor personages, bow passively before the difficulties that confront them, and since they may be said to represent the weaker of the species, they lend balance to the novelist's comprehensive picture of life. On the whole, they are a hardy lot, outwardly defeated perhaps though inwardly gaining stature, never remaining long in a state of rest, and drawn on almost always by newly arising motives. The impression conveyed is that of the unsatisfiable human spirit, which no sooner approaches one objective than it changes it into another.

Whether Galdós became deeply impressed with this aspect of individual character from observing his own creations, from a study of himself, or from a combination of observation with the philosophical and psychological thought of his day, it is certain that he came to think of it as a fundamental of human nature and a dominant trait of his own personality. Like Angel Guerra, he may have envied in others a peaceful conformity with self, which he considered "tal vez el supremo ideal del hombre" (V, 1378). It was, however, an ideal which for him remained always in the future, because it demanded not only a satisfied conscience—in the usual sense of the word—but a constant extension of prior activity. A few of his maturest characters (Nazarín and Benina, for example) reach what seems to be an ideal state of repose, but they do so only at the end of their recorded histories; and we can be sure that if Galdós had carried their stories further, he would have drawn them again into agitation and struggle.

That Galdós saw human experience as a fluid, never-ending succession of stages is confirmed by his own assertions made late in life, when, discussing his novelistic endeavors with Gregorio Marañón, he voices the conviction that a stage of life is but a continuous extension of the past into the future, and that "to live with a full consciousness of life is nothing more than to repeat the yesterday and dream of the morrow."[6] From this viewpoint, life is indeed a game whose activity is a contest between hope and fulfillment, and death is feared primarily because it represents the stoppage of an unfinished work. The life process visualized in this interpretation of the novels is fundamentally one of completion. It may be compared to the writing of a book. There is much groping and frustration, and though the ideal of wholeness is never fully attained, it beckons always and draws the individual on. Thus the individual comes to realize that in his very striving he is enacting a fundamental principle of life—that the striving to attain a goal is even more important than the attainment itself. A state of equilibrium can at best be considered merely a halt in forward movement; for otherwise it would be the beginning of the decay and degeneration which come with a cessation of the dynamic process.

Galdós, who plunged deep into the stream of life, struggled desperately even to the last to carry out his dynamic role. Creative writing became a compulsion, a kind of tyrannical habit that drove him on relentlessly, forcing him to extend himself to the utmost. The desire to lead his country forward never left him, but his writing was also a continuous urge to find and express his true self—in a word, to complete himself. In the process of completion, professional accomplishment was a medium for personality integration. What the writer learned in creating characters, reliving their lives, and in this way living his own life, constitutes perhaps the most essential part of his "message" to posterity.

The importance of this message pertains above all to the individual. This emphasis on the individual is probably not so well understood as the more obvious facts concerning Galdós' role as an apostle of progress and revitalization on a national scale. The lesson is one that grew naturally out of the novelist's own life, and it must be analyzed and constructed anew by him who would know its significance. By undertaking this task of analysis and reorganization, one can see how the author's handling of plot and character comes increasingly to bear on the subject of human dignity—a dignity that lies not so much in a state of permanence as in the individual's ability to earn the prize of worthiness. It calls for a demonstration of the right to freedom by winning freedom from self and entering into a sympathetic communion with the world to which the individual is inseparably joined. This is essentially a moral outlook, and it emphasizes an integrity of experience which combines under self-fulfillment the affirmation of individuality in creative activity, the affirmation of one's fellow man, and the restraint of reason.[7] Man thus is asked to be the master of his own destiny, but in conformity with the belief that self-interest is identified with the interests of others in a total order that is at the same time natural and divine.[8] What is found in the author's outlook, in brief, is a forthright determination to serve life rather than destroy it—a decisive combination of realistic thinking that makes life bearable, and a faith in what may be that makes life worth living.

The message implicit in the novels as a whole is in a sense one of the oldest and simplest. Yet it is one that can be continually repeated without losing its forcefulness, for it is a vitalizing review of the process of growing to maturity. It is especially timely in the present century, when much talk is heard of personality maturity and integration, and when many signs are manifest—in literature—of personality immaturity and disintegration. With his belief in self-creation, Galdós anticipates the Generation of 1898, some of whose members, however, contrast with him in their emphasis on the asocial, isolated self with its cult of will and power. A hostile, aggressive kind of individualism colored with heavy shades of disillusionment stands out prominently at the beginning of the twentieth century. Though stimulated by Nietzsche in particular, it is traceable in part to earlier currents of nineteenth-century thought, such as Romantic egoism and a materialistic application of the doctrine of natural selection. Both of these Galdós vigorously rejected, while reasserting some of the most enduring thought of the centuries. He was the spokesman of an age of optimism and idealism, who stood for the integration of social, moral, and religious experience in an equilibrating personal philosophy.

The spontaneous reaction of one who reads Galdós' novels is often a mixture of sympathy with the author's ideas and of dissatisfaction over questions of form. Let it be remembered, however, that with few exceptions the ideas in the novels grow out of the experience that precedes them; that is, the reader comes into their possession—much as the author does—by first entering into the lives of the characters. The satisfaction of acquiring as one's own the thought incorporated in the portrayal of a flowing stream of life would in any case be a fundamental part of the reader's aesthetic experience. It is especially true in reference to Galdós. His subject is essentially the problem of living a well-integrated life amidst particular social circumstances, and his basic form or method is that of tracing an individual's biography. The form is adequate to the subject, if not, indeed, the most appropriate. For the characters are psychological beings who associate with other psychological beings, struggling with them, learning to live with them, discovering along the way their own strength and their own worth, possibly succumbing to forces from without, but always moving, changing, and reaching out in an effort to possess themselves fully. If the novels lack the finish of painstaking craftsmanship, they consummate something more important for the reader: an image of the life process unfolding itself in successive stages of development. On this image the author places his personal stamp, which encourages belief that life, with all its perverseness, holds a profound justification for him who is courageous enough to seek the justification earnestly. Dynamic message and the portrayal of a dynamic process are thus merged in one.

CHRONOLOGICAL LIST OF NOVELS

La Fontana de Oro, 1867-68

El audaz, 1871

Doña Perfecta, 1876

Gloria, 1876-77

Marianela, 1878

La familia de León Roch, 1878

La desheredada, 1881

El amigo Manso, 1882

El doctor Centeno, 1883

Tormento, 1884

La de Bringas, 1884

Lo prohibido, 1884-85

Fortunata y Jacinta, 1886-87

Miau, 1888

La Incógnita, 1888-89

Torquemada en la hoguera, 1889

Realidad, 1889

Angel Guerra, 1890-91

Tristana, 1892

La loca de la casa, 1892

Torquemada en la cruz, 1893

Torquemada en el purgatorio, 1894

Torquemada y San Pedro, 1895

Nazarín, 1895

Halma, 1895

El abuelo, 1897

Misericordia, 1897

Casandra, 1905

El caballero encantado, 1909

La razón de la sinrazón, 1915

NOTES

CHAPTER ONE

[1] For further and similar discussion of Galdós' early novelistic writing, see my article "The Formative Period of Galdós' Social-Psychological Perspective," *Romantic Review*, XLI (1950), 33-41.

[2] "Nota preliminar," *Obras completas de don Benito Pérez Galdós*, IV (Madrid, 1941), pp. 763-64.

[3] Joaquín Casalduero appropriately calls this Galdós' abstract period: "El desarrollo de la obra de Galdós," *Hispanic Review*, X (1942), 245-46.

[4] Cf. Robert Kirsner, "Pérez Galdós' Vision of Spain in *Torquemada en la hoguera*," *Bulletin of Hispanic Studies*, XXVII (1950), 1-7; also by the same author: "Galdós' Attitude toward Spain as Seen in the Characters of *Fortunata y Jacinta*," *Publications of the Modern Language Association*, LXVI (1951), 124-37.

[5] Cf. Angel del Río, "A Note on *Misericordia*," in the school edition by Angel del Río and McKendree Petty (New York: The Dryden Press, 1946), p. xxi.

[6] "Significado y forma de *Misericordia*," *PMLA*, LIX (1944), 1104-10.

[7] "*Crónica de la quincena*." By Benito Pérez Galdós (Princeton, 1948), pp. 44-45.

CHAPTER TWO

[1] Where Roman and Arabic numerals appear together in parentheses, the reference is to volume and page in Federico Carlos Sáinz de Robles' edition of Galdós' *Obras completas* (Madrid, 1941-42)

[2] Evidence that Galdós was definitely interested in the relation between physiology and psychology as late as 1889 is found in some of his nonfictional writings ("Niñerías," *Obras completas*, VI, 1545-48). Cf. the unpublished Ph.D. dissertation (University of Texas, 1948) by Jasper W. Treat, "Characterization in the Contemporary Novels of Benito Pérez Galdós," pp. 127-30.

[3] See the "prólogo" of P. Lain Entralgo to *La psiquiatría española en el siglo XIX* by Trino Peraza de Ayala (Madrid, 1947), pp. x-xi.

[4] See Peraza de Ayala, *op. cit.*, particularly pp. 82-86 in reference to Juan Drumen's *Patología médica* (1850), and pp. 120-22 in reference to Juan Giné y Partagá's *Tratado de frenopatología* (1876).

[5] Cf. Wilhelm Wundt, *Outlines of Psychology*, trans. Charles Hubbard Judd (Leipzig, 1907), pp. 305 ff. (3rd revised English edition from 7th German edition).

[6] As quoted by Peraza de Ayala, *op. cit.*, pp. 83, 84, 85.

[7] Where only Roman numerals appear in parentheses, the reference is to "Parte" and chapter of the novel in question. In some of the novels the chapters are subdivided. Thus "I, ix, *viii*" means Part I, chapter ix, subdivision *viii.*

[8] This question is discussed here at considerable length because, in my opinion, far too much emphasis has been placed on Galdós' naturalism. Cf. especially Joaquín Casalduero, *Vida y obra de Galdós* (Buenos Aires, 1943).

⁹ For a fuller discussion of this similarity, see my article "A Galdosian Version of Picaresque Psychology," *Modern Language Forum*, XXXVIII (1953), 1-12.

¹⁰ Cf. Leopoldo Alas, *Galdós* (Madrid, 1912), pp. 104-5.

CHAPTER THREE

¹ *The Way of All Flesh*, Modern Library edition, p. 305. "Samuel Butler began to write 'The Way of All Flesh' about the year 1872, and was engaged upon it intermittently until 1884" (introductory note by R. A. Streatfeild).

² The table presented here represents something of a digest and modification of sources, among them: Andras Angyal, *Foundations for a Science of Personality*, New York, 1941; James S. Plant, *Personality and the Cultural Pattern*, New York, 1937; and Gordon W. Allport, *Personality, a Psychological Interpretation*, New York, 1937. I do not mean to maintain that literary criticism can be reduced to tabular form. This kind of systematization, however, is definitely an aid in obtaining a precise view of a writer's character portrayal.

³ Floyd L. Ruch, *Psychology and Life* (Chicago, 1941), p. 91. The terms used by Ruch, which range in order of importance from "appetite-hunger" to "teasing," are too general and inclusive to be of much help in psychological analysis, but they are useful for the purpose of visualizing a writer's perspective of human experience.

⁴ Cf. Sáinz de Robles (V, 1581), who cites opinions of Leopoldo Alas and Emilia Pardo Bazán which suggest the two objectives mentioned here.

⁵ Of interest in this connection is the fact that Augusta has entered a new stage of personality growth when we meet her again in *Torquemada y San Pedro*. Cf. below, p. 143.

⁶ The reader will find ample discussion of the ideas expressed here in such books as George H. Mead, *Mind, Self, and Society*, Chicago, 1934; Andras Angyal, *op. cit.;* Muzafer Sherif and Hadley Cantril, *The Psychology of Ego-Involvements*, New York, 1947.

⁷ The passage quoted is taken from my article "The Treatment of Individual Personality in *Fortunata y Jacinta*" (*Hispanic Review*, XII [1949], 278-79), which touches upon several of the points contained in the present discussion.

CHAPTER FOUR

¹ One could find a closer similarity to Galdós in Pereda's novels of a distinct social quality, such as *Pedro Sánchez, La montálvez, Los hombres de pro*.

² A question of some interest arises in connection with the doña Perfecta who visits María Egipcíaca in *La familia de León Roch* (II, III and II, VII). The author barely mentions the visits and gives no indication of the person's family history, but he apparently thinks of her as being a continuation, symbolically at least, of the central personality in *Doña Perfecta*. Assuming that he does consciously identify the two personalities, we may say that doña Perfecta now appears in a later stage of development, where the imposition of asceticism upon others is a necessity to her integrity.

³ José A. Balseiro, *Novelistas españoles modernos* (New York, 1933), p. 236.

⁴ Joaquín Casalduero, *Vida y obra de Galdós* (Buenos Aires, 1943), pp. 100-1.

⁵ "Nota preliminar" (to *Tormento*), *Obras completas*, IV, 1461.

⁶ See J. Warshaw, "Introduction" to *La loca de la casa* (New York: Henry Holt & Company, Inc., 1924), pp. xxvi-xxviii.

CHAPTER FIVE

¹ See Albion W. Small, *General Sociology* (Chicago, 1905), p. 209.

² Joaquín Casalduero, *Vida y obra de Galdós*, pp. 105-7.

³ Further discussion of this topic will be found in chapter 8.

4 "Characterization in the Contemporary Novels of Benito Pérez Galdós," Ph.D. dissertation (University of Texas, 1948), chapter II.

5 "Observaciones sobre la novela contemporánea en España," *Revista de España*, XV (1870), pp. 162-72.

6 See H. Chonon Berkowitz, *Pérez Galdós. Spanish Liberal Crusader* (Madison, 1948), p. 313.

7 Cf. *ibid.*, chapter XVII.

8 In *Torquemada en el purgatorio* (II, IV) Galdós also uses the vision to reveal the subconscious ratification of a state of mind into which the individual is already drifting: when Valentín tells Torquemada that he wants to take a train ride, thus approving his father's impending submission to Cruz's wish.

9 See Albion W. Small, *op. cit.*, pp. 67-86.

10 Cf. Berkowitz, *op. cit.*, p. 92.

11 This conception of the social process is expressed by Small, *op. cit.*, p. 672.

CHAPTER SIX

1 *El amigo Manso* is discussed, from a philosophical viewpoint, in the next chapter.

2 Cf. in this connection Casalduero's statement that Galdós begins in *Fortunata y Jacinta* his treatment of religion from the viewpoint of the individual: "*Ana Karénina y Realidad*," *Bulletin Hispanique*, XXXIX (1937), 391.

3 *The Two Sources of Morality and Religion*, trans. Audra and Brereton (New York, 1935), p. 218.

4 *Ibid.*, pp. 43, 70.

5 Henri Bergson, *The Creative Mind*, trans. Mabelle L. Andison (New York, 1946), p. 275.

CHAPTER SEVEN

1 *Crónica de la quincena*, ed. William H. Shoemaker (Princeton, 1948), p. 131.

2 "Auguste Comte y *Marianela*," *Smith College Studies in Modern Languages*, XXI (1939-40), 10-25.

3 See his *Análisis del pensamiento racional*, Madrid, 1877; particularly pp. 194-96, and the author's "adición," included in the editors' footnote, p. xxv. This posthumous publication is a set of lectures which, according to the editors, Sanz del Río prepared in 1862-63, and revised for a course that he gave at the University of Madrid in 1863-64. It is considered to be the author's key work in so far as exposition of the Krausist method is concerned.

4 Cf. Joaquín Xirau, "Julián Sanz del Río y el krausismo español," *Cuadernos americanos*, 1944, No. 4, pp. 55-71.

5 As quoted by Mario Méndez Bejarano, *Historia de la filosofía en España hasta el siglo XX* (Madrid, n. d.), p. 477.

6 One of Galdós' friends, José Rodríguez Monrelo, once suggested that Giner de los Ríos was the model for Máximo Manso's characterization; see H. Chonon Berkowitz, "Galdós and Giner: a Literary Friendship," *The Spanish Review*, I (1934), 64. In a recent interpretation of *El amigo Manso*, Robert Kirsner overlooks the story's philosophical aspects, though justifiably emphasizing the point that in this novel, for the first time, the central personage enjoys the role of an autonomous literary character, as compared to Galdós' earlier characters, who are instruments for unfavorable criticism of Spanish society: "Sobre *El amigo Manso*, de Galdós," *Cuadernos de literatura* (julio-diciembre, 1950), pp. 189-200.

7 Cf. Sanz del Río, *op. cit.*, p. 12.

8 Cf. *ibid.*, 33-34, 58, 89.

9 W. H. Shoemaker ("Galdós' Literary Creativity: D. José Ido del Sagrario," *Hispanic Review*, XIX [1951], 221), speaking of another personal relationship in *El*

doctor Centeno, also refers to Don Quijote and Sancho. While commenting on the role of José Ido as sympathetic friend of Felipe and others, he observes that "the whole Ido-Centeno relationship after Alejandro's death" recalls Don Quijote and Sancho.

¹⁰ Since we must assume that Galdós did not read German (though he probably did read French), we are faced with the question of translations. I have been unable to find any record of a nineteenth-century Spanish translation of the *Phenomenology of Mind*. The earliest translation, according to Palau y Dulcet (*Manual del librero hispanoamericano*, IV, 1926), was 1907. The same source lists the *Lógica*, translated by Antonio M. Fabié, Madrid, 1872 (probably the publication to which Galdós refers in his *Crónica de la quincena*, May 15, 1872), and a treatise, *Filosofía del derecho según la doctrina de Hegel*, by Benítez de Lugo, Sevilla, 1878. The *Boletín de la Librería* published by the Librería M. Murillo, Madrid, records a translation of the *Logic* by Antonio Zozaya, Madrid, 1892-1893, which is not listed by Palau y Dulcet, but makes no reference to a translation of the *Phenomenology* in the nineteenth century. There was, however, a French translation, *Philosophie de l'esprit*, by A. Véra, 1867-1869 (Otto Lorenz, *Catalogue de la librairie française*, V, 1876). Granting the possibility that Galdós did not read this work, we must still remember that Hegel's *Logic* (1812-1816) embodies the broad principles expounded in his *Phenomenology*. Even if we assume that the novelist did not read Hegel at all, we still know that he had ample opportunities to become acquainted with the philosopher's writings through Sanz del Río and his followers, who were themselves students of Hegel. Furthermore, there were in the 1870's several Spanish treatises on philosophy which included expositions on Kant and Hegel. The former's writings were more freely translated and apparently more widely read, but the latter also had a number of influential adherents and exponents, among them Francisco Pi y Margall and Emilio Castelar (cf. Méndez Bejarano, *op. cit.*, 457-61).

¹¹ Joaquín Casalduero (*Vida y obra de Galdós*, foreword and p. 59 *et passim*) sees—wrongly, I believe—a marked anti-Hegelian influence of Comte and Taine in Galdós' early works, but recognizes that the novelist, in the period of "el espiritualismo" (from *La loca de la casa* to *El abuelo*), found in Hegel's synthesis of antagonistic forces a way to rise above the contradictions of life. And Angel del Río, who interprets *La loca de la casa* as a demonstration of Galdós' ideal of bringing together the antithetical elements of Spanish society, sees in this novel a possible remote Hegelian influence ("La significación de *La loca de la casa*," *Cuadernos americanos*, 1945, No. 3, p. 238).

¹² Cf. my article "The Treatment of Individual Personality in *Fortunata y Jacinta*," *Hispanic Review*, XVII (1949), 284, 287.

¹³ Cf. Josiah Royce, *The Spirit of Modern Philosophy* (New York, 1892), p. 123.

¹⁴ Angel del Río (*op. cit.*) classifies under the following headings the themes presented in *La loca de la casa*: social (the harmony of classes), economic (the function of money), moral (the problem of good and evil), and religious (mysticism via active service).

¹⁵ Berkowitz (*Pérez Galdós. Spanish Liberal Crusader*, p. 223) asserts that the Fuencarral murder case of 1888-1889 started Galdós thinking on the question of apparent and absolute truth and resulted in his writing *La Incógnita* and *Realidad*.

¹⁶ Although Anna Karenina does not deliberately philosophize as Augusta does, there is a decided similarity between the two personalities (in their subjection to the senses), and this similarity is the main justification for comparing *Anna Karenina* and *Realidad*. That Galdós recalled Tolstoi's novel when he wrote *Realidad* seems almost certain. But when the two works are considered in their entirety, they have little in common, and I agree with Casalduero ("Ana Karénina y Realidad," *Bulletin Hispanique*, XXXIX [1937], 375-96) in his argument with George Portnoff (*La literatura rusa en España* [New York, 1932], pp. 123 ff.) that the question of influence is of little consequence.

¹⁷ *Op. cit.*, p. 224.

¹⁸ Cf. J. Loewenberg, "Introduction" to *Hegel. Selections* (New York, 1929), p. xxxii.

[19] With the characterization of Orozco in mind, read Hegel's *Phenomenology of Mind*, trans. J. B. Baillie, I (London, 1910), pp. 369-80.

[20] *Op. cit.*, pp. xxxv-xliii.

[21] Cf. Andras Angyal, *Foundations for a Science of Personality* (New York, 1941), pp. 24 ff.

[22] Angel del Río, *op. cit.*, pp. 265-67.

[23] Cf. Henri Bergson, *The Two Sources of Morality and Religion* (New York, 1935), p. 52.

[24] I am recalling here a statement by Percy Lubbock on subject and form: *The Craft of Fiction* (New York, n. d.), p. 40.

CHAPTER EIGHT

[1] For biographical details the reader is referred to H. Chonon Berkowitz, *Benito Pérez Galdós. Spanish Liberal Crusader*, Madison, 1948. This biography, the most recent and most complete, contains a large and valuable collection of information. Unfortunately, the author does little in the way of presenting a composite picture of the novelist's personality.

[2] Casalduero (*Vida y obra de Galdós*, pp. 160 ff.), with reference to the last decade of Galdós' life, has pointed out this dreamworld phase of the novelist's development. I would add only that Galdós had always been a dreamer and that he gave himself up to dreaming most decidedly in his late works (after 1904).

[3] Bernard de Voto, *The World of Fiction* (Boston, 1950), p. 43.

[4] *Discursos leídos en las recepciones públicas de la Real Academia Española*, 2nd series, Vol. IV (Madrid, 1948), p. 380.

[5] *The Problems of Philosophy* (New York, n. d.), p. 243.

[6] As reported by Berkowitz, *op. cit.*, p. 345.

[7] Cf. H. A. Overstreet's discussion of the mature mind: *The Mature Mind* (New York, 1949), pp. 101 ff.

[8] Salvador de Madariaga (*Semblanzas literarias contemporáneas* [Barcelona, 1924], p. 76) expresses a general but fundamental truth about Galdós when he says that the novelist's writings make us feel "la cooperación activa de Dios, la Naturaleza, y el destino."

INDEX

WASHINGTON UNIVERSITY STUDIES

Titles in brackets are out of print.

[A Byzantine Paraphrase of Onasander, by Clarence G. Lowe. 1927.]

The Localization of Business Activities in Metropolitan St. Louis, by Lewis F. Thomas. October, 1927. $2.00.

The Mean Velocity of Flow of Water in Open Channels, by Herbert R. Grummann. October, 1928. $1.00.

Ionization of Gases and Vapors by Ultraviolet Light, by Arthur Llewelyn Hughes. August, 1929. 75c.

Oscillations of Compound Springs, by Alexander S. Langsdorf. October, 1929. 50c.

Science and Humanism in University Education, by John D. E. Spaeth. June, 1930. 50c.

Papers on Classical Subjects, in Memory of John Max Wulfing. December, 1930. $1.00.
Contents:
>John Max Wulfing, The Man and Scholar, by George R. Throop; Canidia and Other Witches, by Eugene Tavenner; Restoration Coins, by Thomas S. Duncan; The Lex Data as a Source of Imperial Authority, by Donald McFayden; C. Sosius: His Coins, His Triumph, and His Temple of Apollo, by Frederick W. Shipley; Concerning the Rostra of Julius Caesar, by Frederick W. Shipley.

Faust and Faustus, by Otto Heller. March, 1931. $2.00.

Fire Hazards in Warm Air Ducts, by Alexander S. Langsdorf. July, 1931. 75c.

Three Philosophical Studies. April, 1931. $1.00.
Contents:
>Spinoza and Modern Thought, by Lawson P. Chambers; Existence and Value, by George R. Dodson; The Realm of Necessity, by Charles E. Cory.

Contributions in Chemistry. Edited by Theodore R. Ball. May, 1932. $1.00.
Contents:
>The Electrodeposition of Alloys, by Lawrence E. Stout; The Chemistry of Some Drugs Derived from Anthracene, by John H. Gardner; The Present Status of the Theories of Solution with Special Reference to the Problem of the Solubility of Nonelectrolytes, by H. Lee Ward; The Induced Reaction between Chromic and Hydriodic Acids, by Theodore R. Ball and Edgar H. Bohle.

[Contributions in Geology. Edited by Chester K. Wentworth. October, 1932.]

Contributions in Geology and Geography. Edited by Lewis F. Thomas. October, 1932. $1.50.
Contents:
>The Geographic Landscape of Metropolitan St. Louis, by Lewis F. Thomas; The Geologic Work of Ice Jams in Subarctic Rivers, by Chester K. Wentworth; The Opemiska Granitic Intrusive, Quebec, by Carl Tolman; Synonymy of the Mid-Devonian Rugose Corals of the Fall of the Ohio, by Courtney Werner.

Agrippa's Building Activities in Rome, by Frederick W. Shipley. August, 1933. $1.25.

Criteria for Rejection of Observations, by Paul R. Rider. October. 1933. 75c.

Sociology and the Study of International Relations, by Luther L. Bernard and Jessie Bernard. February, 1934. $1.25.

The Facetiae of the Mensa Philosophica, by Thomas F. Dunn. June, 1934. 75c.

[Ancients and Moderns: A Study of the Background of the *Battle of the Books*, by Richard F. Jones. January, 1936.]

WASHINGTON UNIVERSITY STUDIES

[A Survey of the Labor Market in Missouri in Relation to Unemployment Compensation, by Joseph M. Klamon in collaboration with Russell S. Bauder and Roy A. Prewitt. March, 1937.]

[Contributions in Geology. Edited by Carl Tolman. February, 1936.]

Forms of Address in German (1500-1800), by George J. Metcalf. December, 1938. $2.00.

Charles Sealsfield—Bibliography and Catalogue of Literature, by Otto Heller and Theodore H. Leon. September, 1939. $1.00.

Edmund Burke and His Literary Friends, by Donald Cross Bryant. December, 1939. $2.75.

Émile Zola's Letters to J. Van Santen Kolff. Edited by Robert J. Niess. May, 1940. $1.00.

[Collected Studies of Skin Diseases—Vol. III. Edited by M. F. Engman, Sr., M.D. November, 1940.]

The Weight Field of Force of the Earth, by William H. Roever. September, 1940. $1.50.

Fundamental Theorems of Orthographic Axonometry, by William H. Roever. 1941. $1.00.

The Language of Charles Sealsfield: A Study in Atypical Usage, by Otto Heller assisted by Theodore H. Leon. July, 1941. $1.50.

A Glossary of Mississippi Valley French, 1673-1850, by John Francis McDermott. December, 1941. $1.50.

The Hymn to Demeter and Her Sanctuary at Eleusis, by George Emmanuel Mylonas. March, 1942. $1.00.

Studies in Honor of Frederick W. Shipley. 1942. $3.00.

Contents:

A Constitutional Doctrine Re-examined, by Donald McFayden; The Use of Fire in Greek and Roman Love Magic, by Eugene Tavenner; Thucydides and the Causes of the Peloponnesian War, by Thomas Shearer Duncan; Prehistoric Macedonia, by George E. Mylonas; Classical "Ariels," by Otto Brendel; An Aesopic Allusion in the *Roman D'Alexandre*, by Bateman Edwards; The Poetic Theories of Minturno, by Bernard Weinberg; Pereda's Realism: His Style, by Sherman Eoff; Early English and American Critics of French Symbolism, by Bruce A. Morrissette; Bibliographical Data on Diderot, by Herbert Dieckmann; Rosencrantz and Guildenstern, by W. Roy Mackenzie; The Contemporary Reception of Edmund Burke's Speaking, by Donald Cross Bryant; The Moral Sense of Simplicity, by Richard F. Jones; Imitation as an Aesthetic Norm, by Fred O. Nolte; Immediacy: Its Nature and Value, by Charles E. Cory.

Letters of Mr. and Mrs. Charles Kean Relating to Their American Tours. Edited with Introduction and Notes by William G. B. Carson. August, 1944. $2.50.

Types of Utility Rate Bases under Depreciation Reserve Accounting, by William S. Krebs. 1946. $1.50.

German Literature as Reflected in the German-Language Press of St. Louis Prior to 1898, by Erich P. Hofacker. 1946. $1.50.

The Life and Works of Marie-Catherine Desjardins (1632-1683), by Bruce A. Morrissette. 1947. $3.00.

Le Philosophe: Texts and Interpretation, by Herbert Dieckmann. 1948. $3.00.

On the Edge of the Black Waxy: A Cultural Survey of Bell County, Texas, by Oscar Lewis. 1948. $3.00.

WASHINGTON UNIVERSITY STUDIES

The Political History of Leigh Hunt's *Examiner*, Together with an Account of "The Book," by George D. Stout. 1949. $2.50.

The Wulfing Plates: Products of Prehistoric Americans, by Virginia Drew Watson. 1950. $2.50.

Studies in Memory of Frank Martindale Webster. 1951. $3.50.

Contents:

In Deference to David Hume, by Robert M. Schmitz; Leigh Hunt's Shakespeare: A "Romantic" Concept, by George Dumas Stout; Jeffrey, *Marmion*, and Scott, by Alexander M. Buchan; The Frustrated Opposition: Burke, Barré, and Their Audiences, by Donald C. Bryant; The First Public Address of George W. Cable, Southern Liberal, by Guy A. Cardwell; Linguistic Equations for the Study of Indo-European Culture, by Vladimir Jelinek.

The Soviet Theory of Internationalism, by Merle Kling. 1952. $2.00.

Pope's Windsor Forest 1712, by Robert M. Schmitz. 1952. $4.50.

The Esthetic Intent of Tieck's Fantastic Comedy, by Raymond M. Immerwahr. March, 1953. $3.50.

American Literature and the American Language, by T. S. Eliot. June, 1953. $1.50.

"Our Dear Sarah." An Essay on Sarah Orne Jewett, by A. M. Buchan. November, 1953. $1.50.

The Novels of Pérez Galdós: The Concept of Life as Dynamic Process, by Sherman H. Eoff. November, 1954. $3.00.

Orders for any of these publications should be addressed to the Bookstore, Washington University, St. Louis 5, Mo.